To Herbert with friendship and esteem
October 26, 1997

International Privatization

International Privatization

PUBLISHED UNDER THE AUSPICES

OF THE CENTER FOR INTERNATIONAL LEGAL STUDIES

Editor

Dennis Campbell

Director, Center for International Legal Studies

Salzburg, Austria

LONDON – THE HAGUE – BOSTON

Published by Kluwer Law International Ltd
Sterling House
66 Wilton Road
London SW1V 1DE
United Kingdom

Sold and distributed in the USA
and Canada by Kluwer Law International
675 Massachusetts Avenue
Cambirdge MA 02136
USA

Kluwer Law International Ltd incorporates
the publishing programmes
of Graham & Trotman Ltd,
Kluwer Law & Taxation Publishers
and Martinus Nijhoff Publishers.

In all other countries, sold and distributed
by Kluwer Law International Ltd
P.O. Box 85889
2508 CN The Hague
The Netherlands

© Kluwer Law International Ltd
First published in 1996
ISBN 90 411 0931 5

British Library Cataloguing in Publication Data and
Library of Congress Cataloguing in Publication Data is available.

This publication is protected by international copyright law. All rights reserved. No part of this publication may be reproduced, stored in a retrieval system, or transmitted in any form or by any means, electronic, mechanical, photocopying, recording or otherwise, without the prior permission of the publishers.

Printed and bound by Athenaeum Press, Ltd.,
Gateshead, Tyne & Wear.

Table of Contents

Global Privatization 1
   By Douglas Wardle and Nick Towle

Argentina 29
   By Carlos A. Alemán

Brazil 45
   By José Guilherme Vasi Werner

Bulgaria 63
   By Yavor Vesselinov Manoilov and Arno Artune Mamasian

Croatia 81
   By Stefan Pürner

Germany 91
   By Kerstin Reiserer and Valentin Boll

Hungary 117
   By McKenna Ormai & Co.

Italy 153
   By Emanuele Turco

The Slovak Republic 189
   By Kevin T. Connor and Julian Juhasz

Slovenia 199
   By Peter Grilc and Miha Juhart

United Kingdom 211
   By Robin Brooks

European Community 239
   By Andrzej Kmiecik and Laurence Gourley

Index 263

The Authors

Carlos A. Alemán
Estudio Alberto Lisdero
Buenos Aires, Argentina

Valentin Boll
Melchers, Schubert, Stocker, Sturies
Berlin, Germany

Robin Brooks
Norton Rose
London, England

Kevin T. Connor
Squire, Sanders & Dempsey
Bratislava, Slovak Republic

Laurence Gourley
Van Bael & Bellis
Brussels, Belgium

Peter Grilc
University of Ljubljana, Faculty of Law
Ljubljana, Slovenia

Julian Juhasz
Squire, Sanders & Dempsey
Bratislava, Slovak Republic

Miha Juhart
University of Ljubljana, Faculty of Law
Ljubljana, Slovenia

Andrzej W.J. Kmiecik
Van Bael & Bellis
Brussels, Belgium

Arno Artune Mamasian
Ciela
Sofia, Bulgaria

Yvor Vesselinov Manoilov
Ciela
Sofia, Bulgaria

Stefan Pürner
Rödl & Partner
Zagreb, Croatia

Kerstin Reiserer
Melchers, Schubert, Stocker, Sturies
Berlin, Germany

McKenna Ormai & Co.
Budapest, Hungary

Nick Towle
Watson, Farley & Williams
London, England

Emanuele Turco
Studio Legale Emanuele Turco
Rome, Italy

GLOBAL PRIVATIZATION

Douglas Wardle and Nick Towle
Watson, Farley & Williams
London, England

INTRODUCTION

Many commentators suggest that the origins of privatization trace to the United Kingdom during the late 1970s. In addition, there is little doubt that the Thatcher years imprinted privatization on the public consciousness, both in the United Kingdom and in many other countries. Yet, while "privatization" may well have been a word coined in the recent past, the transfer of state-owned assets to the private sector is rooted in more ancient times. State (or Crown) patronage in many different guises has been a common feature of most recorded civilizations. In other words, privatization has been around for many years and in many different countries. In 1940 in Latvia, at that time (as it is again today) an independent sovereign state, a law on "The Liquidation of State Property" was introduced providing for a system of competitive tenders to transfer state ownership to private individuals. In the United Kingdom, "denationalization", as it was then called, was occurring during the 1950s in response to the Labor Party government's years of nationalization in the late 1940s.

Global Privatization

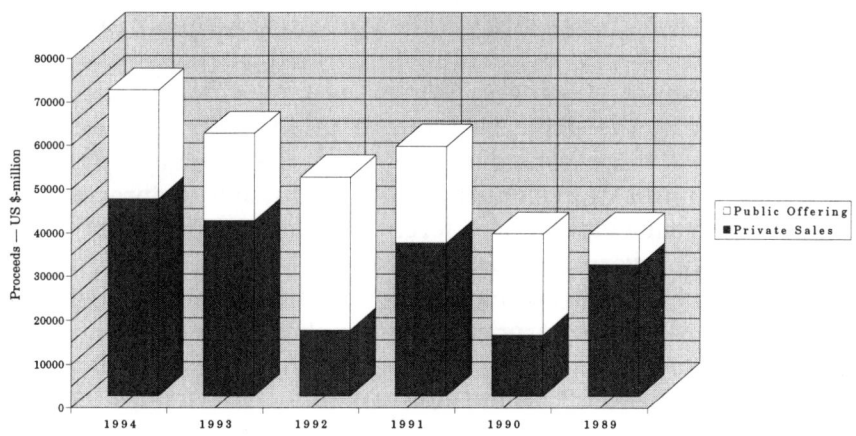

However, it was not until 1979 that privatization developed center stage as an integral element in economic policy, harnessed by a monetarist United Kingdom government to raise revenue, reduce government borrowing, restructure industry and reduce the powers of trade unions. Even today, many countries look to the so-called "United Kingdom model" for privatization inspiration. However, United Kingdom experience is not the only experience and in turn the privatization industry has seen the emergence of alternative systems, notably the spectacular massed tender offerings conducted by the *Treuhandanstalt* in Germany and the voucher privatizations of Eastern Europe, and each of these, in its own way, has a place in the privatization universe. Put another way, a distinction seems to have developed between the approach to privatization in emerging markets and the approach to privatization in developed economies. This should not be so surprising for emerging markets. Developed economies have different priorities, with privatization often being employed for very different reasons:

(1) *Benefits of Competition* — Released from the protective custody of the state, companies in the private sector are subject to the invisible hand of the free market, and conventional wisdom dictates that competition, engendered by market forces and boosted by generous helpings of deregulation and liberalization, results in more efficient and healthier companies. In fact, this is something of a truism since a company operating in the private sector can but fail in the absence of long-term profitability, thereby increasing the average profitability of the pool of remaining companies.

(2) *Industrial Efficiency* — Empirical and comparative studies have demonstrated time and again that the transfer of state-owned assets into the private sector stimulates a more dynamic business ethos within a privatized organization. Proponents of privatization claim that this results from management striving to achieve a more efficient use of resources in the drive to improve profitability and increase dividends to shareholders. However, this is something of an oversimplification since in reality productivity improvements result from a variety of different (and interacting) stimuli, not least the overnight disappearance of "jobs for life", which epitomizes the traditional view of state-owned industry. It should not be too surprising that employees can be encouraged to improve their performance in an environment which dictates the eradication of overmanning.

(3) *Public Finance* — In theory, privatization will reduce a government's current account deficit as responsibility for enterprise funding is transferred to the private sector. Add to this privatization revenues (both in the form of capital payments and, depending on the privatization, license fees) and the prospect of increased revenues from taxation of more profitable enterprises, and a government has in its hands a tool that can yield tax cuts for the populace and/or an increase in government spending in other (politically sensitive) areas such as health, education and law enforcement. These prospects are very attractive to a government seeking reelection.

(4) *Wider Share Ownership* — Wider share ownership is generally regarded as a good thing. There is a belief that spreading participation in a nation's wealth-generating assets in some way creates a more democratic society. This was perhaps the paramount consideration in a newly democratic Czechoslovakia where 1990 saw the government moving with breathtaking speed to achieve wide private ownership, creating a society in which recent reforms became irreversible. For Vaclav Klaus, it also had the benefit of sweeping him back into power in the Czech Republic during the 1992 elections.

(5) *Elimination of Political Interference* — It is often argued that state ownership of industry inevitably subordinates commercial efficacy to political objectives. Phrases such as "political taskmasters" and "level playing fields" frequently crop up in this context. While this too is something of a generalization, there is little doubt that any motivating forces other than pure commercial considerations will serve only to restrain the invisible hand.

(6) *IMF/World Bank Requirements* — In many emerging markets, both the IMF and the World Bank have tied their funding programs to privatization of the state sector (referred to in the jargon as "conditionality"). This has largely been a 1990s response to the third-world debt crisis of the 1980s where funding which was not tied to economic stabilization programs resulted in the major debt-reschedulings and write-offs that have characterized the last ten years of international lending.

If it is possible to encapsulate in one sentence the essence of privatization, it is that privatization is predicated on the assumption that a modern economy will develop more effectively where the free market is allowed to shape decisions on the utilization of productive assets and that for any debtor nation to access world resources it must adhere to this philosophy. As an aside, there is but a thin line between privatization and the use of private sector finance for new projects (typically infrastructure development) which, by convention, is not regarded as "privatization". In many ways, this is an artificial distinction since philosophically there is considerable common ground and the distinction becomes all the more blurred if one accepts the unconventional view that the concession rights which underpin such projects are just another form of intangible state asset.

PRIVATIZATION PROGRAMS

The policies and strategies for employing the various mechanisms for effecting privatization are elaborated in "privatization programs". These are sometimes very integrated, sometimes less so, even bordering on the "ad hoc". Currently received wisdom is that in an emerging economy, where there may be hundreds or even thousands of companies to privatize, a blend of different programs is required. In a developed economy, the programe is more a function of a government's political objectives and the characteristics of that country's economic system.

Pilot Programs

The distinction between privatization in emerging markets and privatization in developed economies is best illustrated in the form of "pilot" privatization programs. Such programs are often introduced at the behest of donor-aid agencies working in emerging markets to "teach-by-doing" the various domestic institutions that will be involved in an ongoing programe of privatization. Typically, several enterprises will be selected and one or more international advisory consortia will be appointed to prepare the enterprises for privatization, determine the individual strategy and implement it in conjunction with those government officials charged with developing the privatization process. The enterprises concerned will usually be drawn from among the largest in the country and there is often a debate between advisers and government as to the most suitable companies to bring in to the programe. The government will sometimes want to involve large, unprofitable "white elephant" industries in the often mistaken belief that foreign investors will for some reason wish to invest in such companies and sort out all their problems at no cost to the state. Conversely, advisers, whose remuneration will often be linked to the success of the privatization, will want good companies in which investors can be expected to show interest.

Typical candidates for a pilot program are enterprises drawn from the tobacco sector, the cement sector and the hotel sector, principally because of their potential to generate privatization revenues and the fact that they do not require specific industry regulation to be in place (as would be the case for utilities). It is also fair to say that investors in these sectors have generally proved to be less risk averse than in many other sectors, offering the prospect of a more successful start to privatization in an embryonic market. Working on pilot programs can be extremely demanding since the advisory group will not only be wrestling with the particular challenges of the relevant enterprise, but they must also educate their local counterparts in the process (for example, valuation techniques, implementation procedures, marketing and negotiating techniques) and frequently become embroiled in fundamental policy and regulatory issues at a government level which must be resolved before the privatization can proceed. A good example is the need to reform import duties and excise taxes in order for an investment in an enterprise producing for the domestic market to be viable. The potential knock-on effect of such regulatory changes can sometimes kill a privatization. Another feature of pilot programs is that they quickly demonstrate conflicts in poorly drafted privatization legislation, conflicts which must be remedied before a privatization can legally proceed. The fact that the government operates under delegated powers and that it will require an amendment in parliament can create friction with governmental figures whose initial reaction is often (and incorrectly) that the problem can be solved by a cabinet resolution.

Fast-Track or Multi-Enterprise Programs

Faced with a large number of companies to privatize and limited resources, there has been a trend over the past two years to develop programs which mirror the successful techniques pioneered by the

Treuhandanstalt in Germany after unification. Notably, the Baltic Republics of Estonia and Latvia have experienced some success through such programs, part-financed by the German Government. Fast-track programs can be summarized as follows:

(1) The enterprises chosen are typically medium-sized, non-strategic concerns with relatively straightforward businesses where the cash commitments of the purchaser can be regarded as the principal selection criterion, both in terms of purchase price and investment into the company.

(2) There is little or no restructuring of the enterprise before privatization.

(3) Only a basic investigation into the company is carried out by the state's advisers and there is heavy reliance on the information produced by the company itself. Such information as is available largely serves a marketing purpose since it is left up to prospective purchasers to investigate the company and draw their own conclusions.

(4) Economies of scale are achieved through conducting the privatizations in waves of twenty to fifty companies at a time, with summary information about all the companies in the wave being advertised in the international press.

(5) The implementation procedures are (in theory) both standardized and streamlined with bids usually being required within six weeks of announcement of the tender and subsequent finalizing of contracts within a short time thereafter.

Such fast-track programs give rise to a rapid transfer of less sophisticated companies into the private sector, the justification being that it is in the national interest for such companies to be free to evolve and adapt to the new market environment in which they are already operating. The price for this less tailored approach is that without a thorough investor search, the quality of bids received will almost certainly suffer.

Mass Privatization Programs

The concept of mass privatization programs first evolved in former Czechoslovakia although it has since been adopted throughout Eastern Europe including, most notably in Russia where the substantial majority of enterprises were transferred into the private sector during 1993 and 1994. As to why it is only a feature of East

European privatization, the answer seems to be that it serves the political purpose of entrenching the break with the past by giving each citizen the opportunity to have a personal stake in their country's income-producing assets, thereby reducing support for any future attempts to nationalize. It also provides an expectant public with a tangible sign of the political changes and compensation for past hardship and deprivation of individual rights. It would not be surprising to see the South African authorities adopting this approach to privatization during the next year for similar reasons.

The programs proceed on the basis that each member of the population is issued with investment vouchers (indeed, in Hungary, they are known as "Compensation Vouchers", underlining the purpose behind their introduction). Depending on the country, the vouchers can be used to acquire an equity interest either directly in former state enterprises offered through the program or in investment funds established as intermediaries for this purpose. The privatization takes place though a series of bidding rounds, organized, depending on the country, through auctions or electronic clearing systems. A common feature of the post-mass privatization environment worth noting is the emergence of secondary markets and financial intermediaries. Together, these serve the important purpose of putting private sector finance and know-how in touch with the new owners of companies.

However, mass privatization programs are not without their problems, being something of a halfway house in terms of what they deliver. What have they achieved?

(1) Immediately following privatization, there is little more than a nominal change of ownership. Indeed, at first sight one can argue that the situation of the companies themselves is even worse since their corporate governance may well be in the hands of myriad small and uninformed shareholders who lack any real finance which can be made available to the companies at a time when they most need it.

(2) Although many mass privatization programs can also accommodate cash purchases in addition to the use of vouchers, not surprisingly for countries with low levels of personal disposable income there is little actual cash directed at such programs (although there is always a vibrant secondary market in investment vouchers).

(3) Worse still are the pressures placed on newly "privatized" companies to pay dividend income to their new owners, again

at a time when such companies need all the retained income they can hold on to in order to finance company development internally.

Mass privatization does not, therefore, deliver finance, know-how, new markets, technology nor effective governance. In other words, once the mass privatization program has been concluded, the hard work has only just begun. However, what it does deliver, more than anything else, is the unshackling of companies from the bureaucracy of the state, a bureaucracy which, in the context of conventional privatization, has resulted time and again in damage to the well-being of companies. The result is that within a matter of a year or two there has been substantial change of ownership as citizens cash in. It means that there are many bargains to be had and, looked at as a whole, the state is likely to have lost out in terms of privatization revenues. However, this must be balanced against what many consider to be the greater benefits to be derived from rapid exposure of the majority of industry to the free market. Certainly, experience from the Czech Republic would appear to bear this out.

Case-by-Case Programs

Whatever the merits of mass privatization, it is not a panacea that can be applied uniformly to all emerging markets. Czech industry is characterized by light industry which one can argue is easier to adapt to a market environment, not least because it requires, as a general rule, lower capital expenditure to develop and re-focus. Where there is a higher concentration of heavy industry (as was the case in the Slovak Republic), mass privatization does not have so wide an application: there is little doubt that heavy industry requires a tailored and controlled approach to privatization, an approach which would be unlikely to be achieved if it were left to the holders of investment vouchers.

Therefore, the tendency is for enterprises which are large, complex, strategic or valuable to be the subject of individual attention and indeed this tends to be an approach not just employed in emerging markets but also in developed economies. Typically, enterprises which fall to be privatized on a case-by-case basis are drawn from non-manufacturing sectors such as telecommunications, utilities, aviation and financial services. Such privatizations tend to follow on some time after conclusion of the pilot programs, reflecting their greater complexity and their dependence on specific regulatory reform. They will frequently be the subject of extensive stabilization and restructuring programs prior to privatization becoming a possibility.

Employee Ownership Programs

Programs aimed at putting companies into the hands of their workforces deserve a special mention. In these cases, management and employees are given preferential assistance in acquiring significant or even controlling stakes in the companies for which they work. Such programs come in many forms:

(1) Buy-outs: conventional management and management/employee buy-outs have been a frequent feature of privatization in many countries, both emerging and developed.
(2) Vouchers: the voucher programs which have been a common feature of many East European countries, have been extended in some countries to give employees a prior right to use their vouchers for the acquisition of equity in the company for which they work.
(3) Discounts: a common feature of privatizations in most countries is the offering of equity to the workforce at a discount, sometimes substantial. Normally, the amount of equity available for privatization in this way and the amount of the discount are regulated by law.
(4) Scrip issues: unusually, Lithuania saw a period during which enterprise profits were converted into equity issued to the workforce. During 1992, this led to a situation in which employee participation in some companies placed them in a majority position, rendering a sale by the state extremely difficult to negotiate. Not surprisingly, employee participation achieved in this way was subsequently scrapped.
(5) Employee share ownership plans: in many countries, the establishment of employee share ownership plans (ESOPs) are a significant requirement to be addressed in investment proposals.

The key thing to observe is that employee participation is generally regarded as a good thing on the basis that it gives the workforce an interest in their own business and increases their motivation. While this is true in principle, it does require a liquid exit route through which employees can realize their share holdings if it is to be of any effective motivational value. This can, of course, be achieved by the establishment of a market in the company's shares or, in the absence of a conventional market, an ability to sell out to a strategic investor, the company itself or to an employees' trust. A problem flowing from employee participation is that, by and large, the workforce cannot be relied on as a source of future financing for the company. Equally, their vested interest in the company for which they work simply creates an additional layer of complexity during privatization negotiations and subsequent restructuring.

Commercialization

Although not privatization as such, the concept of "commercialization" of a state enterprise sometimes comes up when determining the strategy for its future development. It implies no change of ownership of the enterprise but it does require financial and organizational restructuring with a view to allowing it to function as if it were completely independent of the state. Commercialization may extend to using management contracts and may ultimately lead to privatization in much the same way as a conventional restructuring.

IMPLEMENTATION OF PRIVATIZATION

If the introduction of market forces into an economy is the essence of privatization, how is it manifested? Although there exists no precise definition of "privatization", it can (and, in the authors' view, should) be regarded as embracing any process which results in a reduction in state ownership and/or control, howsoever arising. To illustrate the diversity, the Adam Smith Institute, leading proponents of the free market, have identified some twenty-four methods of effecting privatization; however, the most commonly applied are as follows:
(1) Public offerings of shares;
(2) Private sales of shares;
(3) Private investments in state enterprises;
(4) Sales of state or state enterprise assets;
(5) Reorganizations of state enterprises into component parts involving the private sector;
(6) Sales of assets (either directly state-owned or state enterprise-owned);
(7) Management buy-outs;

(8) Management and employee buy-outs;
(9) Leasing arrangements;
(10) Management contracts;
(11) Liquidations;
(12) Joint ventures; and
(13) Concessions or franchises.

While some of the above methods lead to total divestiture or denationalization, a partial approach is often adopted with parliaments frequently entrenching in law state ownership in strategic enterprises where (typically) either a twenty-five per cent (plus one vote) or a fifty per cent (plus one vote) equity holding must be retained.

Often, the privatization strategy for an enterprise will combine several of the above methods, a common example being the restructuring of an enterprise as a prelude to the establishment of a joint venture with a strategic partner and ahead of a public offering on the basis that this will enhance its attractiveness to investors.

In contrast, trade investors wishing to acquire a state enterprise will prefer to make their acquisition without any restructuring (or, at most, limited to "soft" restructuring of the enterprise's balance sheet) on the basis that they will want to reorganize the target in the way that best suits their own group and without paying a premium for the way in which someone else thinks it should be reorganized. As will be obvious from the foregoing, issues arising during implementation vary enormously, depending on the method of privatization to be used. Some of the different methods, many of which will be familiar from other contexts, are outlined below.

Public Offerings

Privatization offerings have principally, but not exclusively, been a feature of privatization in developed markets where stable enterprises with established track records can be prepared relatively easily for access to liquid capital markets. Although such offerings are of existing government-held equities, where finance is also required for the company to be privatized, the offering may also be structured to include the issue of new securities (shares or bonds) by the company itself. The offering process itself is conventional and not covered in detail here.

Suffice to say that the offering prospectus is normally prepared by the investment bank acting for the government. The bank may also, on its own or as part of a syndicate, underwrite the offering which may be on a fixed price or a demand-led basis (whereby the price of the shares is calculated to reflect the strength of demand from the public). The securities may be marketed either domestically or internationally and where it is the first offering of securities of that company, it will often be referred to as an "initial public offering" or "IPO", as opposed to a "secondary public offering".

Having said that the offering process itself is fairly conventional, certain aspects of preparation are more specific to privatization offerings:

(1) Conversion of the corporate form of the legal entity, for example, from a state enterprise to a joint stock company;
(2) Modification of the legislative framework, for example, the creation of privatization laws or laws regulating a monopoly once it is in the private sector;
(3) Financial restructuring of the entity, sometimes including writing off debt owed to the state;
(4) Physical rehabilitation of the enterprise; and
(5) Reorganization of the workforce.

Advantages of public offerings are perceived to include the attainment of widespread share ownership and the general transparency of the process making the privatization more easily acceptable politically. Disadvantages include the associated expense, the delay and the prospect of misjudging investment interest, with the result that the offering is under-subscribed and fails. The prospect of an offering failing leads to the price of securities being marked down to ensure success.

On a privatization, this often gives rise to subsequent political controversy if, as a result, there is material over-subscription and a perceived loss of privatization revenues to the state. Conversely, if the offer price is perfectly matched to market demand, this can give rise to a sluggish after-market (or even a slide in share price) with dissatisfied investors and a privatization which is not perceived to have been successful. Worse, this can have implications for subsequent privatization offerings.

Private Sales of Shares

Under this most popular of techniques, the government sells all or part of its shareholding in a state enterprise to purchasers selected in one of a variety of ways. Open or closed tenders, perhaps with pre-qualification of bidders, are popular, as are auctions for smaller enterprises. Less popular with governments due to uncertainty over the attainment of a fair market price and lack of transparency are directly negotiated sales. As a rule, investors in general view these sales more positively than governments. To meet potential concerns over lack of transparency, many countries have introduced compulsory procedures to be observed for private sales, covering matters such as price-setting, the selection process and terms of payment, particularly relating to payment guarantees or acceptable forms of security where ongoing financing is to be provided by the government.

Private sales are sometimes employed as a first step towards a privatization offering, being a useful method of establishing a core of stable shareholders and improving the company's quality before widening share ownership to the general public.

Sale of Government/Enterprise Assets

An asset sale by government may either take the form of the sale of individual state/state enterprise assets/rights or the sale of all the assets of an enterprise so that its business is disposed of as a going concern. Similar to a direct share sale, the sale of assets can be effected by tender, auction or direct negotiation with a pre-identified party. However, unlike share sales, assets are normally sold without liabilities and it is the ongoing responsibility for any such liabilities that make asset sales, at least in the context of the business of an enterprise, less popular with government.

It may, however, be possible to create a contractual arrangement under which the buyer is obligated to re-hire a portion of the workforce and/or to assume certain liabilities with creditors, although this can be convoluted. Once again, uncertainty over valuation gives rise to considerable concern on the side of the state.

New Private Investment in a State Enterprise

If further investment is required in a particular state enterprise, this will sometimes be achieved through a capital increase whereby the private sector subscribes for fresh equity in the former state enterprise. In this case, the government is not actually disposing of any existing equity but is acquiescing in a dilution of the state's holding and an increase in private sector participation. Most recently, this was how the German government's holding in Lufthansa fell from 51.4 per cent to forty-one per cent following the sale of shares not taken up by the state during a rights issue.

A variation on this theme is the establishment of a new subsidiary company between the state or state enterprise (contributing existing state assets to joint venture capital) and private investors (contributing cash and technology to joint venture capital).

Management and Management/Employee Buy-Outs

A management buy-out (MBO) is the acquisition of a majority shareholding in a company by its management, while a management/employee buy-out (MEBO) additionally involves the employees as shareholders. In many cases, such transactions are highly leveraged, the assets of the company being used as security for funding from financiers. Strong cashflow projections will inevitably be a precondition for financiers making funds available for an MBO/MEBO. Notable instances of successful MEBO privatizations were the trust port privatizations in the United Kingdom during 1992.

Generally, a holding company is incorporated by the management and possibly the employees as subscribers. The holding company then acquires the state enterprise by using the capital of the holding company and/or borrowed funds. The major attraction of MBOs and MEBOs is considered to be the prospective improvement in productivity, and they have been used successfully in cases where the only other alternative was the liquidation of the enterprise due to its bankruptcy. A necessary feature of MBOs and MEBOs is the presence of a competent and intelligent management and a committed workforce. It may nevertheless be necessary to educate the employees as to the nature and benefits of share ownership.

Leases and Management Contracts

Leases and management contracts provide private sector management, skills and technology to a state enterprise without a transfer of ownership. They tend to be used for one of two reasons. First, as a temporary measure, put in place to return a state enterprise to profitability at which point the state enterprise can then be divested by the state. Second, in emerging markets, leasing or even lease-purchasing has been introduced as a means of enabling local entrepreneurs, often management, to achieve an interest in a state enterprise in the absence of their being able to finance an outright purchase.

A management contractor assumes responsibility to manage an enterprise and unlike the lessee (who pays the state for the use of state assets) is normally paid by government to provide management skills while the state continues to bear the full commercial risk in respect of the assets. Under a lease arrangement, the lessee typically assumes full commercial risk in operating the leased assets and hiring its own workforce (which may or may not come from the existing workforce). A lessee therefore has much greater control over the workforce than does a management contractor and total control over the operation of the assets. One consequence is that the lessee is financially responsible for the upkeep of the assets.

A current illustration is the "privatization" of British Rail which will, in the first place, be limited to letting franchises on particular routes to franchise holders who will not own the track. While the master rail restructuring plan involves, as a cardinal principle, the separation of infrastructure from operation, there is already great pressure being exerted by certain franchise bidders to permit them to purchase the track as well.

Restructuring

Deserving of separate mention here is restructuring prior to privatization. This is often employed where a state enterprise pursues activities which, taken together, would not be attractive to potential investors although the individual components may themselves be attractive. Another reason for fragmentation can be to create competition in a sector where a monopoly has previously existed. Having broken a state enterprise into its constituents, the privatization of each of those parts can then be carried out using any of the methods previously described.

A good example of restructuring prior to privatization is the comprehensive program currently being conducted by the government of Bangladesh in relation to the jute and textile industry. The program will financially restructure and divest eighteen jute mills over a three-year period. Twenty textile mills will be sold by the end of 1995. Many of these enterprises are running at a heavy loss and will have to restructure their debt before privatization. Others may need to be liquidated.

PRIVATIZATION PRACTICE

If that is some of the theory, what has been privatization practice during 1994 and what can be expected, looking ahead to 1995 and beyond?

Western Europe

The most notable privatizations of 1994 included France's biggest ever privatization, the sale of a majority holding in the oil company Elf Aquitaine, following on from public offerings for Banque Nationale de Paris and Rhône Poulenc. In Italy, privatization continues to limp along, despite unending political crisis, and companies in both financial and utility sectors remain scheduled for sale.

In the United Kingdom, the privatization of the Post Office has been indefinitely postponed thanks to backbench revolt and the privatization of British Rail continues to be delayed. Current major privatizations include the following:

Austria

The province of Burgenland has announced its intention to sell a 50.6 per cent stake in Bank Burgenland. Both Creditanstalt and Bank Austria are seeking to sell industrial holdings. The state's remaining stake in Vienna Airport was reduced from thirty-six per cent to seventeen per cent.

The state also will sell part of its holding in Austrian Airlines. There may be sales of minority stakes in the regional electricity companies. The state holding company has postponed plans for a secondary offering of shares in oil company OMV.

Belgium

The *Office Central de Crédit Hypothécaire*, Belgium's mortgage bank, has been transferred into state holding company *Société Fédérale de Participations*, paving the way for future privatization prospects.

The government has announced its intention to sell stakes in Belgacom, (possibly as high as forty-nine per cent) which has an estimated value of US $5-billion.

Denmark

Since the victory of the Social Democrats in the autumn 1994 elections, Denmark's privatization program has been on hold.

However, there may be the sale of certain subsidiaries of the national railway concern in the near future.

France

Privatization continues following the re-election of Jaques Chirac with a budgeted US $4.4-billion still on offer. The government has announced its intention to sell Credit Lyonnais within five years. France Telecom is scheduled for corporatization during 1996 to permit share swaps with Deutsche Telekom and Sprint.

A possibility exists for the sale of up to twenty per cent of the corporatized company during 1997. Notable companies still scheduled for privatization include: Thomson, Aerospatiale (part sold), Air France (part sold) aluminum and packaging group Pechiney, and BNP (part sold). Privatization plans for Renault have been postponed.

Germany

An estimated US $10-million worth of new shares in Deutsche Telekom are to be offered in two tranches, the first during November 1996, the second during 1998. State owned shares in the Company will not be available for sale until 2000. A remaining thirty-six per cent stake holding in Lufthansa also has been scheduled for sale during 1996.

Railways restructuring has commenced in anticipation of privatization over a ten year period. A twenty-five per cent stake in Postbank is scheduled for sale during 1998.

Greece

A policy of partial privatization of state utilities has been adopted by the Greek government, to be pursued through flotations of minority stakes on the Athens Stock Exchange. A target of US $3-billion in privatization revenues during the three years to 1997 has been set in response to continuing criticism from the European Commission over the large budget deficit maintained by the Greek government.

A public offering of six to eight per cent of the telecommunications utility, OTE, is likely to occur by early 1996. Flotations of Greece's two largest oil refineries and the public power corporation may also occur in the near future.

Italy

The new government is committed to privatization. The Ministry of Post is to be turned into a public body and will eventually be listed on the Stock Exchange. Rome's electricity and water utility, ACEA, is to be converted into a joint stock company before being partially privatized.

The sale of toll-road operator, Autostrade, may take place before the end of the year. The railways are to be corporatized and divided into a commercial division.

The Netherlands

Part sale of telecommunications operator PTT realized US $3.8-billion reducing the government stake to forty-five per cent. The government are able to re-offer a further thirteen per cent stake from 1 January 1997. The remaining thirty-three per cent is not available until 2004.

NVRCC is scheduled for sale within the next two years and a part sale of Schipol airport in Amsterdam is under discussion. The freight division of the Netherlands railways also is due to be privatized during the next year.

Portugal

Privatization plans are promised to be accelerated under the new Socialist government. The program is currently stagnant and expected to remain so until the 1996 budget is drawn. A twenty per cent stake of UBP and a twenty-five per cent stake of Bonanca are still expected to be sold in the future.

The Portuguese water distribution sector is currently scheduled for immediate privatization. An eighty per cent stake in tobacco company Tabquiera is likely to proceed in 1996 as is a twenty to twenty-five per cent stake in the generation utility CPPE.

Sweden

A thirty per cent stake in Nordbanken worth an estimated US $820-million was marked for sale during September 1995.

United Kingdom

Three subsidiaries of coal, oil, and gas distributor British Fuels are in the process of being sold by tender. The sale of the local authority-owned airports is to be encouraged by central government. The flotation of fifty-one per cent stake in Railtrack was likely to occur in April/May 1996.

In the nuclear energy sector, the government has announced its intention to privatize seven AGR stations and the PWR station at Sizewell during 1996 with liabilities to be transferred to the private sector.

Eastern Europe

Bulgaria

The Bulgarian government, headed by Zhan Videnor, is likely to combine voucher and cash privatizations with internal and external debt/equity conversions. A mass privatization scheme commencing March 1996 is expected to raise US $1.3 billion.

The Hotel Sofia, the Hotel Sheraton Sofia, the Rodina Hotel, Balkan Airlines and the sea and river fleets are on the government list for privatization.

Czech Republic

Fifty-three major companies are still scheduled for sale including major banks and utilities, including SPT Telecom, Komercni Banka, and electrical group CE2. Sale of utilities are unlikely to proceed before the June 1996 elections.

A clarification of the extent of privatization program is expected with a new law identifying those companies not to be listed for privatization.

Estonia

Twenty companies currently listed for privatization. Electricity generation and supply company Eesti Energia, Estonian Rail, and Estonian Telecom are all candidates for privatization.

Hungary

The Hungarian state Privatization Agency's (APV) successful sale of five regional gas distribution gas companies, eight electricity generation and supply companies and shares in oil and gas supplier MOL was undoubtedly 1995's highlight in Central and Eastern Europe. It is understood that APV will receive an estimated combined total of US $2.5-billion for the sales.

Approximately 900 companies, worth an estimated US $15-billion, remain on the privatization agenda. Offerings include stakes in telecommunications company Matav and National Airline Malev.

Kazakhstan

The Mass Privatization Program is proceeding rapidly and effectively. The companies sold are largely from the construction, building materials, machine-building, trading, and distribution and consumer goods sectors.

Latvia

The fourth round of the privatization program was scheduled between 18 December 1995 and 12 January 1996. A twenty-four per cent stake in Latvijas Gaze was to be offered following a government decision regarding the method of sale.

Lithuania

Partial privatization of 18 enterprises of strategic importance including the Lietuvos Dijos gas utility and the Mazeikiai oil refinery are due to proceed.

Poland

With privatization proceeds to October 1995 totaling US $528-million, 1996 is anticipated to bring even greater returns before declining in 1997. A further 101 companies have been added to the Mass Privatization Fund, increasing the total to 514. Mid-December 1995 saw the listing of Bank Gdansk on the Polish Stock Exchange, offering for sale stakes of between 30.2 and 32.9 per cent.

Still to be privatized during 1996 are five tobacco companies, a forty-nine per cent stake in the national airline LOT and ninety per cent of shares in silver and copper giant KGHM. The generating plants and distribution companies also remain scheduled for privatization.

Romania

The second phase of the Mass Privatization Program commenced in October 1995 for a three-month period. This seems likely to be extended after poor domestic participation. Cash investments likely to strengthen after conclusion of the second phase.

Legislation is currently anticipated to privatize two of the six state-owned banks. International privatizations proceeded well in 1995 with strategic sales to Procter & Gamble and Kimberly-Clark.

Russia

One-hundred-thirty-six companies have been noted for sale in the second phase of the privatization program. Ninety per cent of shares will be sold by auction for cash, and ten per cent will be reserved for employees.

The shares for loans scheme which enables the government to trade in shares held in trust (shares the government are legally prevented from selling) has been postponed to 1 September 1996. A forty-nine per cent stake in Aeroflot also is planned for sale.

Slovak Republic

Investment fund operations have been restricted and voucher sales stopped, currently permitting direct sales only. There is a proposal to transfer the privatization process to the government.

Ukraine

A Mass Privatization Program of both medium-sized and large companies has been launched. Vouchers will be used as in the Czech system. The president has stated that 4,000 enterprises should be privatized during the next year.

Latin America

Argentina

The sale of nuclear plants and all other electricity assets is due before the end of 1995. The post office savings bank, the National Mint and the national Grain Board are all due to be sold.

The airports are due to be sold by the end of 1996. Certain gas companies also will be sold.

Brazil

The telecommunications sector will be opened up for investment during the first half of 1996, but full privatization is not expected before 1998. Oil, telecommunications and mining sectors may also be opened up to competition.

Electrobras is expected to privatize unfinished hydro projects. The State of Sao Paulo has commenced a US $41-billion privatization program of almost all its electricity sector.

Columbia

Privatization is continuing under President Ernesto Samper. The privatization of several of Columbia's banks has been postponed by the Constitutional Court pending enabling legislation.

Several electricity power plants are due for privatization, and the state holding company, Instituto Fomento Industrial, is due to sell a majority of its industrial concerns (including chemicals and petrochemicals).

Mexico

An estimated US $6-billion is due to be raised from the sale of power plants. Overall, US $12-billion to US $14-billion may be raised from privatization. The petrochemical and waste water treatment plans are currently for sale.

Plans to privatize public transportation in Mexico City (excluding Metro and light transport) are under discussion. November 1995 saw government guidelines for bidding on railway concessions and rules for investment in the natural gas industry.

Peru

A privatization scheme involving public participation in which payment can be made by installments has been launched. The sale of the three separate generating units of Electroperu has been ordered. Port privatization is planned, as are privatizations in the copper, zinc, and steel industries.

Venezuela

An estimated US $6-billion is expected to be raised from the IMF program during 1996–1997 through the sale of holding company

CVG, the electricity sector and a forty-nine per cent stake in telecoms company CANTV. The re-privatization of several Venezuelan banks has been delayed.

Asia

China

Shandong Power Development, Datang Power, *Guangzhou — Shenzhen* Railway, and China Eastern and Southern Airlines are due to be listed for sale. Several other companies are on the government's list.

India

Indian banks are expected to make plans in the near future to strengthen their capital bases. The government is expected to dilute its stake in Indian Petrochemicals Limited from seventy-two per cent to sixty-three per cent by the issue of convertible debentures.
Tenders have been invited from the private sector for telecoms services and road projects.

Japan

Privatization of the western region of Japan Railways has been postponed due to poor market conditions. The Japanese government is considering the sale of Japan Railways' eastern region.
The government still intends to float part of its remaining stake in NTT (Japan's domestic post and telegraph company), but this also has been suspended due to market conditions.

Malaysia

The government is considering its options for the sale of the second largest bank in Malaysia (*Bank Buymiputera*). The government has expressed its intention to privatize the transport sector by 2000. The Malaysian post office also is due to be privatized during the next year.

The government's majority holding in the Merchant International Shipping Corporation is due to be sold by trade sale. All ports and airports are to be privatized.

The Philippines

The sale of further stakes in the Philippines National Bank has been postponed due to poor market conditions. The gas sector is planned for sale and in the oil sector, Subic Bay oil tank farm is due to be sold.

Singapore

A further stake in Singapore Telecom may be sold. The Singapore post office may be disposed of before the end of 1997. Privatization continues in the gas and electricity sectors.

Changi International Airport has been labeled for future sale and the Port of Singapore Authority is expected to be corporatized within three years.

Taiwan

The electricity enterprise of Taiwan, Taiwan Power, is currently considering its privatization options. Further tranches of China Steel are likely to be sold.

The military will divest Aero Industry Development to the government within two years and privatization is expected within three-and-a-half years. Chinese petroleum will be listed in early 1997.

Thailand

The telephone organization of Thailand is currently being advised as to its most suitable route to privatization. The electricity generating authority of Thailand is due to be listed in 1996.

Thai Oil is due to be listed on the Bangkok Stock Exchange on which twenty-five per cent of its equity will be floated. Ninety-three per cent of Thai Airways also is due to be sold.

Africa

Egypt

The government is due to announce a revised and accelerated privatization program.

Morocco

There have been some public offers in Morocco. The government has expressed its intention to sell telecoms utility ONPT by 1997. Currently, internal disagreement over the structure of the privatization program.

Africa Generally

With the encouragement of the World Bank, most countries in Africa are investigating the possibilities for privatization of state enterprises, irrespective of the political complexion of their governments.

CONCLUSION

Where does the privatization industry go from here? The past five years have seen privatization become truly global with most emerging markets and developed economies at least contemplating the privatization option. Coinciding as it has with the globalization of the world's capital markets, privatization can no longer be regarded as principally a domestic or regional affair and shares in privatized sate enterprises have become an investment sector in their own right.

Yet, despite the launch of privatization specific funds, demand for privatization investment is now so very great that not everyone will be satisfied: failed privatizations can be expected to become an increasing feature of the privatization landscape. The novelty factor has worn off, investors have become more discerning. In short, the privatization industry itself is now the subject of free market theory.[1]

---

[1] Source of Privatization Information: *Privatization International*. Privatization information current to December 1995.

ARGENTINA

Carlos A. Alemán
Estudio Alberto Lisdero
Buenos Aires, Argentina

INTRODUCTION

"The Argentine people have an appointment with history. In order to rise to the occasion we shall have to make a major effort, starting with the restructuring of our National State."

This was part of the closing speech attached to the State Reform Law Bill, sent to the Congress of the Argentine Republic by the executive on 14 July 1989.

SITUATION OF ARGENTINA IN MID — 1989

Halfway through 1989, Argentina was submerged in hyperinflation, the state was in virtual financial bankruptcy and large quantities of capital were being taken out of the country. The development of such a critical situation was primarily due to the fact that, for decades, Argentina carried out activities which should have been within the sphere of the private sector, creating petrochemical, carbochemical, carboniferous, mining, shipping, air transportation, catering trade, industrial and commercial firms, which included areas of no political, geopolitical or strategic interest. In that intense process of state participation, the public sector took charge of the management and absorbed the liabilities of those private firms which had been declared bankrupt or were in composition with creditors. This situation resulted in wasteful management of public funds which, consequently, dwindled to the extent that it became increasingly difficult to cover essential state services. State-owned companies, inadequately administered, underwent serious economic and financial crises, showing cumulative increasing deficits and providing inefficient services.

The state was in no condition to incorporate new technology into the public utilities or to increase their scope in order to reach those people who lacked essential services. Therefore, the state could not accomplish one of its main goals: ensuring the welfare of the people. There were no resources to maintain the essential infrastructure (roads, harbors, airports) which, as a consequence of inadequate maintenance or lack of it, showed signs of premature collapse. The state lacked the resources to efficiently fulfill its primary and fundamental role (in the areas of justice, domestic security, defense and foreign affairs) as well as its public sector role (social welfare, education and health). In the course of time, Argentina suffered a steady distortion in the distribution of resources and functions; the state absorbed activities which should have been channeled both through the provinces and town councils as well as the private sector. In order to revert this situation, it was essential to reformulate the role played by the state and state-owned companies. For President Carlos Saúl Menem, although the state as a political organization with historic category continued to be valid, its activities as businessman, producer, manufacturer and salesman were not effective anymore. Therefore, Menem committed himself in that:

> "... anything that could be done by the private sector on its own would not be done by the national state. Anything that could be done by the provinces on their own would not be done by the national state. Also, anything that could be done by the town councils would not be done by the national state".

STATE-OWNED COMPANY DEFICIT

One of the reasons for the heavy indebtedness accumulated by Argentina has been the absorption of obsolete and inefficient private companies which were taken over with the premise of maintaining job opportunities. As a consequence thereof, the state has transferred on a regular basis huge amounts of currency in order to finance the state-owned companies. This transfer of funds was undoubtedly one of the main causes for the rise of hyperinflation in Argentina in 1989. There was an urgent need to eliminate the deficit suffered by state-owned companies in order to revert the economic impact on the economy. The reduction of public spending through the privatization of companies and state-run activities was one of the instruments used to reduce the fiscal deficit. The goal of reducing the fiscal deficit would be achieved not only by reducing the state-owned companie's deficit but also by using the economic resources derived from their sale.

The government believed that the state reform and transformation should not be concluded with the privatization of only some state-owned companies. Moreover, it was necessary to attain the economic decentralization of the state and a redistribution of economic sectors, favoring the return of private activities and enterprises. In order to do so, it was essential to forget about financial state assistance, which had hindered development, and get used to investing and running risks. In that sense, the administration of President Menem has implemented a new model of growth for the country based on economic openness as well as on fiscal and monetary discipline. The main instruments are a comprehensive structural reform of the public sector, the privatization of state-owned companies, the creation of competitive markets to promote efficient resource allocation, balanced budgets, trade liberalization and deregulation.[1] The following aspects should be noted:

(1) Renegotiation of the foreign debt with the IMF and the committee of creditor banks. A central priority of the government was the re-establishment of the country creditworthiness;
(2) Internal and external obligations have been completely restructured in order to enable the emergence of the economy from the debt crisis in an atmosphere of fiscal order. The framework Brady Plan agreement, covering US $31-billion in debt to commercial banks, was reached in 1992 and a final exchange of old for new debt securities was completed one year later;
(3) Substantial reductions in spending and in fiscal deficit;
(4) Rapid and effective progress in privatizing state-owned companies;
(5) Price, wage, interest rates and exchange controls were eliminated together with a complex network of subsidies and hidden taxes that distorted the markets;

---

[1] The most important aspects of the execution of the state reform plan have been duly noted in the paper entitled "A Compendium for Foreign Investors", prepared by the Undersecretariat of Investment, Ministry of Economy and Public Works and Services of Argentina (November 1993).

(6) A massive deregulation program was undertaken covering regulatory agencies, foreign trade and investment, capital markets, regional products and capital intensive industries, as well as the local market for goods and services;
(7) Liberalization of regulations on foreign investment;
(8) The government re-issued the foreign capital law to include in a single body of legislation the liberalization measures contained in the previous Economic Emergency and State Reform Laws and other executive orders.[2] The law confirms the equal treatment received by domestic and foreign capital invested in Argentina. There are no exchange restrictions of any kind, and dividends are not taxable;
(9) Full freedom has been granted to the currency markets, and all controls on prices, wages and interest rates have been eliminated;
(10) By the end of March 1991, Law 23.929, the Convertibility Law, was passed. According to this law, local currency must be fully backed by foreign reserves and gold at a fixed exchange rate of one peso per dollar; indexation is prohibited; and contracts can be denominated and legally enforced in foreign currencies;
(11) Elimination of distortional taxes;
(12) Numerous government agencies controlling and restricting productive activities have been shut down, and restrictions on hours of operation have been abolished;
(13) The entire social security system has been reformed; and
(14) Inflation in consumer prices has fallen from 5000 per cent in 1989 to around eight per cent in 1993 and continues to fall.

PRINCIPLE OF SWIFTNESS

As pointed out by Juan M. F. Martín,[3] the operations associated with the deregulation and transfer of assets must necessarily be

---

2 Decree 1853 issued on 8 September 1993.

3 *Interacción de los sectores público y privado y la eficiencia global de la economía* (Public and Private Sector Interaction and the Global Efficiency of Economy), *Revista de la CEPAL* N36, December 1988, Santiago de Chile.

carried out with caution and social sensibility. This is necessary because the process may lead to a wide democratization experience or a violent movement towards the concentration of wealth and power. It must be kept in mind that the streamlining of state-owned companies and the decentralization policies which may accompany it are long-term processes with long-term consequences. Due to this, it is necessary to attain, at least, a minimum consensus to assure its sustained existence. This, in turn, requires a wide, well-informed and open discussion. In the privatization process carried out in Argentina from 1989 onwards, it is a moot point whether the above-mentioned factors of sensibility and prudence were observed. In this respect, it is appropriate to note that the first stage of the privatization process was marked by some irregularities and that after the appointment of Dr. Domingo Cavallo as Minister of the Economy, the privatization process was approached in a more orderly manner.

Of course, the situation of the country when Cavallo took office on 28 January 1991 was completely different from that which prevailed in 1989. The new economic cabinet took office in a generally stable environment of macroeconomic variables, almost sound public finance, a funded quasi-fiscal debt (through the 1990 Bonex Plan) and the overt desire of many foreign investors to take part in the Argentinean privatization process. This process was launched with the firm political aim of giving priority to the awarding and transfer of companies and services as soon as possible. The negative effects entailed by the above-mentioned principle of swiftness will be made clear and will be duly graded with the course of time and after having made the corresponding comparisons with other privatization processes carried out in other countries.

COMMUNITY CONSENSUS

It has been noted that the streamlining of state-owned companies and the policies applied to achieve it require a minimum consensus to ensure continuation. This is so because any process of socio-economic change demands the community consensus, since it is the community who will have to pay any possible social cost as a consequence. Although some sectors which favored populist economic and political doctrines (today considered obsolete) such as the *salariazo* and the productive revolution tried, under the slogan "defending national sovereignty", to maintain the dichotomy between nationalism and privatization, the fact is that the reforms and transformations brought about by the official party obtained the initial consensus of a majority of Argentinean society. This included sectors which had not voted for the *Partido Justicialista*, precisely because it was feared that they would apply populist policies.

LEGAL FRAMEWORK FOR STATE REFORM

Law 23.696, of Emergency Management and State-Owned Companies Reform, and Law 23.697, of Economic Emergency, as well as their respective regulatory decrees, provided the appropriate legal framework to initiate the transformation process introduced by the Menem Administration.

Law 23.696 set forth the suitable process to carry out the reform of the state, determining the adequate means and instruments for its implementation. All of these factors are subject to a regime of parliamentary control. As noted by José Roberto Dromi:[4]

> "Law 23.696 is specific as regards the plan; it regulates the conduct which the Executive Power, as administrator, must imperatively observe but which society has the option of approaching from the Legislative Power."

Law 23.696 gives full powers to the executive to privatize or liquidate those companies, partnerships or institutions of the national state subject to privatization, according to the decision of Congress. Moreover, it establishes a series of ways in which the privatizations may be carried out: sale of assets; sale of stock; rent or leasing; management with the option to buy or not; concession; franchise or authorization. This enumeration is not exhaustive, since other methods have also been used, such as, "contract of loan and restitution of realty with option to buy" used in the bidding of two television channels.

One of the most controversial sections of Law 23.696 grants the executive full powers to decide the partial or complete absorption

---

4 *Reforma del Estado y Privatizaciones* (State Reform and Privatizations), T1, p. 66.

by the national state of the liabilities of companies to be privatized. These powers were granted to the executive in order to improve contracting terms and to encourage a greater number of people to take part in privatizations. It is worth noting that, except in specific cases, such as the sale of stock in companies where the state had minor participation, in most of the privatization processes carried out in Argentina, the liabilities corresponding to the stage previous to the transfer were absorbed by the national state. Moreover, with the aim of encouraging the participation of potential interested parties, several measures were adopted. These included the exemption of tax levied on the transference of goods that could be privatized, the guarantee of free disposition of dividends and currency overseas and the elimination of most restrictions connected with the participation of foreign parties. Such measures have undoubtedly helped to raise the interest of foreign investors and operators.

AIMS OF PRIVATIZATION

As noted by Naum Minsburg in *El auge de la privatización en América Latina* (The Boom of Privatizations in Latin America): [5]

> "The wave of privatizations which has stretched throughout Latin America is propelled by two main factors: one, which we could term 'foreign' and consists of the repeatedly mentioned influence exerted by the international financial agencies which actively encourage privatization, mainly by the system of conversion of debt into capital. The second one, generated by 'domestic' causes inherent to the domestic situation of the countries of the region, and which may be synthetically expressed as the need to obtain greater efficiency in the public sector which, obviously, cannot operate non-strategic or non-essential companies. Privatization, it is hoped, will put an end to the technological backwardness suffered by many state-owned companies, which has been one of the reasons

---

5 *Boletín de Información Comercial Española* N 2280, 20–26 May 1991, Madrid, España.

for their lack of competitiveness. It may also put an end to the management by corrupt groups which have used the public sector for their own enrichment. Finally privatization will try to solve, at least partially, budgetary needs."

The conditions under which the state-owned companies carried out business have not been adequate to attain a reasonable level of efficiency — both as regards their operation, as determined by law, and the rules which govern their control. The state-owned companies generally possess several negative global factors which have historically contributed to their deficit, for example, managerial lack of competence, permanent rotation of chief executive officers, lack of training and encouragement of personnel, lack of specific programs for production and development, heavy paper work, excessive personnel and inadequate labor laws and lack of ability and competence on the part of the controlling agencies to exert an adequate supervision and control over the state-owned companies. Modern managerial techniques, executive competence and wise decision-making skills are basic elements which must be possessed by any good manager. The human factor continues to be essential; so much so that there are no legal or regulatory policies or organizational schemes which may guarantee the success of a company if it is not coupled with the competence of its management.

PREVENTION OF MONOPOLISTIC BEHAVIOR

The government made clear that it would approach the privatization program with the aim of attaining adequate safeguards to prevent monopolistic behavior. This policy was intended to boost competition, in order to obtain benefits in general quality and costs, to improve the quality of the services rendered and the allocation of resources and to promote genuine investments by private resources. It is true that private companies, within a framework of competitive markets, are frequently more efficient than governmental bureaucracies; nevertheless, private organizations, without competition and without corresponding supervisory controls, might end up as inefficient organisms which render inadequate services. Although it is undoubtedly necessary to boost competition in order to avoid the substitution of state-owned monopolies by private-owned monopolies, the Argentinean experience shows that this is not an easy process. So much so that the assets of the former ENTEL (*Empresa Nacional de Telecomunicaciones*/National Telecommunications Company) were transferred to two successful bidders under a regime of regional exclusiveness. Even though the exclusiveness conditions under which the exploitation of the telecommunications service was granted may not be extended for more than seven years (after which the service will be absolutely freed), these conditions were severely criticized and gave rise to union disputes. The government claimed the existence of urgent reasons. It asserted that, in order to generate a general consensus, it was necessary to act without delay, passing bills, enacting decrees, working on bidding conditions, setting into motion the bidding process and awarding and transferring the properties sold in unusually short periods.

EFFECTS OF PRIVATIZATION

According to the appraisal made by the government and as a consequence of the privatization process initiated in 1989, during 1994 the national state should only transfer those state-owned companies which still have approximately US $625-million. In comparison with the situation prevailing in 1989, this means an annual saving of US $4,700-million, that is, a saving equivalent to ten times the former expenditure. If this saving is projected in the future, the state should save approximately US $9,000-million every two years. Although it is true that the cash obtained from the sale of the companies is deposited only once in the National Treasury safe and that the government will no longer count on that income, it is also true that the positive impact derived from the saving of the deficit of state-owned companies should be a constant and long-term one. On the other hand, it is important to note that with privatization almost all subsidies deriving from tax exemption of state-owned companies were eliminated. This should also contribute to reduce the state shortfall in tax revenue and to increase tax revenue. The greatest negative impact on the Argentinean economy is generated by the transference of the heavy indebtedness of former state-owned companies to the Public Treasury, which represents almost half the foreign debt of Argentina. Probably, the absorption of liabilities by the state was an unavoidable condition to guarantee the presence of first-rate investors who otherwise might not have taken part.

Economist Pablo Gerchunoff, in his book, *Las privatizaciones en Argentina* (Privatizations in Argentina), points out a series of macroeconomic consequences on which it is interesting to go into detail. As regards the privatization of ENTEL, the national telephone company, Gerchunoff believes there is a constant income for the Treasury, mainly derived from the trade of a market protected by a cheap foreign debt. In the case of the concession of highways, the balance would also be positive for public accounts because upon the instrumentation of a toll system, in which the user finances part of the investment, the state is able to liberate a tax which had a specific allocation. In connection with the sale of verified oil reserves in exchange for cash (no debt exchange), Gerchunoff considers that there is a fiscal loss as a consequence of the reconversion of valuable assets into current expenses. Finally, with reference to the impact caused by the sale of public assets on savings and investment, Gerchunoff explains that privatizations were justified *a priori* because:

> "...the state is undergoing a severe credit restriction while private trusts show financial surplus or have the means to contact foreign financial markets".

INVESTMENTS DERIVED FROM THE PRIVATIZATION PROCESS

In order to guarantee the success of the privatization process, it is vital to have not only an investment commitment but also a specification of the financing methods to be used in order to satisfy this commitment, and in such a way be able to exert an adequate control and follow-up. Official statistics note that while between 1970 and 1980 the mean annual investment was US $3,788-million, between 1981 and 1991 it was reduced to US $3,385-million. Between 1992 and the year 2000, the total projected investment in privatized companies will amount to approximately US $36,600-million, without including the oil sector. At the end of 1993 the level of indebtedness (adding up the issued debt securities, credits received and stock to be offered) of privatized companies was very high: almost US $2,500-million and with an increasing projection.

INVESTMENT FINANCING

An important issue to be taken into account when assessing the privatization process is that of the means used to finance investments. If investment plans were mainly financed with undistributed profits and an increase in prices or tariffs, that would ruin the statement which affirms that privatizations themselves stimulate investments. Although the idea of making the most of the cash flow from public utility companies has probably always been in the mind of buyers and licensees of privatized companies, this has not been possible in practice since the collection has not been enough to cover in due time and form the investments committed. The most frequent financing means used by companies in order to comply with the investments committed has been the indebtedness through credits granted by international financing corporations. The next most frequent financing means is obtaining funds through the issuance of stock and/or debt securities. In practice, this financing alternative has been used less than the aforementioned one due to the fact that, in general, it is advisable to put it into practice when the companies start to show operative profits in their balance sheets, since otherwise it is not easy to appeal to the interest of potential buyers.

Another financing system used to a lesser extent than the two systems already mentioned is the contribution by the partners or stockholders of their own capital. It is important to note that the state, through the corresponding supervising agencies, should have a clear knowledge of the financing means used by the successful bidders in order to comply with the investments committed. It would be dangerous if the state should not be aware of or should not exert the corresponding controls, especially if the companies involved render basic public services. An inadequate or unplanned uptake of financing means could generate a severe economic or financial crisis in the successful bidding company, which should be solved directly by the state or by consumers through an increase in tariffs. In this last case, the consumers would finance the investments committed. In Argentina, some negative experiences have shown that not all private companies are in themselves more efficient than state-owned companies. That was the case with the transference of the stock of *Austral Líneas Aéreas* (an airline) to the national state, pursuant to Decree 1922/80. Formally, this transference was justified by the fact that the company needed capital contributions that the stockholders were not in a condition to furnish and it was not possible to obtain said funds from other private investors. Seven years after its transference to the state, the airline was privatized in an amount approximate to US $15-million. With this transaction the national state lost about US $135-million since it had to absorb liabilities equivalent to US $150-million.

CONCLUSION

Although it is true that the measures adopted pursuant to the State Reform Plan, including privatizations, have contributed to consolidate the socio-economic model proposed by the Menem administration, there are still some issues to be tackled. For example, the use of funds obtained from privatizations in the areas of health, education, housing, justice, defense and security need to be examined. The government has earmarked most of those funds to buy part of the debt, to finance current expenses and to pay social insurance costs. This will probably change as the different electoral processes come closer since these investments have a high rate of return socially.

The question now is whether the community will ratify its initial acceptance of the model and the changes which have occurred since 1989. Ratification will be obtained as the goals originally proposed are fulfilled. These include reduction of public fiscal deficit, improvement of the quality and efficiency of services, genuine investments, destination of funds derived from privatizations to the areas of health, education, housing, justice, defense and security, free supply and demand and a sustained reduction of inflation rates. As Samuelson stated, "the consumer is the king ... and with his choice he has the power to obtain what he wants". In the same way, the community makes its assessment and expresses its approval or disapproval of the governmental policies applied when it exerts its constitutional right, the vote. In the forthcoming elections, in 1995, the Argentinean people will have the choice to say either yes or no to ratifying the political and economic model proposed by the administration of Dr. Carlos S. Menem.

Appendix

DEVELOPMENT OF THE PRIVATIZATION PROCESS

From November 1990, when the privatization of ENTEL and *Aerolíneas Argentinas* took place, until the end of 1992, more than thirty state-owned companies were privatized, either by sale or license.

The areas covered were:
Television, radio, railway, petrochemical, hydroelectric, grain elevators, racetracks, hotels, parts of *Yacimientos Petrolíferos Fiscales* (YPF), central and marginal oil areas, 10,000 km of highway and 529 properties.

PRIVATIZATIONS CONCLUDED IN 1990

Companies sold:
Six — Polisur, Petropol, Induclor, Monómeros vinícolos, ENTEL, Aerolíneas.

Leased Services\Companies:
Three — LS 84 Channel 11, television station; LS 85 Channel 13, television station; 10,000 km of national highways.

Oil leases:
Twenty-eight marginal areas (first lot).

During this period, the Argentine companies had the greatest participation in the privatization process with a 40.25 per cent share, followed by Spanish companies (14.76 per cent), American companies (11.98 per cent), Italian companies (8.76 per cent), French companies (6.92 per cent), Chilean companies (5.89 per cent), Canadian companies (2.58 per cent), British companies (2.30 per cent), Belgian companies (0.54 per cent), Swiss companies (0.51 per cent), and others with a participation inferior to one per cent.

Among the Argentine companies, Perez Companc was in first place with a relative participation amounting to 11.50 per cent, followed by Techint (seven per cent), Astra (5.17 per cent), Sideco Americana (2.56 per cent), etc.

PRIVATIZATIONS CONCLUDED IN 1991

Companies sold:
Two — Llao Llao Hotel, Tandanor Naval Shops.

Leased Services/Companies:
Seven — six radio stations; *Rosario-Bahía Blanca* Railway branch (5.287 km).

Oil leases:
Twenty-eight marginal areas (second lot).

Sale of stock of privatized companies:
One — sale of thirty per cent of *Telefónica de Argentina* stock.

YPF SA:
Partnership contracts in four central areas (*Puesto Hernández, Vizcacheras, El Huemul, Tordillo*) and the subsequent enlargement of private participation in these areas and in the central area of Santa Cruz I (*Austral Oil Basin*).

PRIVATIZATIONS CARRIED OUT BETWEEN 1992–1994

1992 was a year of intense privatization:
Fourteen companies sold, nine awarded for operation, twenty-two oil leases and five partnership contracts.

In November and December of this year SOMISA, EDELAP (the power generation company of La Plata), YPF's northeast basin, and Gas del Estado were privatized.

Total income in US $ million:
Cash: 2,335.1
Debt Securities: 41.8 at standard values and 1,089 in its equivalent in cash.

As a consequence of the privatization process, in the period between 1990 and 1994 the Public Treasury collected more than US $9,700-million in cash. At the same time, a substantial reduction in public debt was obtained through the payment of the assets transferred. The state received more than US $6,700-million of foreign debt securities and domestic and foreign public debt securities amounting to approximately US $3,400-million in cash. In addition, the government transferred to the successful bidders the liabilities of the state-owned companies, which amounted to approximately US $2,600-million.

As regards the sale of assets up to July 1994, the participation of Argentinean capital increased to 40.26 per cent, followed by American capital (16.19 per cent), Spanish capital (12.44 per cent), Chilean capital (7.64 per cent), Italian capital (7.47 per cent), French capital (5.84 per cent), Canadian capital (3.17 per cent) and British capital (2.33 per cent). The remaining assets sold correspond to Mutual Investment Funds and to Australian, Swiss, Belgian and Panamanian capital.

Another characteristic of the Argentinean privatization process has been the important participation of European public utilities companies, most of them state-owned companies: Spain (*Iberia, Repsol*, Gas *Natural, Telefónica*), France (*Electricité de France, Cable et Radio*), and Italy (*Stet, Italgas*).

The most interested parties in privatizations have been the state, national and international holding companies, banks providing foreign debt securities and the consultant companies which work for all parties. According to official estimates, consultancy expenses reached US $25-million by the end of 1992, mostly financed by the World Bank. This organization not only provided part of the capital but also took part in the approval of the consultant firms proposed and selected.

BRAZIL

José Guilherme Vasi Werner
Pinheiro Neto — Advogados
Rio de Janeiro, Brazil

INTRODUCTION

Denationalization Program

In the last ten years, the political leaders of almost all developing countries have increasingly regarded privatization of public companies as a prime way of reducing public expenditure and permitting the use of available resources in those sectors of the economy which are in great need of support. Brazil has been no different, despite the long-standing state presence in the economy. This presence, unlike the situation in other countries that underwent privatization, arose at the very outset of the development of basic economic activities. A lack of adequate private capital to build up the infrastructure meant that the major companies in the basic sectors of the economy were mainly state-owned enterprises such as *Banco do Brasil* SA, founded in the early 1800's, and Lloyd Brasileiro, the government-owned shipping company which dates back nearly a century. Many other companies were set up in the first half of this century for the development of activities deemed to be of national interest.

Industrial Development

Brazilian industrial development burgeoned during the 1960s, 1970s and early 1980s, taking firm root under the administration of President Juscelino Kubitscheck, the founder of the city of Brasília, and continuing during the military government regime of 1964 to 1985. During this period, the majority of existing state-owned companies were created by the government either, to serve areas of the economy deemed to be under state monopoly, or to foster the development of certain vital economic areas. Presently, the total number of companies owned by the federal government is quite extensive with some 600 companies. State-owned companies are organized into groups, having in many cases a holding company for those groups which share the same area of activity. The government has accepted minority shareholders in most of the state-owned companies. In addition, non-voting shares in some of these companies are traded on the principal Brazilian stock exchanges.

Only in the last decade has the Brazilian Government taken the privatization issue seriously. In 1981, the administration launched a plan to reduce bureaucracy which set the ground rules for the transfer of state-owned companies to private control. Some privatizations did occur in the period from 1981 to 1984, but only involving companies engaged in less important areas, such as *Companhia Indústrias Brasileiras de Papel* (INBRAPEL) (production of paper) and three subsidiaries of *Petroquisa* (in turn held by *Petrobrás*) in the petrochemical sector. Privatization was implemented by selling shares by either public tender or direct negotiation with the buyer. In 1985, after twenty-one years of military government, a civilian president took office in Brazil. President Sarney launched an ambitious privatization program, establishing that privatization would be achieved by means of freeing capital, selling shares, or liquidation of certain companies. The net result of this privatization program, however, was not significant: only some smaller companies were privatized, such as *Companhia Melhoramentos Blumenau* (hotels) and *Usina Siderúrgica da Bahia — Usiba* (steel production).

The Collor Administration

It was on 15 March 1990 that privatization received the necessary boost. On that date the first president elected by a direct vote in nearly thirty years took office: Fernando Collor de Mello. Collor enacted a number of measures that introduced far-reaching changes in various sectors of the economy, with a view to bringing Brazil into the developed world while also achieving modernity. In fact, President Collor was responsible for the liberalization of the Brazilian economy, which had traditionally suffered from an excessive number of tariff barriers. One of the most important contributions of the Collor administration was undoubtedly the Brazilian Denationalization Program (PND), a well-designed set of rules for loosening state control of the economy. After overcoming initial criticism and distrust engendered in certain sectors, the

PND succeeded in achieving a consensus as regards its efficiency and its importance to the economy. The privatization of companies is now recognized as being one of the principal means of bringing Brazil onto the international scene, redefining priorities so as to benefit those sectors which had previously been overlooked.

LEGAL STRUCTURE

The Brazilian Denationalization Program (PND) was created by Provisional Measure Number 155, subsequently converted into Law Number 8031 of 12 April 1990. Its regulations were issued by Decree Number 99463 of 16 August 1990, and later replaced and repealed by Decree Number 1024 of 29 July 1994.[1] Law Number 8031 and Decree Number 1024 provide the foundation for the legal structure of the PND, based on the following objectives:

(1) Redefinition of the state's strategic position within the Brazilian economy, transferring certain activities needlessly performed by the public sector to private enterprise;
(2) Reduction in public debt, thus strengthening the public sector;
(3) Resumption of investments in any companies and activities transferred to private enterprise;
(4) Modernization of Brazilian industry, boosting its competition and business capacity in the various sectors of the economy;
(5) Concentration of the efforts of the public administration in those activities in which the presence of the state is pivotal to the achievement of national priorities; and
(6) Enhancement of the capital market by widening the availability of securities and democratization of capital ownership in companies involved in the program.

These objectives will be pursued through terminating federal government participation in certain public companies in the public sector. Exception will be made for those companies engaged in activities in areas that are state monopolies. These include communications,

---

1 Decree Number 1024 of 29 July 1994 was replaced by Provisional Measure Number 1070 of 28 July 1995.

telecommunications, mining, and extraction and refining of petroleum, pursuant to the 1988 Federal Constitution, in addition to *Banco do Brasil* SA and the official reinsurance agency.[2] Although the termination of corporate participation through distribution to the public has to date been the sole approach to achieving the PND objectives, privatization may also be effected as follows:[3]

(1) Opening-up of corporate capital;
(2) Increasing the corporate capital of the respective companies, with total or partial waiver or assignment of subscription rights by the federal government or the respective controlling entity;
(3) Corporate transformation, incorporation, merger or splitting;
(4) Disposal, leasing, rental, arrangements for gratuitous use or assignment of corporate holdings or facilities; and
(5) Winding-up of the company or partial deactivation with the resultant disposal of a portion of the holdings.

Privatization Procedures

Whatever the approach, the transfer of public investments to private ownership must follow certain legal procedures. Standardizing the privatization process was selected as an alternative to the issuance of rules on a case-by-case basis, which has occurred in privatizations in other countries. This standardization will permit more effective control over privatization proceedings based on pre-determined rules and regulations. Privatization procedures involve a number of well-defined stages and the participation of various agents, and take an average of 274 days from inclusion of the company in the PND to the actual auction of the state shares to the private sector. The procedure is relatively simple and relies on the function of two agencies which are essential to the Denationalization Program: the PND Directive Committee and the PND Manager.

---

2 Some of the state monopolies mentioned above are presently under review through a series of amendments to the constitution subject to the approval of the congress. Although no changes have been made regarding privatization, some restrictions may be eliminated in the course of 1995.

3 Decree 1024/94, Article 5.

The Directive Committee

The Directive Committee of the Brazilian Denationalization Program is the government agency set up to coordinate execution of the PND and to supervise privatization proceedings in general. Due to recent changes in Brazilian privatization regulations,[4] the Directive Committee became the National Privatization Council (*Conselho Nacional de Desestatização*). The functions and prerogatives of the Directive Committee were not substantially changed.

The National Privatization Council is responsible for indicating to the President of the Republic which companies are to be included under the PND, and for stipulating any adjustments in the conditions for each ongoing privatization. The Council is required to examine and appraise the reports and studies produced by the evaluation teams and the Manager of the Denationalization Fund, defining and approving the best way of carrying out the privatization projects. The Council is mainly responsible for:[5]

(1) Submitting proposals to the President of the Republic for:
   (a) Inclusion of the respective company in the PND;
   (b) The public institution to be appointed Manager;
   (c) The minimum percentage to be paid in cash, against the price of the shares, assets, entitlements or valuables to be disposed of; and
   (d) The criteria to be observed regarding the participation by foreign individuals or corporate entities;
(2) Approving:
   (a) Privatization projects, including definition of the best way to implement them;
   (b) Operational, accounting or legal adjustments and financial rehabilitation of companies required for setting up procedures for disposal, subject to preliminary agreement by the Ministry of Finance;
   (c) The general conditions for disposal of shares, blocks of controlling stock, minority shareholders and other holdings and entitlements of the company, including the minimum price payable for the assets, rights and securities; and

---

4 These changes were implemented by Provisional Measure Number 1070 of 28 July 1995, which replaced Decree Number 1024 of 29 July 1994.

5 Provisional Measure Number 1070 of 28 July 1995.

(d) The terms of incorporation, form of spin-off and transformation of a company included in the PND, when this is the method selected for denationalization;
(3) Deciding on:
(a) Winding-up and liquidating companies included in the PND, or partial deactivation; and the terms for conveyance of assets and payment of the respective corporate commitments; and
(b) The terms of conveyance, leasing, rental, arrangements for free lease or assignment of corporate assets and facilities included in the PND;
(4) Appraising the accounts rendered by the Manager;
(5) Supervising each privatization process, including the conveyances stipulated therein while also ensuring they are clear; and
(6) Suggesting to the President of the Republic the adoption of special activities and the matters thereunder.

The National Privatization Council, despite its quite broad powers, serves in practice to coordinate and supervise. It is politically biased and leaves the task of carrying out and monitoring the progress of the privatization proceedings to the Fund Manager. The Council is directly under the influence of the President of the Republic and is technically connected with the Ministry of Finance. It is composed of only four members who are ministries of state, chaired by the Ministry of Planning. The Chairman of the Council is entitled to cast not only a personal vote but a tie-breaking vote. The Council meets ordinarily once a month and extraordinarily whenever deemed necessary. The quorum for meetings is a majority of the members of the Council and decisions are adopted by a majority vote of those at the meeting. These are then converted into resolutions by the Council and published in the *Official Gazette*.

Denationalization Fund Manager

It is also the responsibility of the National Privatization Council to propose to the President of the Republic the name of the institution to be appointed as Manager of the Brazilian Denationalization Fund. This fund comprises the deposits of corporate shareholdings in companies included in the Brazilian Denationalization Program, and held directly or indirectly by the federal government.[6] The activities of the Manager, currently being performed by the Brazilian Economic and Social Development Bank (BNDES), which is the agency responsible for fostering the administration's macro-economic policies, transcend management of the Fund. The Manager is required to provide supporting services and the information required for decisions by the National Privatization Council. In this respect, the Manager has quite broad powers, ranging from provision of secretarial services to the Council to recommendations as to the best way of paying for the participations to be disposed of. Responsibilities also include operating, accounting or legal procedures required for implementation of the privatization procedures.

Listing economic consultancy and auditing companies for evaluation of the participations to be privatized and following up on the respective reports is another duty of the Manager. In practice, it is the Manager who carries out and arranges for others to comply with the resolutions of the National Privatization Council. The following are the main responsibilities of the Manager:

(1) To provide administrative and operating support for the Council;
(2) To provide any information which might be required by the Council;
(3) To fully disclose all privatization proceedings and to provide any information called for by the authorities;
(4) To submit for preliminary approval by the Council the form and terms of sale of corporate controlling stock, minority stock participations, and other holdings and entitlements, including the minimum price and the proportion of the assets or securities to be paid for in cash;
(5) To recommend to the Council the way in which the assets and securities to be disposed of are to be paid for;
(6) To recommend to the Council the purposes for which the resources from such disposals are to be earmarked;
(7) To arrange for full liaison with the security distribution system and the stock exchanges, so as to foster greater capital distribution of companies included in the PND;
(8) To recommend to the Council which operating, accounting or legal procedures are required for implementing privatization proceedings;

---

6 Provisional Measure Number 1070 of 28 July 1995.

(9) To recommend to the Council, as applicable, the establishment of special categories of shares and subjects that might entail vetoes; and
(10) To recommend to the Council the terms for employee participation in purchasing stock in those companies included in the PND.

The Manager's activities are closely linked to the activities of the Council. The Council defines privatization projects based on expert opinions and studies presented by the Manager. In most cases, the Council has made decisions in line with the alternatives proposed by the technicians and specialized staff of the BNDES, acting as the Manager.

The President of the Republic

Apart from the National Privatization Council and the Manager, the participation of the President of the Republic in decisions on certain matters involved in the PND should be mentioned. The scope of his decision-making authority usually involves the appointment of members to the Council, the inclusion of companies in the PND, and the creation of special category shares ("Golden Shares"). Under Article 10 of Decree 1024/94, the President is also entitled at any time to take cognizance of and decide on any subjects within the scope of the PND, at his exclusive discretion.

The Procedure

The Council and the Manager participate in the privatization proceedings from the moment when the company to be privatized is included in the PND. The company to be privatized is included in the PND by Presidential Decree after being designated for that purpose by the Council. The company receives a Stock Deposit Receipt (RDA), which is non-transferable and non-negotiable. The Manager issues the RDA and, in turn, receives from the depositor mandatory powers to dispose of the stock on the conditions approved by the Directive Committee. If the company to be privatized is a limited liability company, the shareholder will merely be issued a receipt for the instrument granting powers to dispose thereof. The next stage involves contracting by way of a public call for tenders of the groups that are to appraise the company to be privatized. Although it is not actually mandatory to contract third parties for this purpose, this has been the practice in the main privatization proceedings to date.

Independent Appraisals

Each company or business under privatization is subject to at least two independent appraisals by consulting firms with proven economic experience. One consulting company will perform the "A" Assignment, which entails the economic/financial evaluation of the company, evaluation of its market competitiveness, identification and analysis of investment alternatives and recommendations as to the minimum sale price. The consulting company responsible for the "B" Assignment carries out practically the same task as in the "A" Assignment, plus identification of the critical factors in privatization and presentation of model proposals. This second company will also act as the privatization agent, meeting with interested parties and participating in negotiations with creditors.

Since 1993 there has also been a requirement that a "C" Assignment be contracted for. This entails evaluation of holdings and accounting audits plus due diligence investigations. These tasks were previously included in the "B" Assignment. The work of the respective appraisers is monitored by the Manager and, in line with instructions from the National Privatization Council, the Manager determines the form of execution, adapting it until such time as the sale model is approved by the Council. After the privatization proposal has been approved, it is then the responsibility of the Manager to publicly disclose information concerning the company to be privatized. This information takes the form of a public announcement in the *Official Gazette* of the Federal Executive. Furthermore, two newspapers circulated nationwide must contain a variety of information on the company, including data from the appraisal surveys and the form of disposal. The disposal is usually carried out by public auction at a special trading session. The auction in question is open only to qualified investors represented by their brokers. Their tenders must contain an indication as to payment in cash or by means of privatization scrip, which refers to various types of government debt. Although privatization scrips are generally overvalued, purchasers have usually opted to use them.

Forms of Payment

According to Decree 1024/94, apart from the Brazilian legal tender ("real"), all net and certain credits with the federal government or entities controlled thereby (including some entities already extinguished, provided they are eligible for guarantees or cosigning by the National Treasury and can be renegotiated by the Ministry of Finance) are acceptable forms of payment for government purchase of corporate holdings. Credits already accepted at auctions held previously are also acceptable. In specific cases, however, the President of the Republic is entitled to stipulate the means of payment to be accepted for the conveyance of holdings, and determine the inclusion of new means of payment.

Currency and Scrip

The following privatization currency and scrip are currently accepted as forms of payment:
(1)   Cash;
(2)   Secured federal debts, guaranteed by the Treasury;
(3)   Privatization certificates;
(4)   Debentures of Siderurgia Brasileira SA — *Siderbrás*;
(5)   Agrarian debt securities;
(6)   Securities issued by the Brazilian Development Fund;
(7)   Mortgage notes issued by *Caixa Econômica Federal* (a state investment bank); and
(8)   Foreign debt securities.

Inclusion among the types of privatization currencies of a number of federal debt securities reflects the administration's willingness to resort to considerable offsetting of credits. This is achieved via the exchange of government debts for corporate participation in the privatized companies. Acceptance of more than a single quasi-currency (with often unrealistic face values) has engendered the need for discounting the face values so that all such currencies can be used on an equal footing. The practical upshot was that some foreign debt ^securities were subject to a twenty-five per cent discount on their face value. Prominent among the forms of payment accepted in denationalization proceedings are the government's domestic debt securities. These represent foreign debt privatization certificates (CPs) and were created for the specific purpose of ensuring the marketability of companies to be privatized and to help compensate for excess liquidity.

Privatization Certificates (CPs)

CPs are certified securities issued by the National Treasury that are not negotiable and have no stated date of redemption. To force holders to use them in privatization proceedings, the law stipulates that they have a substantial medium and long-term index of devaluation. Purchase of the first CP was mandatory for financial institutions, open and closed private social welfare entities, and insurance and capitalization companies, thereby inducing the transfer of net revenue from these entities to the privatization effort.

Foreign Debt Securities

Acceptance of foreign debt securities played an important role in paving the way for converting debt into investments in privatized companies. In certain cases, acceptance of the securities was linked to a discount of twenty-five per cent on their face value, as in the case of the Depositary Facility Agreements (DFAs), and to the keeping of funds invested in Brazil for a twelve-year period. Securities will be regulated on a case-by-case basis, through a resolution of the Brazilian Monetary Council (CMN), which is also charged with stipulating the discount level to be adopted. Under Decree 1024/94, the lock-in term on funds invested in Brazil via conversion of foreign debt bonds was reduced to six years. It should be noted that the participation of foreign interests in privatization proceedings, previously restricted to forty per cent of the total voting capital of the company under privatization, can now be up to 100 per cent of the voting stock, except if specifically ruled otherwise by the Executive Branch. Foreign capital is still subject to restrictions in certain economic sectors, and may therefore be restricted in privatization proceedings involving companies operating in such sectors.

Privatization Funds

The establishment of the currencies and scrip that are acceptable as forms of payment for privatized participations has given rise to the development of privatization funds. These funds, set up with a view to attracting investors to the PND, may be compared with mutual stock investment funds and bring together investors holding certain kinds of privatization currencies. There are currently funds in existence for practically all privatization currencies and the relevant rules are defined by the Brazilian Securities Commission (CVM).

Earmarking of Privatization Funds

Privatization funds must be earmarked by their holder for settlement of the latter's debts to the public sector.[7] More specifically, cash and credit funds received in payment of holdings disposed of under the PND are required to be earmarked for the purchase of National Treasury notes, and must be used for repayment of the funded federal public debt issued by the National Treasury. They must also be utilized for defraying programs and projects in the areas of science and technology, public health, national defense, public security and the environment. The earmarking of privatization funds reflects the concern of the legislative branch in ensuring compliance with the PND objectives by directing both efforts and funds toward less economically developed sectors and activities.

Employee Participation

A major PND goal is to foster employee participation within the companies to be denationalized. In an attempt to achieve this, a certain number of shares representing control of the company is offered to both current and retired employees. In certain cases, the remaining stock left over after having been offered to the employees is made available to social security foundations or employee associations. This employee participation occurs in cases involving control conveyance, and is encouraged in order to more widely distribute corporate capital and to strengthen the capital market pursuant to the PND objectives.

---

7 Decree 1024/94, Article 41.

Means for Ensuring Compliance with PND Objectives

As mentioned above, Brazil has adopted a system of privatization founded on special legislation applicable to all privatization proceedings, with a view to ensuring more transparent proceedings and more efficient results. The legislation accordingly contains certain provisions that, apart from establishing strict rules and procedures to be followed in each privatization process, permit both internal and external control mechanisms to regulate the actual privatization proceedings. All such control mechanisms, though differing to some extent in nature and scope, serve a common purpose, i.e., they ensure that the PND objectives are achieved. Of course, certain PND agencies exert, to the extent that is feasible, continuing control over privatization proceedings. Such control, however, is routine by nature, resulting from strict observance of the prerogatives of each agency, but without the intervention of special mechanisms such as external auditing and enactment of special stock categories.

External Auditing of Privatization Proceedings

Pursuant to PND legislation, all privatization proceedings must be audited by an independent outside auditor registered with the CVM and contracted through a public auction. It is the responsibility of the external auditors to check and certify compliance with the rules established in the public announcement of share disposal for all of those involved in the proceedings. Auditors are further required to draw up the report for the National Privatization Council.

Creating Special Stock Categories

Another system of checks has been set up by the legislative branch so as to ensure in certain cases the lasting effects of the objectives achieved by the PND. This system entails the authority vested in the President of the Republic to decide on the creation of special shares (Golden Shares) in the corporate capital of an already privatized company. The specific purpose of the system is to give the federal government veto powers over certain public interest topics. As stipulated by law, Golden Shares may be created only when clearly justified, and the public interest must always be respected.

Only the federal government may subscribe for such Golden Shares. It is the duty of the National Privatization Council to suggest when Golden Shares should be created, specifying the exact number to be issued and the topics subject to veto, plus the manner in which these shares are to be acquired. The Council must seek expert advice when taking any decisions in this regard. Only one of the privatization proceedings concluded to date (*Companhia Eletromecânica Celma*) has used Golden Shares. This was done to ensure that the company would continue to operate in the strategic sector of design, construction, repair and checking of aircraft engines, tooling, instruments, parts and components for a further ten years at least.

Subordination to the Ministry of Finance

In addition to the aforesaid methods of ensuring compliance with the PND objectives and proper performance of the respective proceedings, legislation also provides for the subordination of the companies under the PND to the Ministry of Finance. This subordination was intended to avoid the undue influence of certain activities on the amount and conditions of the companies to be privatized. Therefore, administrators of a company holding a company under the PND require express authorization from the Ministry of Finance to:[8]

(1) Open capital for public subscription;
(2) Increase corporate capital through subscription for new shares;
(3) Waive subscription rights;
(4) Float stock-convertible debentures or issue any other securities in Brazil or abroad;
(5) Promote spin-offs, mergers or incorporations;
(6) Sign shareholders' agreements or any corporate commitments, or waive any entitlements stipulated thereunder;
(7) Sign or reformulate financing contracts or commercial agreements for a term of more than three months, or any other transactions that do not correspond to normal corporate operations; and

---

8 Decree Number 1024/94.

(8) Acquire or dispose of those assets which exceed five per cent of the company's net worth.

CONCLUSION

Despite all the precautions adopted and the detailed nature of the legislation, the Brazilian privatization program has not been free from problems, especially in view of the fact that its results affect employees, professional categories and leadership entities in the various sectors of the economy, and above all public interests. On occasion, certain minority factions (with greater and lesser influence) have felt jeopardized by the transformations imposed by the PND, and have availed themselves of all means in their power to try and delay or even halt privatization. Though some programs have been held up or canceled at the behest of the administration or of the President of the Republic, the reaction against the PND has mainly taken the form of court actions. According to the 1993 Directive Committee Annual Report these have primarily been lodged by minority groups on the grounds of:
(1) The legitimacy of the PND's power to issue regulations;
(2) The absence of provisions regarding the allocation of resources;
(3) The failure to recoup public funds;
(4) The conversion of domestic debt securities at face value;
(5) The sale of shares to employees at a discount;
(6) The lack of democratization of the capital involved; and
(7) The utilization of privatization currencies.

Notwithstanding these minority pressures, the Brazilian Denationalization Program has produced quite positive results to date. Since 1991, shares in the corporate capital of thirty-two different companies have been disposed of, with profits equivalent to US $8-billion. In eighteen of these privatizations, stock offers were made to employees, who acquired nearly US $300-million in minority holdings in the companies where they had been working. In Brazil, privatized companies under the control of private enterprise have shown better results than when under state control.

The PND has been definitively consolidated, and has helped reduce and redistribute public debt on a quite significant scale. The increased competitiveness of the privatized companies and the democratization of their capital are already showing noteworthy results. One good example of this is the iron and steel sector, previously state-owned but now almost entirely privatized, which has displayed excellent results in terms of productivity and efficiency, and which is no longer a drain on Brazilian taxpayers. Undoubtedly, the greatest merit of the PND lies in its achievement of a well-organized and ongoing effort toward reducing government presence in the economy for the first time in the history of Brazil. This alone represents significant progress.

Brazil is currently a nation in quite an optimistic frame of mind. Its economy is rated among the ten largest in the world and, despite serious domestic and foreign problems such as inflation, external debt, graft, outsized bureaucracy and extremely disproportionate income distribution, it has been growing at a steadily impressive rate. In 1993, for instance, notwithstanding inflation of 2,497.15 per cent, the GNP grew by 4.96 per cent. Since July 1994, when the Real Plan sponsored by the then Minister of Finance made its debut, Brazil has succeeded in slashing inflation, thereby permitting the resumption of long-range strategic planning and the entry of additional foreign investment. This has been facilitated by the concomitant gradual liberalization of the economy which started under the Collor administration.

With inflation apparently under control and implementation of the Real Plan ensured by the election of its original author, Fernando Henrique Cardoso, to the Presidency, expectations for the next few years are very high. Under the new administration, Brazil will now commence the quest to consolidate its position among the most modern and efficient economies in the world. One of the main instruments for achievement of this objective will undoubtedly be the privatization program already under way. The Cardoso administration is promising to put new life into the PND, extending it to all sectors of the economy and to public utilities, so as to meet the need for investing in the infrastructure, especially in the sectors of railroad transportation and distribution of electric energy.

Ultimately, prospects are highly favorable. State monopolies are now under serious attack. Despite the difficulty of abolishing them or even eliminating some of the restrictions on foreign capital, there are unmistakable signs that the new administration will spare no political effort in its attempt to do away with these traditional roadblocks to a free economy. It is a bit premature to engage in speculation, but it is to be hoped that the PND will play a key role in Brazilian economic growth over the next few years, both ensuring the funding needed for new investments and contributing to the modernization and development of certain sectors of the economy. It is also somewhat premature to conclude that those factions hostile to the PND have abandoned their efforts to undermine the privatization program, and there will undoubtedly be future attempts to halt privatization, mainly through the courts. However, it is a certainty that any litigation will be countered by an administration that is deeply committed to fostering the development of Brazil in all possible ways.

BULGARIA

Yavor Vesselinov Manoilov and
Arno Artune Mamasian
Ciela
Sofia, Bulgaria

INTRODUCTION

The privatization legislative system in Bulgaria dates back to 1992 with the passing of the Law on Transformation and Privatization of State-Owned and Municipal Enterprises. Until now, this law has undergone only one considerable amendment, adopted in June 1994.

It should be pointed out that the Bulgarian privatization legislation is not contained solely in the basic privatization law. The Council of Ministers has adopted a number of statutory acts supplementary to the law under legislative delegation. These statutory acts are in conformity with the rules and the essential principles of the privatization law. They detail the privatization process from both the point of view of the competencies of the state administration and also from the point of view of the legal opportunities of the physical persons and private legal entities who shall bear the rights and assume the obligations in connection with the privatization of state-owned and municipal property.

Bearing in mind that the subject matter of each privatization transaction is state-owned and municipal property, the following is a brief *resumé* explaining the legal and organizational means by which the state is carrying out its economic activities.

By virtue of Article 61 of the Trade Law, a state-owned and municipal enterprise can be set up in the form of a one-man limited liability company or a one-man joint-stock company. According to Paragraph One of the additional provisions of the Law on Transformation and Privatization of State-Owned and Municipal Enterprises, "State-Owned" and "Municipal Enterprises" within the meaning of this law shall mean a legal entity carrying out business activities and whose capital is owned by the state or a municipality. In the same sense as the Trade Law, it is pointed out that state and municipal enterprises also have the right to set up other commercial companies or groups of companies. The conclusion is that the legal means for the execution of economic activities by the state are through commercial companies in the form settled by the Bulgarian Trade Law. Of course, along with the general provisions provided for the commercial companies there are some provided as special regulations (*lex specialis*) which define the legal status of these companies.

As a rule, the state-owned and municipal enterprises can be in the form of one-man limited liability companies or one-man joint-stock companies. These are named "one-man" companies since their capital as a whole is the property of a single owner, that is, the state. The latter is a logical corollary from the fact that these companies originate from previous enterprises, which were entirely state-owned properties.

Of course, there will be no obstacle to the formation of joint ventures with respect to property and in that case the state will not hold the majority block of shares. There are some companies of this kind and their legal regime resembles the status of companies with a total state participation or the status of private commercial companies, depending on the percentage proportion between the share of the state and that of the other participants, shareholders or partners.

It is of great importance to point out that, after the formation of the commercial companies in which the state is the only shareholder or partner, a substantial amendment in the legal status of state-owned property was introduced. Until the reformation of the state-owned enterprises into one-man commercial companies, the state was the sole owner of a property complex such as the state-owned enterprises basically were. When the one-man state-owned companies were established, the state lost its owner's rights over the property of the enterprise. In Bulgarian law, just like in most European legal systems, a commercial company holds the capacity of a trader, no matter what the subject of its activities.[1]

As the property rights over the real estate of the enterprises changes, the state becomes a sole shareholder and a partner in the newly set up companies. This evolves from the logical conclusion of Article 1, Paragraph 3 of the Law on the Transformation and Privatization of State-Owned and Municipal Enterprises which specifies the legal definition of the term "privatization". According to this law:

> "... the privatization of state-owned and municipal enterprises is the transferring to physical and corporate entities of the following:

---

[1] Trade Law, Article 63.

"(1) Shares and stocks, property of the state, of municipalities and commercial companies;

"(2) Entire enterprises or separate parts thereof and property of liquidated enterprises or sites under construction;

"(3) State or municipal premises not used for living purposes except flats, apartments, houses and those premises not included in the structure of the state; and

"(4) Municipal enterprises which are designated for certain economic activities such as shops, work rooms, stores, service parlors and department stores."

As a consequence, there follows the conclusion that the entity which the state, on behalf of its authorized representatives, has the right to transfer in compliance with the terms of the privatization transaction, and which happens to be the subject matter of the same transaction, are the stocks and shares from the state-owned enterprises or such concrete subjects as buildings, together with the stock-in-hand and the machines left over from the liquidated enterprises or properties as a whole, taken from the economic unit. Certainly, it should immediately be stated that the state, in accordance with the privatization transaction, also has the right to transfer the property over to the commercial enterprise as a whole. The Bulgarian Trade Law defines the commercial enterprise not as a subject but as an object of the law.[2]

STATE DECISION-MAKING AUTHORITIES

Generally speaking, as far as the privatization of state property is concerned, it is necessary to be precise about who, in fact, is a party to the privatization transaction on behalf of the state, that is, who expresses the will for the transfer of the state-owned property to a third person? In accordance with Bulgarian Privatization Law, the decision-making authorities who are able to

---

[2] Trade Law, Article 15.

proceed with the possible privatization of a particular state-owned enterprise and who can conclude the privatization transaction are as follows:
(1) Unified branch ministries and committees which, by virtue of Decree Number 155,[3] constitute owners on behalf of the state of the capital of the state-owned commercial companies. For example, these are the Ministry of Trade and the Ministry of Heavy and Light Industry.
(2) The Privatization Agency, which is a specialized institution on privatization, functioning as an organizer and supervisor in the process of privatization;
(3) The Privatization Agency after the approval of the Council of Ministers;
(4) The Council of Ministers with respect to the enterprises included in the list for mass privatization.

The criteria for the distribution of responsibilities is the balance sheet value of the long-term assets of the companies. If the balance sheet value of the long-term assets is not more than Leva (L) 70-million, the competence is a matter of the branch ministries and, in the case of the balance sheet value exceeding L 70-million the specialized institution in charge of that privatization transaction shall be the Privatization Agency. For a certain number of enterprises, determined by the Council of Ministers, the competence of the Privatization Agency shall be subordinated to the approval of the Council of Ministers. This latter body, as mentioned above, is the decision-making institution authorized to include a certain company in the program for mass privatization.

INVESTORS

As for the other party to the transaction, that is, the investor, this could be either a Bulgarian physical or corporate entity, or a foreign one. Regarding Bulgarian corporate entities, there is one limitation

---

3 Issued on 14 August 1992, *State Gazette*, Number 68, 21 August 1992, Article 2, as amended by Decree Number 29, 11 February 1993, *State Gazette*, Number 14, 19 February 1993, passed by the Council of Ministers as to enterprises within their respective specialized areas of responsibility.

in Article 5, Paragraph 4, of the Law on Transformation and Privatization of State-Owned and Municipal Enterprises. The latter reads:

> "Corporate entities with more than fifty per cent state or municipal participation shall not take part in the privatization of the state-owned enterprises unless they have previously received the written consent of the Privatization Agency for each case."

Two major points for discussion should be mentioned:
(1) There are no obstacles for a foreign corporate entity with more than fifty per cent participation to take part in the privatization process; and
(2) The limitation of Article 5, Paragraph 4, from the law shall not be valid in the cases when a certain corporate entity, included in that limitation, receives the consent of the Privatization Agency. In compliance with Article 2 of the Law on Economic Activities of Foreign Persons and Protection of Foreign Investments (LEAFPPFI), a foreign person is defined as:
  (a) A corporate entity, registered abroad;
  (b) A company other than a corporate entity, registered abroad; or
  (c) A person holding foreign citizenship and a permanent residence abroad.

The fact that a certain person has foreign status is of importance in relation to Article 9 of LEAFPPFI, which defines foreign investments as being:
(1) Stocks and shares, property of a commercial company;
(2) Property rights and limited real estate property rights;
(3) Ownership of an enterprise;
(4) Deposits in banks;
(5) Bonds, treasury bonds and other securities, issued by the state or Bulgarian corporate entities; and
(6) Credit, borrowed for more than five years.

FOREIGN INVESTMENT PROVISIONS

In compliance with Article 9, Paragraph 2, of LEAFPPFI, the ownership of real estate properties by foreign companies with an

interest of more than fifty per cent is deemed to be a foreign investment. This could be interpreted in two separate ways:
(1) LEAFPPFI makes a provision for the registration regime of foreign investments to be applied for through the Ministry of Finance; or
(2) The activities enumerated in Article 9 of LEAFPPFI, which the law considers to be foreign investments, are the regular legal means used during the privatization of state-owned enterprises, that is, buying stocks from the enterprise when privatization is ongoing and buying a commercial enterprise as an entity of rights.

It is important to point out that in LEAFPPFI there are provisions which aim to protect foreign investments. One of the guarantees for the protection of foreign investments is the provision that the property of a foreign person can only be expropriated by the state in times of national emergency when no other alternative exists.

The privatization transaction is the last element of the whole process of privatization and is the culmination of considerable legal work. With regards to the legal work which precedes the privatization transaction it should be noted that it is the precondition for the conclusion of a valid privatization transaction.

THE PRIVATIZATION PROCESS

The first step necessary in the privatization process is for the authorities to institute proceedings for the privatization of a certain enterprise. The proceedings shall start after the issue of a decision or an order which are liable to promulgation in the *State Gazette* and in at least two major daily newspapers. The act by which the privatization proceedings shall be instituted is a matter of decision by the privatization competence of the authority in charge.

The law defines who can authorize the commencement of privatization proceedings in a certain enterprise. This includes the authorities in charge of the management of the companies (the manager in a limited liability company or the board of directors in a joint-stock company), the employers and officers of the company and the Privatization Agency. If the Privatization Agency is not the competent authority for the particular enterprise, the authority then rests with the leaseholders and lessees.

Without doubt, there should be no problem for a person intending to invest in a certain enterprise to make a request to the duly authorized institution for privatization. There is no requirement for the referred authority to make a decision within a one-month term and, respectively, there shall be no requirement for that same authority to give a reasonable motive. On the other hand, the above requirements are obligatory when there is an initiative for starting the privatization proceedings by those persons mentioned in Article 4, Paragraph 2, of the Law on the Transformation and Privatization of State-Owned and Municipal Enterprises.

EVALUATION OF ASSETS

After the privatization proceedings are instituted, there follows a legal analysis of the state-owned enterprise concerned and an evaluation of its assets. The legal analysis contains research on the documentation of the enterprise which is aimed at revealing the legal state of the enterprise and any legal problems related to it. This legal analysis will also include suggestions for the solution of existing problems.

The evaluation of the enterprise by the methods determined in the law and the by-laws.[4] The evaluation shall be made by authorized persons appointed by the Privatization Agency and is an extremely important element of the privatization proceedings.

Article 27 of the Law on the Transformation and Privatization of State-Owned and Municipal Enterprises makes provisions that the initial selling price of the shares, the initial price at the auctions and the offered price for the organization of tenders or negotiations shall be defined on the basis of the evaluation price of the enterprise.

As already mentioned, the privatization transaction might have for its subject shares and stocks from the commercial company, that is, an entity of rights, obligations and actual relations. A

---

4 Regulations on the evaluation of the sites in proceedings of privatization, Law on the Transformation and Privatization of State-Owned and Municipal Enterprises, Article 5.

subject matter of the transaction could also be separate from an enterprise in privatization proceedings.[5]

Chapter 5 of the Law on the Transformation and Privatization of State-Owned and Municipal Enterprises is entitled, "Sale of Shares and Stocks Owned by the State and Municipalities". From the title it might be assumed that this chapter represents only one commercial/privatization transaction, namely the sale of shares of limited liability companies or stocks from joint-stock companies. However, this chapter includes some Paragraphs which have a more general meaning and could be applied also in the sale of a commercial enterprise. For example, Article 21 of the Law on the Transformation and Privatization of State-Owned and Munucipal Enterprises states that after the passing of the privatization decision it might be prohibited to complete regulatory transactions with the long-term assets of the enterprise, the conclusion of contracts for shareholding, co-operative work, guarantees for takings and contracts for credit, except with the permission of the respective authority pursuant to Article 3. These provisions refer to all the cases when privatization proceedings are instituted and have the purpose of blocking the possibility for transfer of the property rights belonging to the company for the period from the beginning of the privatization proceedings until the sale of that property. The latter is a guarantee for the potential buyers and serves to obviate the risk of gaining less than initially declared in the transaction.

INSTRUMENTS OF PRIVATIZATION

Article 25 of the Law on the Transformation and Privatization of State-Owned and Municipal Enterprises determines the privatization instruments by which property rights owned by the state should be transferred when privatization takes place. These instruments are as follows:
(1)   An open offering;
(2)   A public auction of the block of shares;
(3)   A publicly invited tender;

---

5 Law on the Transformation and Privatization of State-Owned and Municipal Enterprises, Article 1, Paragraph 3.

(4) Negotiations with potential buyers; and
(5) Purchase of the company or a part of it by the officers and the workers through the sale of blocks of shares according to a contractually defined schedule in ten-year stages.

A closer look at some of these techniques of the privatization process is necessary.

A Public Auctioning of Blocks of Shares

This technique is legally regulated and has been adopted by the Council of Ministers.[6] The privatization technique will be subject to the decision of the authority holding the privatization competence. The actual site to be privatized is decided by a duly appointed act or decision which has to be issued within one month from the proclamation of the privatization evaluation.[7]

Public Auction

The decision for public auction must contain the following:
(1) The name and description of the subject of privatization;
(2) The type of auction;
(3) The initial price;
(4) The amount of the deposit; and
(5) The method of payment and required collateral.

The regulation on auctions obliges the respective authority to publish an announcement for that auction in one local, two national and daily newspapers. The announcement has to contain the items mentioned above and the information about the fee for the auction documentation, the place and the terms for inspection of the site and the place, date and time of the auction.[8] The auction must take place after thirty

---

6 Regulation on auctions, promulgated in the *State Gazette*, Number 50, 1992, amended and supplemented in Numbers 9 and 30, 1993.

7 The Law on the Transformation and Privatization of State-Owned and Municipal Enterprises, Article 20.

8 Regulation on Auctions, Article 4, Paragraph 1.

days from the last publication of the announcement. It is of interest to point out the content of Article 6, Paragraph 2 of the regulation on auctions. It states that if only a single person attends the auction, it shall be postponed for one hour and should no other person appear after that time, the auction may not take place and a written record of that should be drawn up. Should this happen, a new auction must be organized and the terms and the circumstances of it must be defined by the authority in charge. If only one person attends the second auction, by virtue of Article 6, Paragraph 5 of the regulation on auctions, that same person shall be declared the winner of the auction.

The auction might be conducted through an open or a secret bidding. As a rule, the auction winner shall be the one who offers the highest price regardless of whether he has given that price secretly in an envelope or openly by bidding the highest price. The contract for sale shall be concluded with the person who has won the auction within two weeks after the auction has taken place. That term shall be extended if a complaint is lodged by another participant at the auction claiming an irregularity in the auctioning procedures.

THE PUBLICLY INVITED TENDER

The publicly invited tender is one of the most commonly used privatization techniques. The Council of Ministers has adopted a regulation on tenders[9] which specifies the order and the terms for holding tenders. In compliance with Article 2, Paragraph 1, of the Regulation, the decision for privatization by a tender must be given by the competent privatization authority. The name and description of the object of the tender must be stated and the terms of the tender must be made explicit. These include the following:
(1)   The obligation to preserve the economic activities and the same productivity functions of the enterprise;
(2)   The obligation to preserve and increase employment;
(3)   The making of new investments;

---

9 Promulgated in the *State Gazette*, Number 68, 1992, and amended in Number 30, 1993.

(4) The obligation to keep and recover the environment;
(5) The type of privatization and the time period for the complete transfer of the property; and
(6) The period during which the new owner shall be forbidden to transfer the property.

The terms of the tender are decided by the relevant authorities and are considered to be complete. Generally, in the present privatization practice in Bulgaria, the terms of the tender are a question of consideration for the authorities in charge of the privatization. As to the privatization proceedings, particular stress is placed on the period during which the new owner has no right to sell the object of the privatization. From a juridical point of view, that means a prohibition for further dispositions with the object of the privatization. Moreover, this prohibition for disposal also covers the prohibition for institution of mortgage on the real estate property included in the enterprise, in other words, a pledge of chattels. The purpose here is to stop any speculation with the privatized object through rapid resale at a higher price. From another point of view, such prohibitive clauses happen to be the most difficult ones for the managers of the enterprises since they are deprived of the opportunity to receive credits which could effectively be secured by a mortgage or a pledge on the properties and chattels of the enterprise.

NOTIFICATION AND DOCUMENTATION

It should be emphasized that the competent authority is obliged to publish a notification in at least two national and one local newspapers. It is obligatory that the notification state the term for the submission of the tender offerings, the amount (or fee) for receiving the documentation of the tender, the amount of the deposit and the place and the method for inspection of the site.

The documentation for the tender shall contain the offered price corresponding to the objective of the tender.[10] In accordance with the regulations, the tender offers shall be submitted in a sealed envelope. It is of great importance for the participant in the tender

---

10 Regulation on Tenders, Article 4, Paragraph 2.

to know what the content of the offer is. Article 6 of the regulations on tenders requires the following to be included in the offer:
(1) Representation of the candidate;
(2) Name of the object of the tender;
(3) Details of the requirements for participation in the tender;
(4) A projection for the economic development of the object including marketing, technology, organization, social and ecological policy in order to explain how development will be realized;
(5) Price and terms of payment; and
(6) Type of privatization and the period for the full transfer of the property if these are not specified in the decision for privatization.

The authority which is competent to announce the winner in the tender is the privatization authority. The assessment shall be made on the basis of the official report of the tender committee.[11]

The tender, being one of the privatization instruments, is certainly a much more flexible way of doing business. The major criterion for the announcement of the potential buyer is not the highest price offered for the object. On the contrary, it might be the case that the tender is won by a candidate who offers a lower price but has included in his offer more industrious plans for the development of the enterprise with regards to more investments in it and plans for preserving and increasing employment.

As for the contract of sale, it must be concluded in written form. No state or local fees for the transmission of the property need be paid.[12]

NEGOTIATIONS WITH BUYERS

Negotiations with a potential buyer represent one of the most common instruments in the privatization practice of Bulgaria up to now. As a characteristic feature it can be said that this kind of privatization instrument is not regulated by a duly appointed legal act as with auctions and tenders. To a certain extent, the negotiations with a potential buyer representing a privatization

---

[11] Regulation on Tenders, Article 11, Paragraph 1.
[12] Regulation on Tenders, Article 14 .

instrument have something in common with the elements involved for the execution of the tender. The elements necessary for the execution of negotiations are: an offer from the persons interested, the price offered by them, the terms of payment, the business plan for the enterprise and all the other important elements from the future privatization transaction. The final assessment of the privatization authority shall be based on all the statements of the potential buyer.

OPEN OFFERING

As far as open offering is concerned, it should be mentioned that this privatization instrument ranks as the least successful experience in the privatization practice. Essentially, it refers to the trading off of blocks of shares on the stock market or to their open offering to corporate and physical bodies either by using a bank or another financial institution. The relations between the bank and the privatization authority shall be arranged according to the provisions of the mandatory contract.

Usually that instrument is combined with another one as, for example, with the tender. In that case the privatization authority privatizes the monitoring block of shares in favor of a buyer who is selected according to the terms of a competition, and the rest of the shares of the company shall be traded off by means of an open offering. Here it should be observed that except for the Privatization Agency, all the other privatization authorities have the right to use the open offering as a privatization instrument only after the approval of the Privatization Agency.

MANAGEMENT BUY-OUT

Together with the other instruments, there is another element in the law. Article 25, Paragraph 1, item 5, from the Law on the Transformation and Privatization of State-Owned and Municipal Enterprises regulates the opportunity for a company's officers and workers to buy the company or a part of it. A block of shares is sold to them according to a contractually prescribed schedule. Evidently this is not another instrument of the privatization but a type of privatization which gives the chance to the officers and the workers from the enterprise. They become the buyers of that enterprise and thus the law provides the possibility of a gradual purchase of blocks of shares.

Together with the acquisition of stocks and shares by means of a privatization transaction, the law provides a possibility for the acquisition of stocks and shares under preferential terms or as a compensation for private property that has been expropriated by the state in the past.

The first case makes it possible that about twenty per cent of the shares and stocks of the company can be acquired by the workers and the officials, bearing in mind that the latter should have worked in the company for a minimum period of time defined by the law. In this case, the shares and stocks shall be sold with a reduction in the price.

With regards to the acquisition of shares and stocks as a compensation, it should be noted that this is a kind of alternative to the restitution of industrial property nationalized after World War II.

The privatization law contains a chapter entitled "Special types of privatization of state-owned and municipal enterprises and separate parts thereof". For the purpose of this law, Paragraph 2 from the Additional Provisions gives the following meaning of a separate part:

> "... a separate part shall mean an organizational structure within an enterprise which is capable of carrying out business activities independently. This includes shops, studios, ships, work-shops, restaurants and hotels".

Article 34 from that chapter states that:

> "State-owned and municipal enterprises may be transferred through:
>
> "(1) Letting for a period of less than 25 years with a purchase option;
> "(2) A management contract with a purchase option or sale to a third party;
> "(3) A different payments sale by pactum reservati domini; and
> "(4) Sale under dilatory or peremptory conditions, such as preserving the subject of the establishment, the number of employees, making investments and meeting concrete business targets."

Although the law considers the items hitherto as a special type of privatization, there is nothing particularly remarkable about them. Here, as in all other types of privatization it is necessary that privatization proceedings be instituted and consequently a legal analysis and evaluation of the assets of the company should be carried out. The privatization law determines that in these cases the buyer of the enterprise shall be elected only through a tender or negotiations and this, in fact, is the only peculiarity.

The privatization transactions listed in Article 34, as already stated above, are not of great peculiarity from the point of view of the prerequisites for their conclusion. The specification here is the content itself, that is, the clauses, of the transaction which regulate certain intricacies as to the contract relations between the state, represented by the privatization authority, and the buyer of the enterprise. These intricacies are different for each kind of transaction listed in Article 34 of the Privatization Law.

LETTING FOR LESS THAN TWENTY-FIVE YEARS WITH PURCHASE OPTION

The most essential point to note in this type of privatization is that the transferring effect is absent, that is, the act of transition of the enterprise's property shall not take place. On the other hand, at the time of the conclusion of the transaction the investor is granted the right to use the movable and immovable property of the enterprise in his capacity as a lessee for the term of twenty-five years and also to direct the management of the enterprise. The difficulties arising from this are two-fold:
(1) The person is a lessee of the enterprise and manages it and, on the other hand, the state preserves the property rights till the moment of the final sale of the enterprise. The state, being the owner, can control the assets of the company and as a whole can execute the supervising control over it which obviously contradicts the interests of the investor; and
(2) Transactions of this kind evidently reveal the legal effect of a composition of two contracts, namely a contract for lease and a preliminary contract for sale of the enterprise. It is most important that the transaction answer the basic question concerning the price at which the lessee shall buy the enterprise. It could be either a price based on the evaluation made just before the conclusion of the contract for the privatization transaction or

that based on the evaluation performed at the moment of the final purchase which could be valued up to twenty-five years from the conclusion of the privatization transaction.

One other element should be noted. The relevant parties to the contract should make it clear whether the lease price paid during the lease period shall be included in the future sale price of the enterprise.

MANAGEMENT CONTRACT WITH OPTION TO PURCHASE OR SELL THIRD PARTIES

As to the practical application of this kind of transaction, there is not a great difference between it and the previously mentioned one. The reason the lessee leases the enterprise is that he wants to exercise control over it with respect to its future purchase. The state preserves the property until the moment of its transmission. This is then followed by what is called by the law a clause for purchase.

It is possible that the relations referring to the management of the enterprise shall be arranged by a mandatory contract, including many specific items. This supplies the guarantee for preserving the interests of the management from the investor's side until the final purchase of the enterprise. This is the same as the letting with a purchase option, that is, the matter of price at which the managed enterprise shall be purchased.

SALE BY PACTUM RESERVATI DOMINI

This type of transaction seems to be performed with less problems. The state preserves the property until the final payment of the enterprise. The property is transmitted to the buyer *ipso jure* after he makes the last payment. This type of privatization lessens the burden on the buyer since he is not obliged to pay the whole price of the enterprise at the time of its purchase.

SALE UNDER DILATORY OR PEREMPTORY TERMS

Transactions of this type subordinate their legal effect to some extent. Essentially, the terms and conditions shall be enforced *ipso jure* whether or not either executed. Bearing in mind the number of difficulties that this type of privatization presents from a legal perspective, it is not very common despite presenting great advantages to the potential investors.

In the same chapter of the Privatization Law where special types of privatization are listed, one essential preferential term used in the privatization process is regulated and is of importance in the smallest enterprises, that is, those which have a balance sheet value not exceeding L 10-million.

The preferential term pursuant to Article 35 from the Privatization Law expresses the possibility that leaseholders and the lessees of the enterprise can purchase the enterprise without an auction or tender. Contracts up to 15 October 1993 must have been concluded and the period of the contract may not have expired at the date of applying for the institution of privatization procedures.[13] Apart from having the right to buy the enterprise under preferential terms, they also have the right to apply for a long-term payment regulated by the Privatization Law.

OBLIGATION TO DECLARE FINANCES

Those persons who take part in the privatization process in compliance with the Privatization Law are obliged to declare the origin of the finances they use when buying enterprises. That obligation is defined in Paragraph 9 of the Transitional and Concluding Provisions of the Law, which reads:

> "Physical bodies and representatives of legal entities shall submit declarations concerning the origin of the funds used in the privatization. They must also submit declarations for income tax, property tax and tax on profits. This declaration outlines financial stability and gives a complete picture of their purchasing power. These persons shall also submit a written agreement to supply all necessary information to the authorities concerning the data in the declarations. Submission of a declaration with false content shall involve criminal liability under the Penal Code."

---

13 The Law on the Transformation and Privatization of State-Owned and Municipal Enterprises, Article 35.

PRIVATIZATION BY INVESTMENT BONDS

The Bulgarian Privatization Law also regulates privatization by means of investment bonds. Privatization by means of investment bonds concerns the transmission of rights over the stocks and shares owned by the companies whose capital is a state property as a whole. Potential investors must satisfy all the requirements detailed by the law and all the other conditions for taking part in that type of privatization process. The privatization by means of investment bonds excludes the principle of market-sale in the selection of the buyer of stocks and shares. Every citizen of Bulgaria residing permanently in the country has the right to buy investment bonds.

In accordance with the privatization law the investment bonds are issued in the form of bond cards. The bond cards themselves are issued by the Council of Ministers. The law regulates that the investment bond should be issued as nominative securities similar to the nominative shares. The special thing in that type of privatization process is that the acquisition of stocks and shares is performed directly through centralized public auctions or through investment funds.

Pursuant to Paragraph 8(b) of the Privatization Law, investment funds may exist in the form of joint-stock companies or co-operative societies. The same law states that citizens have the right to deposit their investment bonds in the investment funds, at their nominative value. The Privatization Law states that, until the passing of the law on investment funds, all investment activities shall be regulated by an Ordinance passed by the Council of Ministers. To date, neither an Ordinance nor a law on investment funds has been passed.

CROATIA

Stefan Pürner
Rödl & Partner
Zagreb, Croatia

INTRODUCTION

Since August 1995, Croatia has regained sovereignty over almost all of its territory. By regaining Slavonia in May 1995 and the Krajina in August 1995, important traffic connections and tourist areas (such as the Plitvice Lakes) were once more brought under the control of the Zagreb government. This will improve economic growth and make privatization in Croatia more interesting to foreign investors. Up to now, foreign business investors had mainly come to Croatia for ventures involving commercial building construction, road construction, and the energy sectors. However, the overall amount of foreign investment is very small in comparison to other former socialist states. Among these countries, Croatia holds the second last place with respect to net foreign capital investments. Only Albania, which is much smaller than Croatia, received less foreign investment.[1]

Presumably, these investments are not only aimed at the Croatian market, but are also aimed at future activities in other parts of ex-Yugoslavia. In addition, the market and its spin-offs are also of great interest. In connection with this, it must be pointed out that Istria, which along with Dalmacija is one of the two main tourist areas located by the sea, in 1994 had already attained the number of tourists it had prior to the war. Taking into consideration Croatia's adverse competition situation among the other former socialist countries, caused by the war, the country would normally offer attractive legal and business conditions for foreign investors. However, this is not the case at present. The Croatian privatization

---

1 Pürner, "Zum Stand der Reform des Wirtschaftsrechts in Kroatien, Teil 2", (The Current Situation of the Reform of Croatian Economic Law, Part 2), *Wirtschaft und Recht in Osteuropa*, (*Economy and Law in Eastern Europe*) 1995, pages 248ff.

system is considered to be less attractive than privatization systems in other Eastern European Countries. For most prospective investors, cases of irregularities in some privatization procedures have caused much concern.

SELF-MANAGEMENT ECONOMY AND SOCIAL OWNERSHIP

To explain Croatia's privatization system it is necessary to take a look back at the Yugoslav workers' self-management system, because this privatization concept is an attempt to overcome the system. However, it often seems that some of the basic ideas of this former system have not yet vanished. The basic concept of the Yugoslav self-management system was that the only justification for decision-making was the actual work performed in the enterprises.[2] Therefore, capital investment as the justification for decision-making in economic matters was excluded until 1988 when capital invested in a company was declared "former work". On the other hand, Yugoslav theory claimed that state property and state-owned enterprises would lead to an even greater exploitation of the workers than private property and private enterprises in the so-called "capitalist" countries.

Therefore, a unique form of ownership was invented. The so-called "social" property should not be owned by one individual but by everyone in order to create the "association of free producers" mentioned in the Communist Manifesto. This social ownership was thus a "non-ownership" without owner. The only property right which could be acquired was a "right to use". As a consequence of this, the decision-making in the state-owned enterprises was, at least formally, transferred to the workers. Depending on the matter in question, the workers decided either through the worker's council or by direct voting. Furthermore, they decided on the use of income. For example, it was under their control to decide whether this income should be reinvested or paid to the workers.

This all led to one significant problem which contrasted with most other former socialist countries where the state was the

---

2 For details on the self-management system and social ownership's effects on enterprise, see Pürner, *Die GmbH als neugeschaffene Investitionsform in Jugoslawien* (*The Limited Liability Company as a New Form of Investment in Yugoslavia*), Regensburg, 1991.

owner. In Croatia, an owner of the enterprises had to be found before the ownership could be transferred to new shareholders. This is the reason why Croatia decided to include the workers in the transformation process of the enterprise. According to the Croatian concept, this transformation is not only the changing of the legal form from a state-owned enterprise to a capital company but also a partial privatization.[3]

THE CROATIAN CONCEPT OF PRIVATIZATION

The following text will refer to share deals only, because up to now no asset deals have occurred in the privatization practice. It must be pointed out that, at least up to now, no former state-owned enterprise has been liquidated.

Nor were any bankruptcy proceedings started, although there were cases in which illiquidity was more than obvious, for example, in the case of the shipyard "3 Maj" in Rijeka which, according to newspaper reports, was without energy for several days in August 1994 since it was unable to pay its energy bill.

Mixed Ownership

Owing to the fact that the workers have been involved in a kind of ownership of the enterprises and have contributed to its current value the Croatian privatization concept stipulates that a part of the value of these enterprises must be transferred to the workers as a form of restitution for their labors. This is in sharp contrast to the well-known East German transformation from state ownership to privatization, where the Treuhandanstalt became 100 per cent owner of the former state-owned enterprises.[4]

---

3 *See* Pürner, "Zum Stand der Reform des Wirtschaftsrechts in Kroatien, Teil 2", (The Current Situation of the Reform of Croatian Economic Law, Part 2), *Wirtschaft und Recht in Osteuropa*, (*Economy and Law in Eastern Europe*) 1995, pages 248ff.

4 Section 1, Paragraph 4, *Gesetz zur Privatisierung und Reorganization des volkseigenen Vermögens* (Act on the Privatization and Reorganization of Publicly-Owned Property).

The Variety of Shareholders

In Croatia, the shareholding structure of the enterprises to be privatized is mixed. The following groups of shareholders normally hold the shares of the enterprise which are earmarked for sale:

Workers and Former Workers

These persons are allowed to buy shares under special conditions.[5]

A second way for the workers to buy shares of former state-owned enterprises was the so-called "transformation of old foreign currency savings". This process had its roots in the fact that many Yugoslav citizens held foreign currency accounts, especially in German marks. This foreign currency was kept by the National Bank in Belgrade. Therefore, after the splitting up of Yugoslavia into several states, this currency was "out of reach". Croatia decided to solve this problem in the future on a state-to-state level. As restitution for their lost savings, the workers received the right to obtain shares for the counter value of their hard currency savings. Furthermore, persons working in state organizations and other institutions which will not be privatized were given the right to buy shares of former state-owned enterprises.[6] Additionally, the possibility to acquire shares in the transformation process was later extended to those citizens injured or crippled during the war.[7] Due to the lack of financial means to restitute these persons for the injuries they suffered, the Croatian Parliament decided that compensation

---

5 Article 5, Paragraph 1, of *Zakon o pretvorbi drustvenih poduteca* (Act on the Transformation of State-Owned Enterprises or the Transformation Act); a partly German translation of this Law by Mirko Bogdanovic/Stefan Pürner is contained in the *Handbuch Wirtschaft und Recht in Osteuropa* (Guide to Economy and Law in Eastern Europe (edited by Stephan Breidenbach, Munich, 1992)). Depending on the time they have worked in the enterprise, the workers were guaranteed lower prices for shares than the nominal value of the shares. In addition, they were allowed to pay in installments.

6 Transformation Act, Article 5, Paragraph 2.

7 Act on Changes and Completions of the Transformation Act, Article 11.

would be given via the privatization process. Recently, there have been plans to develop a similar scheme for refugees of the war.

Pension Funds

The selling of cheaper shares to the workers may be considered as recognition of their former position as joint owners of the enterprise on an individual level. The dispensing of shares to the pension funds for workers and pension funds for individual farmers[8] may be considered as recognition of this common ownership on a more general level. The funds finance their work by the capital they received in the transformation process.

Croatian Privatization Fund

For the privatization process, the most important of the current shareholders is the Croatian Privatization Fund. The Croatian Privatization Fund's tasks and its organization are regulated by the Law on the Croatian Privatization Funds.[9] The Croationa Privatization Fund is obliged by law to sell its shares under Article 31 of the Transformation Act. Concerning the percentage of shares held by the Croationa Privatization Fund, there is no standard percentage. The enterprises had the opportunity to transform autonomously, especially through selling as much of the shares as possible to the workers under Article 7 of the Transformation Act.[10] If an enterprise failed to develop a transformation plan in time, the transformation plan in time, the transformation was performed by

---

8 Transformation Act, Article 5, Paragraph 5.

9 A German translation by the author is contained in the *Handbuch Wirtschaft und Recht in Osteuropa*, (*Guide to Economy and Law in Eastern Europe*), edited by Stephan Breidenbach, Munich, 1992.

10 There are two major works on the transformation of former state-owned enterprises: Jaksa Barbic, Vladimir Kopun, Zoran Parac, *Pretvorba drustvenih poduzeca* (*Transformation of State-Owned Enterprises*), Zagreb, 1992, and *Prirucnik za pretvorbu drustvenih poduzeca* (Guide to the Transformation of State-Owned Enterprises), edited by the Croatian Agency for Reconstruction and Development and the Croatian Chamber of Commerce, Zagreb, 1992.

the Croationa Privatization Fund under Article 9 of the Transformation Act. This led to a great variety in the structure of shareholders in those Croatian enterprises to be privatized. As a rule, it may be said that those enterprises which have a small percentage of workers' shares are either (even by their own workers) considered to be unattractive or that it is very likely that they have a "lazy" management. Bearing in mind that the widespread holding of shares is not very conducive for a take over, it may be said that privatization in Croatia is characterized by a paradox: the easier it is to gain a majority of shares (or even 100 per cent), the less attractive the enterprise seems. If the enterprise is very attractive, the investor will have to negotiate with a number of current shareholders if he wants to acquire a majority of the share capital.

Purchase of Shares from the Croatian Privatization Fund

The shares of small shareholders can be bought either directly from them or at the Zagreb Stock Exchange.[11] The shares held by the Croatian Privatization Fund may be bought either in a public auction or after a public tender.[12] If a company's value is less than the counter value of DM 5-million, the Croatian Privatization Fund may negotiate directly with individual buyers without public auction or public tender.[13]

Concerning enterprises with a value that exceeds the mentioned amount, the Croatian Privatization Fund is permitted to conduct direct negotiations only when a public auction or a public tender did not lead to success. This might change in the future since a number of modifications to the law are currently being discussed. The decision about who to sell the enterprise to must be made on a basis of the following criteria:
(1) Purchase price offered by the buyer;
(2) Currency and terms of payment;

---

11 The Zagreb Stock Exchange has been established but is not yet fully working.
12 Detailed information on the public tender procedure is contained in the brochure *Javno prikupljanje ponude* (Public Collection of Offers), *Male stranice Informatora*, Number 4122–4123, 8 and 9 September 1993.
13 Transformation Act, Article 14, Section 2.

(3) Eventual investment guarantees; and
(4) Development program for the enterprise and its effects on employment.[14]

Practical Problems in Practice

Xenophobia and Political Influence

Theoretically, foreign investors are guaranteed the same treatment as nationals under Article 14 of the Transformation Act. However, it is a "public secret" that Croatian buyers with political connections receive preference. According to the German *Nachrichten für Außenhandel*,[15] edited by the *Bundesstelle für Außenhandelsinformation* (Federal Office for Foreign Trade Information), foreign investors are regularly passed over as far as "the interests of important members of the governing party are involved". This is the case particularly in the tourism industry. The Croatian business magazine *Profit*,[16] reported on the xenophobic feelings surrounding "Italian irredentists collecting Croatian hotels" and on this being a form of economic colonization of Croatia.

Evaluation and Inflexibility in Contract Price Negotiations

In addition, the Croatian Privatization Fund shows no great flexibility in negotiations concerning the contract price. This is of special importance because the contract price suggested by the Croatian Privatization Fund is built on the basis of its own evaluation of the enterprises which has been, at least in a number of cases, unrealistic. Experience shows that the Croatian privatization funds and the companies themselves tend to neglect eventual problems in the enterprises' legal relations, especially as far as real estate is involved. Owing to this, *Nema problema* (no problem)

---

14 Act on Changes and Completions of the Transformation Act, Article 1.
15 *Foreign Trade News*, 8 July 1994.
16 Raic Zasto, *inozemni investori izbjegavaju ulaganje u Hrvatsku* (Why Foreign Investors Avoid Investments in Croatia), August 1994, page 28.

mentality prevalent among the Croatian authorities, it is highly recommendable to perform one's own due diligence research before acquiring a Croatian enterprise.

Unresolved Restitution

Furthermore, the legal situation of real estate is sometimes very unclear. The land registers are very often incomplete or out of date.[17] This is of major importance since Croatia has not yet brought a law on restitution into force. Doing so would resolve the question of real estate expropriated during the Socialist period. Up to now, only a draft of such a law was published.[18] However, this law has been criticized by several authors.[19]

Therefore, major changes of this draft may not be excluded in the further law-making process. Because of this, it is not easy to predict which cases of past ownership will be considered as cases of restitution. In addition, no definite statements on the legal consequences (restitution in nature or in money?) can be made. Therefore, it is highly recommendable to insist on an exemption clause in contracts with the Croatian Privatization Fund.

Purchasing Subsidiaries of State-Owned Enterprises

A second possibility to acquire (parts of) former state-owned enterprises is the buying of shares of subsidiary companies. The former state-owned enterprises were big concerns which performed a widespread variety of activities. To make these different parts of the

---

17 Ivica Grcar Kako, "najbolje zastiti potrazivanje", (How to Secure Claims in the Best Way) *Poslovni svijet* (Business World) 30 August 1995.

18 *Privreda i pravo (Economy and Law)* 1992, page 455.

19 Mladen Zuvela, "Biljeske uz Nacrt Zakona o denacionalizaciji nekretnina", (Annotations to the Law on the Denationalization of Real Estate), *Privreda i pravo* 1992, page 461, and Jadranko Crnic, *Kako se vratiti oduzeto nacionalizacijom, konfiskacijom, agrarnom reformom,* (How to Return What Has Been Taken Away by Nationalization, Confiscation and Land Reform); both authors are judges of the Croatian Constitutional Court.

enterprise more effective in a certain number of cases, subsidiary companies were founded. Most of these companies were organized as limited liability companies. Therefore, it is possible to acquire shares in these enterprises. The main advantage hereby is that these shares are 100 per cent owned by the parent companies. Therefore, the previously mentioned problems caused by the shareholder structure of the former state-owned enterprises themselves can be avoided. Furthermore, the necessary financial investment is smaller in these cases.

However, the business practice between the holding company and the other subsidiaries should be carefully examined. In some cases, the business practice between the various enterprises in the holding have led to disadvantages for the sudsidiaries. For example, sometimes other subsidiaries are, without any necessity, involved in contract relations to third parties. On the other hand, sometimes advantageous delivery or other relations are performed without any fixed contract. In all of these cases, the investor should urge sensible regulation of the various relations within the group.

Conclusion

Unfortunately, it must be stated that already the theoretical concept of privatization in Croatia is not too attractive for foreign investors. In addition, the aforementioned "practical exercises" complicate the acquisition of shares for foreign investors. However, the actual situation could be improved, at least with regard to some of the above-mentioned problems, since major changes to the Transformation Act (or even a new Privatization Act) are being prepared now. Other legal regulations are being discussed whereby the Croatian Privatization Fund will have to show more flexibility in connection with negotiations on the contract price. On the other hand, there are ongoing talks suggesting that a voucher privatization system, inspired by the Czech privatization system, should be introduced.

Evidently, if the current obstacles are removed, Croatia could become a very attractive market for foreign investors. The country offers a widespread variety of industry ranging from tourism to chemical and electric enterprises. The Croatian workforce is relatively highly qualified. Due to the large number of Croats who have worked abroad, knowledge of foreign languages and of Western business is to be found among a great number of citizens. In addition, due to its geographical position, Croatia will most likely become the entrance door to the entire market in former Yugoslavia.

GERMANY

Kerstin Reiserer and Valentin Boll
Melchers, Schubert, Stocker, Sturies
Berlin, Germany

THE URGENT CALL FOR PRIVATIZATION

Anyone who raises the issue of privatization is in good company at the moment. The call for privatization is being made on all governmental levels. The Federal Minister of Finance has referred to situations in which privatization will secure growth and jobs and create new fields of activity, while contributing to capital formation among large sections of the population. The Federal Minister of Economics has advocated a stronger drive towards the privatization of public companies and functions in order to improve Germany's economic position. Due to budget constraints, the former and newly elected government coalition does not see any alternative to privatization. In 1993, the German Social Democratic Party declared before the Bundes-SKG committee that the functions of the communities must be privatized in view of the strained budgetary situation in the communities.

In the past, legal science rarely succeeded in influencing the discussion about privatization of administrative tasks and in objectifying the arguments. On the contrary, politics and economics control the current discussion.[1] If lawyers ask for legal preconditions about decisions on privatization, these so-called "legal sceptics" are discredited as opponents of privatization.

Efforts toward privatization are aimed at various fields as the following examples illustrate: at the national level, the privatization of air traffic control,[2] the privatization of the Bundespost and Telekom,[3] and the privatization of the Deutsche

---

1 Schoch, "Privatisierung von Verwaltungsaufgaben", *DVBl* 1994, pp. 962, 965.
2 Act for amending the Constitution of 14 July 1992, BGBl I, p. 1254 and the Act for amending the Air Traffic Act of 23 July 1992, BGBl I, p. 1370.
3 Bill for reorganization of the post and telecommunications, BT–DR 12/7270.

Bahnen.[4] Furthermore, part of the interests in Lufthansa AG have already been sold, the shares in Telekom will be issued at the beginning of 1995, the Post AG will be sold in 1998 and the Bahn AG is already being prepared for trading on the stock exchange. These are only a few examples of the move toward privatization. The scope of privatization on the national level extends from partial privatization of employment agencies to subsidiary enterprises of the motorways to the field of transportation, particularly the Rhein-Main-Donau-AG.

At local level, the discussion about privatization of public services still continues. Since 1981, the share of public utility undertakings joining in the Association of Local Companies (VKU) and having the legal form of a corporation has increased from one-third to one-half. Accordingly, the share of municipal undertakings by local authorities has decreased from sixty-five per cent to just under forty-five per cent.[5] However, at local level, the capacity for privatization has not yet been exhausted. According to research conducted by *Deutsche Bank Research in Frankfurt* (DB Research), up to eighty per cent of local services can be privatized on a long-term basis with the catalogue of services extending from waste disposal to zoos. DB Research illustrates that there is a developing trend of services which are being forced to privatize. Commercial cleaning and slaughter-houses are the first chosen for privatization. Today, the shift of tasks is extending more and more to sewage disposal, swimming pools, maintenance of green areas, zoos and construction facilities.[6]

In analyzing the arguments in favor of privatizing public enterprises and services, there are, on the one hand, aspects of public order involved and, on the other hand, fiscal aspects which have come to the fore. With regard to public order, there is a link to the structural features and advantages of the market economy. The fiscal aspect refers to the "dictates of limited financial resources", which normally deem private companies to be more economical than public authorities.

---

4 Act for amending the Constitution of 20 December 1993, BGBl I, p. 2089 and the Act for Reorganization of the Railway of 27 December 1993, BGBl I, p. 2378.

5 Koch, "Kommunale Unternehmen im Konzern", *DVBl* 1994, p. 667.

6 Report in *Frankfurter Allgemeine Zeitung*, 26 November 1994: "Kommunen sollen Dienste privatisieren".

A report on the status of privatization in the Federal Republic of Germany would be incomplete if it did not include the peculiarities that have arisen as a result of the integration of the new *Länder* in the economic and social structure of the country. The desired adjustment of the living conditions and economic development in the new *Länder* confronted economic policy with the task of transforming the main part of productive industrial property of the former GDR into private property without delay. This is an essential condition for the operation of a market economy. The purpose of the Trust Act of 17 June 1990 is to fulfill this goal and provide the legal authority to transform the socialistic economy into a private enterprise system and thus change the organizational form under private law.

As a consequence of the revolutionary swing, this legislative decision was to abolish substantial structural elements of the socialistic economic order. Thus, the preamble to this law sets forth the legislative purpose: "to reduce business transactions of the state by way of privatization as soon as possible and to the extent most possible", which is converted into the concise legal mandate in Section 1, Subsection 1, of the Trust Act: "The nationalized property is to be privatized". In this respect, privatization has three meanings:

(1) The transformation of former community-owned enterprises and state-owned enterprises into companies limited by shares;
(2) The provision of sufficient capital resources to these companies; and
(3) The privatization of stock, that is, acquisition by private investment companies.

THE MEANING OF PRIVATIZATION

Although reference is generally made to the single term "privatization", this term encompasses more than one meaning. In current literature. Four basic privatization models are classified as follows:[7]

(1) Organizational privatization comes about where public authorities use the instruments of private law to organize a

---

7 Schoch, "Privatisierung von Verwaltungsaufgaben", *DVBl* 1994, p. 962; von Hageneister, *Die Privatisierung öffentlicher Aufgaben*, 1992, pp. 33 *et seq*.

private institution (GmbH or AG) as a municipal undertaking; since this form of privatization preserves the function as a public function and only changes the form under which it is effectuated, it is referred to as "formal privatization". By replacing the budget system of a state economy with private accounting methods, the efficiency of the function is thought to increase. The right of supervision, however, remains with the public authorities;

(2) Operational privatization is the transfer of operations that were traditionally under the jurisdiction of the public sector to the private sector. State or local enterprises are converted to a private legal form with the option to sell such interests to private parties, either immediately or at some later date. Since this substantive privatization leads to a real reduction of the services offered by the public administration, it is referred to as "real" privatization;

(3) Asset privatization arises when state or locally owned government property is transferred to private entities. This kind of privatization relates mainly to real estate and business enterprises. Public authorities gradually separate themselves from their property by selling their industrial holdings;

(4) Functional privatization is used in situations where both the jurisdiction and responsibility for a particular function remain with the public institution and only the execution of the function is transferred to an administrative agent subject to private law. This model of partial privatization is particularly suitable for the compulsory functions of a community.

Of course, the four basic types of privatization listed above are not exclusive of one another. Any number of variations is possible. Furthermore, all four basic models are also suitable for partial privatizations. Consequently, it is conceivable that the state will separate itself from only a part of its holdings in a company, or that an administrative agency will not establish a municipal enterprise, but rather cooperate with private parties as a GmbH or AG, so that a mixed enterprise will ultimately result. In the course of the discussion about privatization, the idea of partial privatization is of immense importance because it avoids an "all or nothing" solution. The specific jurisdiction of the administrative institution may be preserved while allowing the institution to take advantage of important private resources, for example, financial, technical and management expertise.

CAPACITY FOR PRIVATIZATION AND ITS LEGAL STANDING

The potential for privatization seems almost unlimited. It is the prevailing opinion that, apart from the classic fields like administration of justice, police, military, foreign affairs and administration of finances, all other fields and functions can be privatized.[8] Since it is theoretically possible to obtain by means of privatization vast sums for reorganizing the budget, it is no wonder that the move toward privatization will continue for budgetary reasons.

Privatization of National Property

At the national level, privatization mostly results in transferring state-owned property to private parties. In its February 1994 report on Reduction of Federal Holdings,[9] the federal government maintained that since 1982 it has privatized holdings in the amount of DM 11.6-billion (including special property). As important examples of privatization in the 1980's, the federal government refers to the disposition of industrial companies such as Veba AG, Viag AG, Volkswagen AG, Salzgitter AG, Industrieverwaltungsgesellschaft AG, Deutsche Pfandbrief- und Hypothekenbank AG, Berliner Industriebank AG, as well as Lufthansa AG. Reputable banks estimated the realization of shares in Telekom starting in 1995 at about DM 50-billion. Together with postal service, post bank and railway and the remaining shares in Lufthansa AG, these experts estimate the figure to reach DM 100-billion. The same experts, however, have doubts about whether these amounts can be ultimately absorbed by the German stock market, since it is not used to such volume. Since 1980, shares were issued in an amount between DM 5 and 25-billion annually. The market could reach DM 30-billion for 1994. Amounts of some DM 100-billion are inconceivable for these experts, unless the legislature supports the

---

8 Wagner, "Privatisierung öffentlicher Aufgaben", *KPBl* 1994, p. 359.
9 BT–Dr. 12/6889.

distribution of the shares among private shareholders. It has been suggested that tax privileges like the current regulations for life insurance could set things in motion.[10]

Privatization of Tasks on the Local Level

Particularly at the local level, the model of performing tasks by involving private enterprises relating to compulsory functions of self-government of the local governments plays a role and shows a number of varieties. As a rule, the communities are free to decide which tasks they want to tackle for promoting the common good of the inhabitants and at which point in time. The fact that they not only decide how to handle their tasks, but also whether and at which time they consider it necessary to start them, is an essential part of their right to self-government, which is protected by the constitution. However, to an increasing degree there are exemptions to this principle for complying with a rather extended uniformity of the standard of living and it is provided by law to fulfill certain tasks, for example, construction of schools and fire prevention facilities. These functions of the communities, which are deemed to be compulsory by law, are partly exempted from privatization. The responsible local authorities may only use a subject of private law for performing the task. The responsibility, however, remains with the community. In the field of waste disposal, this kind of privatization has become more and more significant. Throughout Germany an increasing number of tasks of private waste management are transferred to private enterprises, notwithstanding the unanswered questions relating to waste law, local bylaws, law on competition and, not least, constitutional law.[11]

Opposition to Privatization

The continuous trend toward privatization also causes opposition. There is concern that the privatization euphoria in Germany will

---

10 *Wirtschaftswoche* of 14 October 1994, p. 3.

11 Beckmann, "Abfallrechtliche Aspekte bei der Gründung einer kommunalen Entsorgungsgesellschaft", *DVBl* 1993, p. 9.

lead to an extreme liberalist economic situation by disregarding those parties affected by privatization whose rights were previously secure. Thus, the German Post Office Workers' Union has unanimously opposed the privatization of the postal service.

A variety of examinations were made at the commencement of the privatization efforts to determine whether there are direct constitutional barriers against privatization measures.[12] To a large extent, what the results of these examinations have in common is that the constitution provides neither a mandate for nor a prohibition against privatization. As a rule, the decision of privatization is rather incumbent on the legislature and the administration within the legal barriers. Some constitutional considerations, however, are worth noting:

As briefly mentioned above, the question of the legitimacy of privatization at the local level always refers to the local right to self-government.[13] In particular, the so-called compulsory functions, that is, those matters that a community has to take over within the scope of its local self-government, cannot be privatized without limitations.[14]

In addition, a particular privatization measure may also give rise to peripheral constitutional problems. For example, the privatization of the postal service raises problems relating to the confidentiality of mail and telecommunications under Article 10 of the constitution.[15] Nevertheless, the principle prevails that civil law systems neither offer effective protection against the state using services of private parties, nor do they provide a basis for a private party claim against the transfer of administrative functions. Nor do they prevent the withdrawal of public functions that were previously performed by private parties.[16]

Opposition to privatization is often of a political nature. Particularly in large cities with more than 100,000 inhabitants, a

---

12 Grabbe, *Verfassungsrechtliche Grenzen der Privatisierung kommunaler Aufgaben*, 1979, p. 50; Däubler, *Privatisierung als Rechtsproblem* (1980), pp. 70 et seq.

13 Article 28, Subsection 2 of the German Constitution.

14 Püttner, *Zur Wahl der Privatrechtsform für kommunale Unternehmen und Einrichtungen* (1993), pp. 28 et seq.

15 For discussion in the postal committee of the German *Bundestag*, *WEB* 94, p. 58.

16 Ossenbühl, VVDStRL 29 (1971), pp. 137 and 175 et seq.

comprehensive privatization of services is rarely found. Since the *Länder* and local communities are concerned about losing political influence and finding services for citizens restricted, they often handle privatization possibilities with restraint.

At the national level, the privatization measures at issue have a very high profile. The federal government not only declares privatization at national, *Länder* and local levels as a decisive element for guaranteeing the status of Germany in the future, but also tries to bring about preliminary strategic privatization decisions by means of legislative measures. At the national level, suitable instruments turn out to be the budget and tax laws.

In order to make better use of the potential for privatization in the *Länder* and local communities, the budget law should be amended in a way that the administration will be bound to examine whether private solutions will be more economical.[17] It is an open question whether the federal "compulsory privatization" strived for complies with the constitution. The question remains whether the additional expenses arising from the examination of private solutions will compensate the budget as expected.

The federal government sees the tax law as a means to prevent the *Länder* and local communities from becoming tired of privatization. By imposing standard tax rates on public and private organizational forms, particularly in the field of waste, the public service undertakings would no longer enjoy tax advantages.

A brief overview shows that there is a considerable polarization in the discussion of privatization of administrative tasks between opponents and supporters of privatization, with the latter having, undoubtedly, the upper hand. In view of the hardened positions, however, it will not be easy to weigh up the arguments brought forward.

As Schoch sets forward correctly in his paper about the privatization of administrative functions,[18] the prevailing considerations of the government cannot be given serious reflection. The very premise they expound, either intentionally or unconsciously, caricatures reality: The impression is given implicitly that not only in the new *Länder*, but in Western Germany as well state and economy

---

17 BT–Ds 12/6720.

18 *DVBl* 1994, pp. 962 and 966.

must be transformed from a socialistic to a free market system. It will not be possible to realistically evaluate the prospects for privatization and its related risks until the debate on this area, with the presumption that public performance of functions is more expensive than private performance, is no longer interpreted as an exclusive result of cost considerations.

LABOR ISSUES ARISING FROM PRIVATIZATION OF PUBLIC INSTITUTIONS

Legal Transfer of a Company

As set forth above, as a rule there are no legal objections to the decision to carry out privatization measures. Neither the constitution nor other simple legal rules provide a prohibition against privatization. However, it does appear that within certain fields, such as local government, the decision for privatization is subject to some legal barriers.

With increasing frequency, legal questions arise after the decision to privatize has been made. Legal difficulties may occur, particularly if tasks previously carried out by public service undertakings are transferred to private operators. This is carried out by transferring the enterprise of the administrative institution to a private transferee, as is the case with "real" privatization of tasks.

The starting point for the labor issues is Section 613(a) of the German Civil Code (BGB), which regulates the transfer of a company or a part thereof to another owner by way of legal transaction and which is also applied to the sale of a company by the state. The transfer of a company results in the transferee succeeding to the rights and obligations of the employment relationships, that is, the new employer takes over the employment relationships as they existed prior to the transfer. Thus, the private transferee succeeds to the contract of employment to the full extent as it was concluded with the public institution before. All contractual agreements will be maintained and existing provisions collectively agreed will continue to exist for another year after transfer of the company. Any dismissal of an employee due to such a transfer is ineffective.

Retirement Provision

Since the labor law for the civil service is mainly regulated by collective bargaining provisions, the private employer will be subject to such provisions after privatization, including the German statutory salary scale (BAT). Even if this scale will not be effective as such, it will become part of the contract of employment and may not be amended to the disadvantage of the employees prior to one year after privatization. All collectively bargained regulations such as longer terms of notice or contractually agreed permanent positions for aged employees will be preserved.

Besides the additional and special protection against dismissal for civil servants, the pension system provided by the state by means of a supplementary pension fund is a problem discussed time and again. Since the private employer, like any other transferee, will also succeed to the employees' qualification for retirement pension within the scope of Section 613(a) BGB, there might arise substantial financial burdens for the private employer, which often question the success of a privatization. In addition, the difference between the pension systems of the public sector, on the one hand, and the company pension scheme of private employers, on the other hand, will turn out to be a special problem for the private employer when taking over a company within the scope of privatization. While every private operator has to make pension provisions, the pension scheme for the civil service is based on a system whereby retired employees will receive a pension resulting from payments made by today's employees to supplementary pension funds by way of a contribution procedure. Thus, the public employer does not have to make pension reserves. If the private employer will succeed to the employment relationship of the public employer according to Section 613(a) BGB, it will also take over the accrued pension rights. It must treat the employees the same way as if they were still civil servants.[19]

Since the private employer cannot just be a member of a supplementary pension fund, it may become necessary for the private employer to raise future pension payments on its own. The Federal Labor Court did not agree with private employers who attempted

---

[19] Schipp, "Arbeitsrechtliche Probleme bei der Privatisierung öffentlicher Einrichtungen", *NZA* 1994, pp. 865 *et seq*.

to withdraw from obligations under the pension provisions by arguing that the public employer does not owe pension provisions, but merely has to provide supplementary pension fund insurance for the employee, which in turn is barred by statute to private employers. The employee, rather, has a right to pension provisions, which the private employer has to take over pursuant to Section 613(a) BGB.[20]

The supplementary pension funds realized that they needed to act in order to prevent a *de facto* failure of privatization due to the transfer of pension obligations to the private employer. If the private employer is required to take over high pension payments, the burden of such pension provisions might prove to be excessive. The private employer would want to deduct this sum from the purchase price, otherwise privatization would fail. Therefore, the supplementary pension funds amended their statutes to allow private employers to become members in the public supplementary pension funds, provided the private employer is a legal entity subject to public law.[21] This provides the supplementary pension funds additional security, since they understandably have limited confidence in the financial capacity of private employers. Finally, the supplementary pension funds require that the private employer continue to honor the existing collective agreements concerning pension provisions.[22] This will prevent the private employer from denying pension obligations for future employees.

Labor Codetermination

The question as to, what will happen to the codetermination of labor after privatization is of special significance. The codetermination body in public authorities is the staff council. Private enterprises, however, have a works council. The question is what will happen now to the workers' representation in case of privatization.

In the event of the company of a private employer being transferred to another owner, the works council will always continue in office and will continue its rights and obligations with the new employer as before. The situation is different in the event of a public

---

20 Federal Labor Court, NJW 1993, p. 874.
21 For example, Section 10, Subsection 3 of the Statutes of the *ZVK Bayern*.
22 For example, Section 10, Subsection 2 of the Statutes of the *ZVK Bayern*.

department being transferred to a private institution. In the latter instance, the right of staff representation is terminated with the staff council losing its office.[23] Neither is the staff council automatically transferred to a works council, nor has the staff council at least a remaining term of office, nor an interim office for a limited period of time.[24] Recently, it has been suggested that the staff council may at least prepare the election of a works council so that there is not a gap in workers' representation after privatization. This consideration is based on regulations provided by the legislature. By statute,[25] the works council is granted an interim office for a limited period of time in case of the break-up or merger of companies in the former GDR. In addition, in privatizing the railway system, the legislature passed special rules providing for an interim office for staff councils.[26] Opponents to such an interim office of the staff council correctly point out that had it been the intent of the legislature to provide for general legal provisions for an interim office of the staff council it would have done so, rather than limiting such provisions to particular instances such as the railway. Thus, it is likely that the current prevailing interpretation denying an interim office will also prevail in the future.

Finally, the question shall be discussed as to what extent the staff council is to be integrated in a privatization and possibly prevent such a privatization. Some of the *Länder* laws concerning staff representation define privatization as an element of codetermination. Section 81, Subsection 1, of the Hessian staff administrative act (HessPersVG), for instance, provides that "privatization of works or tasks previously performed by employees of the department" are subject to the codetermination of the staff council. The Higher Administrative Court in Kassel set forth in its order of 1 June 1994 that even the transformation of the municipal enterprise of public utilities into a limited liability company is subject to codetermination pursuant to Section 81, Subsection 1, HessPersVG, and granted the staff council a right of

---

23 Federal Labor Court, NJW 1992, p. 1894.
24 Federal Labor Court, NZA 1989, p. 433.
25 Section 13 SpTrUG and Section 6 b IX VermG.
26 Section 15 of the law for establishing the German railways corporation DBGrG of 21 December 1993, BGBl I, pp. 238 f.

codetermination in the case of the transfer of functions of a legal entity under public law to an institution under private law. In this case, it was sufficient for defining the term of privatization that the municipality took over all shares of the new company for the time being.[27] In the end, staff councils cannot prevent privatization, since privatization measures are constitutionally protected. A staff council may only delay such measures.

SELECTED ISSUES OF PRIVATIZATION

From among the large number of privatizations carried out during the past years, the privatization of the German Federal Postal Administration and of the German Federal Railways shall be briefly outlined for illustrative purposes.

Privatization of the German Federal Postal Administration

On 1 July 1989 the so-called Post Reform I took effect. This was the first step toward privatizing the German postal enterprise. At this time, the German Federal Postal Administration was removed from direct political supervision and its operational and entrepreneurial functions transferred to the three public enterprises: Deutsche Bundespost Postdienst (postal service); Deutsche Bundespost Postbank (banking); and Deutsche Bundespost Telekom (telecommunications). Nevertheless, the sovereign functions such as the telephone services, network and postal services monopolies were still subject to state control. The official structures of the three enterprises did not change either.

With the passing of the law for reorganizing the postal service and telecommunications on 14 September 1994, the Post Reform II was completed. Despite the separation of the German Federal Postal Administration into three public enterprises, the newly established enterprises lacked the decisive scope of action necessary to compete with private competitors. At the same time, the competition for postal and telecommunication services intensified worldwide. Furthermore, the European Union adopted a policy providing for

---

27 *NZA* 1994, p. 903.

the abolition or restriction of state postal monopolies. In order to be prepared for such a change in conditions, the German legislature needed to react. Consequently, Post Reform II was established.

The main goal of the Post Reform II is to improve the international competitiveness of the postal enterprises through private sector involvement. Other goals included increasing the range and quality of services through heightened competition, providing more customer-oriented services, and providing performance-based salaries as well as advancement opportunities for employees. The Post Reform II will be achieved by the following steps:

(1) Transforming the three postal enterprises into public limited companies;
(2) Establishing opportunities for private management;
(3) Establishing a public federal institution in which the federal government will perform its rights and obligations related to the public limited companies;
(4) Securing the state's obligation to provide infrastructure; and
(5) Guaranteeing a legally secured transition for civil servants to the public limited company and the preservation of their status and benefits through the so-called "loan pattern".

An essential condition for the Post Reform II was an amendment to the constitution. The amended version of Article 87 of the constitution provides that postal services will no longer be a state task but a private task. Article 143(b) of the constitution secures the transformation of the postal administration into public limited companies as well as the transfer of the civil servants to the public limited company. Article 33 of the constitution, which guarantees civil servant status, was not changed. The concrete legal form of the Post Reform II was finally achieved by the law for reorganizing the postal and telecommunication services (*Postneuordnungsgesetz*), which consolidates seven new laws as well as all amendments.

On 1 January 1995, the three enterprises comprising the Deutsche Bundespost will become public limited companies. With this transformation, the companies will obtain full entrepreneurial sovereignty with all shares being transferred to the federal government for the time being.[28]

---

28 Section 3(1) of the law for transforming the enterprises of the Deutsche Bundespost into a public limited company (*Postumwandlungsgesetz*).

Reorganization of the Federal Railways

Since 1989 the structural reform of the railways has been on the agenda. After much discussion between the federal government and the *Länder*, the necessary bills were passed, that is, the law for amending the constitution of 20 December 1993[29] and the law for reorganizing the railways (ENeuOG) of 27 December 1993.[30] The majority of provisions took effect on 1 January 1994. For other regulations, transitional periods were provided.

As intended by its initiators, this structural reform shall enable the German railways to be more competitive than before, since they will become more flexible. The reform was launched by the legislature pursuant to the report of the government commission for federal railways and the Directive of the European Communities of 29 July 1991 for the development of the Communities' railway enterprises.[31] The essential parts of this structural reform are:

(1) The separation of the entrepreneurial part of the federal railways from their assets, and their transformation into the Deutsche Bahn AG (DBAG), which must provide railway services, on the one hand, and operate railway infrastructures, on the other. At a minimum, the areas of "local passenger transport", "longer distance passenger transport", "cargo traffic" and "motor ways" must be separated both organizationally and financially and, within five years, divided between newly established companies.[32] As demanded by the *Länder*, the sale of the shares in Fahrweg AG is possible only under authority of law as voted on by the Federal Council, and provided the majority interest remains with the federal government;[33]

(2) Compulsory fares and rates will continue for passenger transport only;[34]

(3) Civil servants of federal railway holdings who will not retire or cannot be suspended may be assigned to the DBAG by law;[35]

---

29 BGBl I, p. 2089.
30 BGBl I, p. 2378.
31 91/440/EEC.
32 Section 25 of the DBGrG.
33 Article 87(e)(3) and (5) of the Constitution.
34 Article 5, ENeuOG — Sections 10, 11, Subsection 2a EG.
35 Article 143a(1) of the Constitution.

(4) For the remaining administrative tasks, the federal government will establish a Federal Railways Institute as superior federal authority which will perform those sovereign tasks that were previously performed by the federal railway institutions of West and East Germany (DB and RB), unless the remaining holdings of the federal railways remain in charge. The Federal Railways Institute will be a controlling and licensing authority for the federal railways and German railway enterprises domiciled in other states. In particular, it will be responsible for the planning of the federal railway network as well as for issuing and revoking licenses;

(5) The construction and maintenance of railways, as well as the operation and security systems, will be regulated by the railways infrastructure enterprise. Ownership of the rails will be transferred to it. The infrastructure, which will be open to all railway enterprises, can be used against payment of charges; and

(6) Finally, the responsibility for tasks and expenses for the local passenger transport will be allocated to the *Länder*, effective as of 1 January 1996.

These laws relating to the structural reform of the railways could only be legally realized after changing important constitutional provisions. By deleting the words "The Federal Railways" in Article 87, Subsection 1 of the constitution and the regulation of Article 87(e), Subsection 3 of the constitution, which provides that the federal railways, "be managed as private business enterprises", the question arises whether or not the new organization of the German railways can be safeguarded by the constitution in the future.[36]

PRIVATIZATION IN THE FORMER GDR

The Unification Treaty and the Law for Privatizing and Reorganizing state-owned assets of 17 June 1990 (Trust Act) created the *Treuhandanstalt* to provide a commercial structure for former state-owned enterprises and to privatize them.[37] Therefore, the

---

36 Fromm, "Die Reorganisation der Deutschen Bahnen", *DVBl* 1994, p. 187.

37 Article 25 of the Unification Treaty.

Treuhandanstalt serves as the means for privatizing and capitalizing the state-owned assets according to the principles of a social market economy.[38] It must promote the structural adaptation of the economy to the requirements of the market[39] and shall assist in creating marketable enterprises, and thus an efficient economic structure, by reasonably decentralizing entrepreneurial structures.

To say that the privatization responsibility of the *Treuhand* in the new *Länder* was simply the transfer of former socialist property to private owners does not do justice to the overall process of transformation of the former socialist GDR into the social market economy of the Federal Republic of Germany. Rather, the political aspects of its responsibilities must be considered. The political purposes are evident in the cooperation principles between the federal government, the new *Länder* and the *Treuhandanstalt*, which were established in March 1991 and modified and renewed in 1992 by the federal government together with the new *Länder* and the *Treuhandanstalt*. It is from these cooperation principles that the phrase "surge in East Germany" comes. These principles provide that the *Treuhandanstalt*, in its efforts toward privatization, must examine whether a particular proposal or solution is preferable to other solutions that might be more expensive in the beginning but more economical in the long run and more considerate to the labor market. When closing down companies or parts thereof, the *Treuhandanstalt*, the *Länder* and the federal government should attempt to reduce the disadvantages for employees, the labor market and the region as a whole. Furthermore, they must explain why these steps are being taken and to provide incentives for the creation of new jobs.

Legislative Procedures Preceding the Passage of the Trust Act

The law for privatizing and reorganizing the state-owned assets (the Trust Act), which took effect in the German Democratic Republic on 1 July 1990, was preceded by a hectic legislative process. Soon after passing the Transformation Regulation of 1 March 1990, pursuant to which the socialistic economic units were given a

---

38 Section 2(1), THG.
39 Section 2(6), THG.

private organizational structure, and after the corresponding resolutions of the Council of Ministers under Mr. Modrow relating to the establishment and statutes of the *Treuhandanstalt* on 1 March through 15 March 1990, it was determined that the process for transforming economic units of the GDR into corporations was progressing too slowly. Upon the suggestion of the responsible politicians, new drafts were worked out in East and West Germany. The federal government raised further considerations before the Council of Ministers to the People's Chamber on 6 June 1990, which were first discussed in parliament on 7 June, 1990. On 16 June 1990 the economic committee of the People's Chamber of the GDR agreed on a final recommendation. After the second reading was interrupted on 15 June 1990 for the above reason, the law was passed in a continued second reading on Sunday, 17 June 1990.

Thus, the Transformation Regulations were replaced by the Trust Act. As of 1 July 1990, all economic units were transformed into corporations according to Section 11(2) of the Trust Act. The assets held in trust by the *Treuhandanstalt* that were intended for privatization comprised the shares in the corporations, which were established from the transformation of state-owned ventures, enterprises, institutions and other legally independent economic units,[40] as well as holdings in trust from former state-owned assets. These assets emanated from state-owned farms, state-owned agricultural and forestry areas that were owned by cooperatives or individual persons, special assets of the Ministry for the State Security Police and the assets of the parties and social organizations.

Guidelines for the Policy of Privatization

The legislature gave the *Treuhandanstalt* full authority to specify its targets and to set priorities. The following guidelines were set up for the work of the *Treuhandanstalt*:[41]
(1) Viable enterprises, or parts thereof, must be privatized as soon as possible;

---

40 Section 1(4), THG.

41 Opinion of the scientific council of the Ministry for Economics on problems of privatization in the new *Länder*, 16 February 1991.

(2) Non-viable enterprises, or parts thereof, must be closed down as soon as possible. The existing assets, particularly real property assets, shall be transferred to private ownership. It does not serve the purposes of privatization for the *Treuhandanstalt* to be left holding a large number of enterprises incapable of being privatized;

(3) The reorganization of enterprises targeted for privatization is, as a rule, the responsibility of the purchaser, and is only in exceptional circumstances the responsibility of the *Treuhandanstalt*;

(4) The aim of privatizing enterprises, or parts thereof, is always to continue their business as commercial economic units. It may not be ruled out, however, that privatization be followed by a liquidation or partial liquidation of assets. The purchaser may not be barred from this option if efforts for reorganization fail;

(5) If possible, privatization shall secure a competitive purchase price. The fair market value of the assets less any liabilities (including prior pollution charges and labor obligations such as a social compensation plan) will mark the minimum claim. In the case of taking over former pollution charges by the purchaser, a negative purchase price can be taken into consideration;

(6) Whenever possible, privatization shall help to bring about competitive market structures. It is not the aim of privatization policy to increase the privatization proceeds for providing monopolistic or similar market positions for the purchaser;

(7) Local policy or social policy is not the responsibility of the *Treuhandanstalt*. If due to regional policy or social conditions considerations other than those already mentioned are required, the competent fields of politics are called for. An exception should only be made if it can be realized by setting high standards in such a way that a limited additional help for survival by the *Treuhandanstalt* or a deduction of the privatization proceeds would be the cheapest possibility to avoid severe regional or social problems in a reliable way. A permanent subsidization by the *Treuhandanstalt* is not permitted;

(8) A general debt relief of an enterprise is not recommended. To do so would be a disincentive to efficiency and would pave the way to eventual liquidation. This rule can be deviated from if the prior debt relief is the precondition for taking over a viable enterprise by an entrepreneur with the propensity to invest.

The Demand for Urgency

From the very beginning, the demand for urgency was deemed to be the most important rule when carrying out privatization, since without privatization, promising reorganization concepts could not be realized in most cases. Also, without privatization on a broader scale, decisions about future debts, particularly in collective wage agreements, would be made by individuals who would not have to accept responsibility later on.

According to the Federal Ministry for Economics, quick decisions on closing down non-viable enterprises had a double function. Firstly, they protected the *Treuhandanstalt* from expenses that would not raise sufficient proceeds. Secondly, the closing down, that is, total liquidation (the bankruptcy proceedings in the new *Länder*), released productive resources still bound to these enterprises, particularly labor and real estate, for applications with a promising future.

The *Treuhandanstalt* should always make decisions on closing down enterprises for reasons of private economy. Again and again, it must resist the common pressures to avoid unemployment. This would not be the way of the market economy.

In view of the outlined problems, it is very impressive how fast the enormous job of privatization has been dealt with, to a large extent by the end of 1994. Although the high speed of privatization and the interest in high proceeds came into conflict with each other again and again, the principle of urgency was accepted. The fact that the performance of these tasks had to be linked with the unavoidable elimination of a great number of unproductive laborers underlines their difficulties and significance without diminishing them. In economic terms, it was impossible to preserve these jobs.

Execution of Privatization

Although the Trust Act already took effect on 1 July 1990, intensified privatization actions could only be noted at the end of the summer of 1990 when the Monetary, Economic and Social Union was introduced and reunification was certain. The *Treuhandgesellschaft*, which was partly occupied by staff who seemed not to be suitable due to their functions in socialism or due to lack of knowledge regarding privatization, was reorganized and agencies were established. Effective privatization did not begin until the end of 1990. Before the very eyes of a critical and impatient public, the speed of privatization increased, and from 1991 to 1993 the largest part of this task (about ninety per cent) had been resolved.[42] By 31 January 1993, the *Treuhandanstalt* counted a total of 11,234 privatizations.

Admittedly, the real success of privatization can only be seen by the further development of the privatized enterprises; particularly by their ability to permanently preserve jobs and to create new ones. It will remain uncertain for some years whether the commitment to jobs made by the purchasers when taking over the enterprises can be kept. During the past years, subsequent negotiations about such commitments between the *Treuhandanstalt* and the purchaser of the enterprise have become commonplace, particularly about the scope and time of payment of contractual penalties.

From the very beginning, it was feared that the activities of the *Treuhandanstalt* could turn out to be a "subsidizing event" despite all good intentions. Under the headlines "aid for survival and reorganization in the course of planned privatizations" and "reduction of privatization proceeds due to saved jobs", large amounts could be spent. Particularly inconspicuous (even for the *Treuhandanstalt*) but no less worrisome is the practice of selling a company's assets to cover losses that could only be avoided by quickly closing down the enterprise. The fear that the *Treuhandanstalt* will suddenly become a poor institution that is a liability to the state instead of contributing to the reorganization of the state budget, and subsequently increasing saving in the former GDR, has already materialized. According to official notes of the Ministry for Economics, the massive debt that the *Treuhandanstalt* will leave to the Federal Republic after completing its tasks is still growing.

Principle of Restitution as an Obstacle to Privatization

The socialistic property that formed the foundation of the collapsed socialistic economic system of the former GDR was mainly derived from former private property and was obtained by expropriation.

---

42 Horn, *Das Zivil und Wirtschaftsrecht im neuen Bundesgebiet* (2nd ed.), pp. 794 *et seq.*

Apart from private persons, legal entities under private law, particularly corporations, were victims of expropriation. A large part of the expropriations were carried out before establishment of the GDR on 7 October 1949. Between 1945 and 1949, acts of expropriation were carried out by the occupation forces, that is, in the Soviet occupation zone by the local Soviet Military Administration for Germany (SMAD).

With the establishment of the German Democratic Republic in 1949, further expropriations were carried out by German authorities on the basis of German regulations. A number of legislative measures of the GDR in economic terms served to restrict the property rights of self-employed tradesmen and put economic pressure on them to give up their work as self-employed persons. At the beginning of 1952, the compulsory collectivization of agriculture was initiated with the aim of establishing agricultural producers' cooperatives. The agricultural producers' cooperatives law of 1959 called for the collectivization of agriculture on a voluntary basis.

The subsequent collectivization, however, was achieved in a very short time through massive propaganda and intimidation. Besides this, the issue of refugees' property gained importance. This referred to those persons who left the territory of the GDR or East Berlin without authorization after 8 May 1945. After appointing curators for absent persons in the beginning, the regulation for securing property of 1952 ordered its confiscation. Owners of houses, too, were confronted with economic pressure due to the housing control, controlled rent and compulsory housing laws. These owners were often forced to renounce ownership of the property and to transfer it to the state, since they were no longer able to bear the costs of maintenance. In view of this policy of expropriation by the GDR, it is understandable that the legal and political topic of expropriation, particularly the question of annulment of expropriations within the scope of the reunification of both German states, has been of substantial significance. The "common statement for clarifying open questions of property" by the governments of the Federal Republic and the GDR of 15 June 1990 was made part of the Reunification Treaty as annex III and is specially protected according to Article 41(3) of the Reunification Treaty. It is the basis for laws passed and still to be passed with respect to restitution and compensations for expropriations. Although only a general principle, it establishes the basis for further legislative decisions. Only expropriations "on the basis of occupation law or occupational sovereignty" (1945–1949) are exempted from restitution according to the above rules. In April 1991, the Federal Constitutional Court decided that this regulation is constitutional.[43]

In order to limit the consequences of the decision to grant "restitution before compensation", at least for those fields wherein entrepreneurs have an interest and a propensity to invest, the investment law of 29 September 1990, extended by the investment priority law of 29 July 1992, was introduced by the legislature. It created a legal possibility to exclude the claims of entitled persons for retransfer and to award to the person entitled the proceeds of the property subject to certain conditions. So, public authorities (*Treuhandanstalt*, regional authorities) may grant an investment priority order, according to which property rights to real estate cannot be retransferred if the real estate in question is required for urgent investment purposes to be defined in detail.[44]

The aim of these investment priority laws was simply to promote investments. Unclear or pending property relationships which could only have been clarified gradually and over a longer period of time by executing the property law were and still are an obstacle to investments in the new *Länder*. The legislation concerning investment priority thus prefers a general interest in new investments to interests of former proprietors in restitution.

The legal claims arising from the principle of restitution resulted in extreme difficulties for the privatization efforts of the *Treuhandanstalt* and its enterprises. As far as restitution claims were made by former proprietors, the privatization measures were in danger of failing to proceed. With regard to the restitution claims for real estate, there was not a general restraint on alienation. Even the conclusion of long-term leasing contracts remained inadmissible without approval of the person entitled to restitution. Real estate, which is often the most important asset of the enterprises to be sold, could not be transferred. Due to the unsecured property situation, the communities could not be provided industrial zones by the *Treuhandanstalt* either, which, as a consequence, resulted in the non-location of enterprises. In turn, the persons entitled to

---

43 BVerfGE 84, p. 90.

44 Horn, *Das Zivil- und Wirtschaftsrecht im neuen Bundesgebiet* (2nd ed.), pp. 650 *et seq*.

restitution could not dispose of their real estate for the time being. Therefore, assets remained economically stagnant until the time-consuming and often expensive administrative procedures were completed. Some of them have still not been completed. The result was that privatization was heavily blocked, at least in the beginning, and that the necessary economic growth started sluggishly.

Transformation of Cooperatives and Other Economic Units

A large number of former socialistic economic units in the new *Länder* were not subject to privatization according to the Trust Act. They were, however, transformed to another organizational form with respect to private law and to another legal basis.

Firstly, there are the former socialistic cooperatives, the most popular representative of which is the agricultural cooperative. These former socialistic cooperatives cannot be subject to the Trust Act, because this law only comprises state-owned property and the property of cooperatives is a different form of socialistic property. Secondly, there are special areas like local enterprises and institutions. These are expressly exempted from the Trust Act and its scope of application.

The removal of compulsory collectivization and the reorganization of property relationships in the agricultural producers' cooperatives (LPG) was dealt with by the legislator in March 1990 for the first time. An amendment of the LPG law allowed farmers in cooperatives to sell their real estate interests contributed to the LPG with the LPG having a right of first refusal. However, only with the abolition of the comprehensive right of the LPG to use the soil contributed,[45] as defined by the State Treaty, were the property rights of the LPG farmers to the soil contributed partly restored. The law for adaptation of agriculture of 29 June 1990 created a comprehensive legal basis for the legal reorganization of the agricultural enterprises. The legal principle was to restore and guarantee the private property to land as the basis for agriculture and forestry. The first and second amendments of the law for adaptation of agriculture of 7 July 1991 and 1 January 1992 were supposed to facilitate the transformation of the LPG into the legal

---

45 Section 18, LPG Law.

form of a partnership. By annulling the law concerning the LPG,[46] the former LPG was no longer able to exist in its former property order. The LPG and cooperative institutions, which were not transformed into cooperative societies, partnerships or corporations by 31 December 1991, were dissolved by law.

The legal situation described led to a fast and comprehensive abolition of old organizational forms of socialistic cooperatives which were replaced by new legal forms. About seventy-five per cent of 4,500 agricultural producers' cooperatives were split up and transformed. The remaining quarter went into liquidation without legal succession or initiated the total execution.[47]

CONCLUSION

The analysis of privatization in the Federal Republic of Germany shows that the significance of privatization of public functions, public organizations and public capital has steadily increased. In the opinion of the federal government and the federal legislature, all forms of privatization should contribute to the removal or, at least, the moderation of problems of mobility which are noticeable everywhere. In addition, there are fiscal considerations in view of empty cash boxes at national, *Länder* and local levels. Whether the aims of privatization will lead to the effects desired such as gaining time when performing tasks, saving public budgets, increasing efficiency and saving costs for citizens as well as better cost management, would be worth a separate examination. Also, the disadvantages of increasing privatization such as public functions not being fulfilled anymore or the withdrawal of the state (particularly in the case of privatizing traffic enterprises and postal service) must be considered in detail.

A totally different conclusion is reached with regard to the former GDR. By the end of 1994, the *Treuhandanstalt* complied with its privatization mandate to a large extent. According to experts, there remains only 100 enterprises, some large, which will

---

46 LPG Law of 31 December 1991.

47 Horn, *Das Zivil- und Wirtschaftsrecht im neuen Bundesgebiet* (2nd ed.), pp. 997 *et seq.*; Turner, Karst, "Die Umwandlung Landwirtschaftlicher Produktionsgenossenschaften", *DtZ* 1992, pp. 33 *et seq.*

need a longer reorganization stage. As a consequence, the *Treuhandanstalt* ceased its main activities at the end of 1994. The remaining tasks, particularly the winding up of the existing liquidation proceedings, will be handled according to the amended provisions of the Trust Act on the basis of a new financing plan by a considerably reduced organization.

HUNGARY

McKenna Ormai & Co.
Budapest, Hungary

INTRODUCTION

The privatization process in Hungary was initiated through the Transformation Act of 1989. This cleared the way for around 2,200 state-owned enterprises (then worth some US $37-billion) to be put up for sale either wholly or partially, subject always to the need for supplementary legislation depending on the industry to be privatized (particularly where the privatizations have involved former state monopolies passing into private hands, such as in the telecommunications and energy sectors).

Hungary's approach to the privatization process has been markedly different to that of its Central European neighbors. While its neighbors have tended to favor systems of distribution of assets through vouchers or the restitution of assets, Hungary has based its privatization program much more on the direct sale of assets and shares. This approach has been supported by the development of a legal and economic framework geared to facilitate the introduction of foreign capital — Hungary was one of the first countries in the region to introduce a law on foreign investments, Act XXIV of 1988 on Investments of Foreigners in Hungary, providing for equal treatment between foreigners and local investors and guaranteeing that the investments of foreigners enjoy complete protection and security and that investments and profits can be fully repatriated. In addition, Hungary has well-established corporate, foreign exchange, securities, competition, corporate tax, environmental and employment regulations. Against this background, by mid-1995 some fifty per cent of the Hungarian state's assets, representing sixty per cent of the economy in terms of gross domestic product had passed into the private sector.

However, the privatization process in Hungary, while securing substantial inward investment since 1988 (some US $8-billion between 1989 and the end of 1994, representing over half of the total investment made in the region) and facilitating the introduction of significant levels of capital, technology and management and marketing expertise, has also been subject to frequent and diverse criticism as to the manner of and delays experienced in the privatization process, In July 1995, for example, the state still held over 800 companies worth more than HUF 1,300-billion (US $10-billion). Out of this over HUF 1,000 billion is concentrated in the commercial banking sector and five big utility companies — MOL Rt (the state oil and gas conglomerate), MATAV Rt (the state telephone company), MVM Rt (the state electricity holding company), Antenna Hungaria (the state broadcasting company) and the regional gas distribution companies.

In response to such criticism, there have been a number of attempts to refine the privatization process, which have met with varying degrees of success, culminating in the long-awaited passing of the Privatization Act 1995.[1] The Privatization Act had been scheduled to be enacted by the end of 1994, but was finally passed only in Mid-May 1995, entering force on 16 June 1995. The Privatization Act substantially supersedes the previous legislation and has been portrayed by the ruling Socialist/Free Democratic coalition as a prerequisite to continuing, accelerating and completing the privatization process in Hungary, which had lain in somewhat of a stasis since the coalition took power in April 1994.

In the year following the election, for example, there was no privatization of significance and during that time opposition within Hungary to privatization to overseas investors became significantly stronger. The government's expressed aim as at Summer 1995 was to complete privatization by 1998 by which time around twenty-five per cent of ownership would remain in state hands.

BODIES RESPONSIBLE FOR PRIVATIZATION: 1990–1994

Although privatization had begun in Hungary under the last communist government from the late 1980s onwards, many transactions were stigmatized as being a type of asset stripping, based on concerns that national assets were being sold off to non-Hungarians for significantly less than their estimated value and that Communist-appointed company managers were being unduly enriched by the transfers. In response to these concerns the incoming government, elected through the first free elections in forty years, created in January 1990 the State Property Agency and required it to approve all major transfers.

---

[1] Act Number 39/35.

State Property Agency

The principal task of the State Property Agency was to administer and encourage both foreign investment and domestic participation in the privatization of the state-owned enterprises and other assets, particularly land, under its control. The State Property Agency was also responsible for all aspects of contract negotiations and supervising the intermediate management of those companies and assets.

Under the First Privatization Program, which began in September 1990, the State Property Agency attempted to privatize quickly twenty or so of the country's most attractive companies. The Second Privatization Program, launched in 1991, covered the remaining 2,000 or so companies under the State Property Agency's control. It particularly encouraged acquisitions by investors working in the same industry as the target company, so as to secure for the companies in question direct access to capital, up to date technology and management techniques specific to that industry. Such sales commonly involved an offer of shares through competitive tender invitation although occasionally sales were effected by a public offer of shares or by private placements with institutional investors.

The State Property Agency, however, was the subject of much public criticism over the speed and manner of its conduct of the privatization program and, in particular, for permitting political considerations to influence its decisions and to slow down the privatization process. While the State Property Agency responded to this criticism by decentralizing the privatization process to outside advisers, often limiting its involvement to the final approval of the transaction, continuing criticism led to a shift in emphasis in the privatization strategy with the establishment in October 1992 of the State Asset Holding Company as a sister agency to the State Property Agency.

State Asset Holding Company

In contrast to the State Property Agency, the State Asset Holding Company's function was to hold and manage the state's interests in shares in 163 key industries (whose total asset value in 1992 totaled some US $22-billion) in which it was deemed essential for the state to retain a minimum interest. The sectors involved included banking, chemicals, engineering, pharmaceuticals and the utility services (oil, gas, electricity and water). The State Property Agency meanwhile continued to be responsible for enterprises in which the state would not hold any long term interest. The government sought at the time to justify this distinction on the basis that the industries in question were of a strategic nature, but it seems likely that an important consideration in this regard was burgeoning public opinion opposing privatization of Hungarian entities where control was passing to non-Hungarian investors. In addition, it was hoped that this strategy would allow the import of managerial and technical expertise and capital at the cost of a partial interest in a company, which expertise would then enable the State Asset Holding Company to enjoy an increase in value of the rump interest for a later sale.

However, both the State Property Agency and the State Asset Holding Company, despite their efforts to improve by becoming more professional through the recruitment of better quality staff continued to be the subject of much criticism over the slow pace and inefficiency of the privatization program. Both organizations were the subject of a number of withering attacks by the State Audit Office, which, while acknowledging some improvements in internal controls and their databases, highlighted a catalogue of failures, for example, in relation to the collection of company and bank dividends and the defective preparation of business plans and privatization strategies.

Moreover, frequent politically inspired changes in the senior management of the state bodies charged with effecting privatization undoubtedly led to their staffs being diverted from focusing on their real task of carrying out the preparatory work for privatization; gradually all the senior figures of the two agencies who had been appointed by the previous government have been eased out, culminating in October 1994 with a wholesale dismissal of the board of the State Asset Holding Company.

PRIVATIZATION PROCESS

Transformation of State Enterprises

Before beginning the process of selling state enterprises to private investors, each state enterprise first had to be transformed into a corporate form within Act VI of 1988 on Business Organizations (Companies Act), a process that is now largely complete. There are two principal forms of corporate entity into which state-owned enterprises have been transformed: the *Részvénytársaság* (Rt) or company limited by shares (which is similar to a United Kingdom public limited company or German *Aktiengesellschaft*) and the *Korlátolt Felelösségü Társaság* (Kft) or limited liability company without shares (which is similar to a United Kingdom limited company or a German *Gesellschaft mit beschränkter Haftung*). Frequently the Rt has been chosen as the transformation vehicle for larger privatizations because the intention will have been for the transformed entity to seek a listing on the Stock Exchange once the necessary accounting track record has been established. The structure and management of Rts and Kfts are regulated by the Companies Act.

Transformation could take place in any of three ways:
(1) Spontaneously, i.e., at the initiative of the state enterprise itself;
(2) Actively, i.e., State Property Agency-initiated transformation, which would usually involve reorganization of the state enterprise prior to transformation; or
(3) By simplified transformation, whereby the State Property Agency would authorize experts to privatize particular companies.

From a legal point of view, the transformed company is deemed to be the general successor to the state enterprise and has the rights, but is subject to the obligations of the predecessor state enterprise.

On transformation, the successor companies became owned by the various governmental agencies charged from time to time with effecting the sale of state assets. Often, municipal governments and/or other investors, including creditors or a combination of such parties, would obtain a minority shareholding; municipalities are, by law, entitled to a number of shares in the transformed company corresponding to the value of land, located in its area, which becomes an asset of the company. Employees may also be allocated shares.

Once a company has been transformed, various means of privatization are available to the various government agencies under the legislation. The breadth of techniques adopted reflects partly the fact that at the outset of the process of economic transition, a number of the countries in Central and Eastern Europe were advised by international financial advice agencies of the need to have available multiple methods of privatization because different methods might be more readily applicable depending on the company or industrial sector to be privatized. These methods have now largely been consolidated in the Privatization Act.

Privatization Schemes in 1990–1994

With an election looming in Spring 1994 and the ruling coalition government continuing to occupy low ratings in the polls, the eighteen months leading up to that election witnessed much development in the government's privatization strategy. This change was generated principally by the twin factors of the perceived needs to persuade the electorate that the government had begun to get the economy under control and to demonstrate that the country's "family silver" was not being gifted to overseas investors. Between 1992 and 1994, the following refinements were introduced into the Hungarian privatization process:

Compensation Coupon Scheme

The compensation coupon scheme, established under the Compensation Act 1992, was aimed at broadening domestic share ownership. Unlike its Eastern European neighbors, Hungary decided not to restore state-owned property, nationalized state enterprises or collectivized land to its citizens. Instead, it elected to compensate persons and their direct descendants who had suffered from the state's actions prior to the fall of communism and persons who had lost their property during the 1949 nationalization by awarding transferable bonds or compensation coupons for the value of the holder's claim against the state, but in no case in excess of HUF 5-million (then US $82,000) per claimant. Coupons can be used either to purchase land or to invest in the state companies that are gradually being privatized. Former owners of farmland were also entitled to repurchase their previously nationalized land at an open auction if they agree to farm it themselves for five years. The deadline for applications for compensation under the scheme has now passed.

A direct benefit of having embarked on a program of compensation rather than restitution has been that Hungary has been better able to avoid the difficulties experienced in other Central and Eastern

European countries where the title to land and other assets has been rendered under by claims for restitution. The principal philosophy behind the coupons was, however, not only to provide compensation, but also to create a competitive secondary market for them by couponholders being able to sell the coupons to another party for cash; compensation coupons are negotiable securities and since 1992 have been tradable on the Stock Exchange.

However, while the privatization policy of the previous government placed particular emphasis on maintaining the value of compensation coupons, by trying to ensure an ongoing supply of property to be offered in exchange therefor, under the current government the value of such coupons has declined due to the reduced number of privatizations and, with the shift in emphasis in 1995 towards further preference being given to cash, the tradable value of compensation coupons is set to decline still further. Nevertheless, the government's aim is to ensure that at least two-thirds of compensation coupons in circulation at the start of 1995 (estimated at some HUF 130-billion in nominal value and representing a significant element of public debt which the government is keen to reduce) are exchanged for private property by the end of 1995, particularly through the privatizations in the energy sector and including some HUF 25-billion worth of shares in the food industry.

Credit Consolidation Program

Recognition of the need to make companies more attractive for privatization led to the creation in 1993 of a credit consolidation program. Under this program, the government conducted detailed audits of the debt portfolios of twelve of the larger state-owned debt-laden companies with a view to determining how best to reduce their debt burden. These companies represent twelve per cent of Hungary's industrial net reserves and twenty-five per cent of its exports. To date, some HUF 15-billion worth of debt has either been wiped off these companies' balance sheets, converted into shares or rescheduled. However, notwithstanding that in late 1993 both the State Property Agency and the State Asset Holding Company signed a protocol with the European Bank for Reconstruction and Development recognizing the need to engage in more corporate reconstructions in advance of future sell-offs, by 1995 the general philosophy had altered so that restructuring is now only to be regarded as appropriate in exceptional cases, given the dire need of many Hungarian companies for capital injections and the rapid ongoing decline in value of such companies.

Small Investor Credit Program (Preferential Share Purchase Program)

In autumn 1993, a new mass privatization initiative was announced which was directed at broadening the base of domestic share-ownership in Hungary beyond the foreign investors and state company management that had dominated the first four years of the country's privatization program. The declared aim was to create a share-buying market and a share-owning public of up to one-million new Hungarian investors, which would allow the process of privatization to be accelerated.

The system involved each investor over the age of eighteen paying a registration fee of HUF 2,000 in return for which a private investment facility was made available in the form of a numbered account credited with HUF 100,000. These credits could be used to buy designated shares in forthcoming flotations. Where any particular issue was oversubscribed, smaller investors would receive preferential treatment. Incentives, such as additional shares, could also be offered on a case-by-case basis. Although the investor became the nominal owner of any shares bought, the shares could not be traded until the credit with which they were bought was repaid to the government.

As such, no security is required beyond the purchased shares themselves. The aim was thereby to inhibit speculation, but equally this meant that, unlike compensation coupons, such credit would not be a tradable instrument. The credit is repayable in five annual or ten semi-annual installments and, provided the installment deadlines are met, no interest will be payable. Installments may be paid not only in cash but also in compensation coupons issued under the government's compensation coupon scheme. Dividends are also used to reduce the installment payments.

While this scheme represented Hungary's first foray into the realms of "mass" privatization, the scheme only ever envisaged that shares worth some HUF 10-billion (then UK £682-million) in seventy companies would be handled by the scheme (small therefore in comparison to the Czech mass privatization scheme whose first wave alone involved more than 1,000 companies valued at

US $7-billion). Moreover, the scheme would have only made available minority stakes and those normally in companies that were already under the management of an industrial investor and in relatively profitable sectors such as hotels, utilities, the producers of consumer goods and retailers. Equally, while the companies slated to participate in the scheme were generally sound companies, the 163 companies managed by the State Asset Holding Company were excluded from this program. Accordingly, unlike the Czech Republic where voucher privatization has handed the corporate reins to the investment funds, the Hungarian program would have had little effect on corporate governance given that the companies in the program were largely already managed or majority-owned by foreign investors.

The launch of the scheme in April 1994 in the run up to the general election was, however, widely viewed as an electoral ploy to get away from the image of privatization having largely benefited foreign investors and managers and entrepreneurs rather than the general public. Correspondingly, this made the scheme a natural target for the incoming socialist government, notwithstanding that it was estimated that by May 1994 the scheme had attracted some 30,000 new investors, thereby more than doubling the number of retail investors in Hungary's population of 10-million (previously about 25,000).

However, an Organization for Economic Cooperation and Development report also concluded that the scheme was "seriously flawed" because it could leave the government holding the risk and ultimate ownership of the shares that were sold; if the loans are not repaid, for example, because the value of the shares had declined over the five year period, the government would be forced to repossess the shares thereby being counter-productive to the privatization effort. Based on this and despite the first issues of shares under the scheme being over-subscribed, the scheme was scrapped by the incoming government.

Subsidies for Purchase of Assets of State-Owned Companies

Following the Bankruptcy Act of 1991, many companies have gone into liquidation. A potential investor may purchase part of a liquidated company directly from the liquidator appointed by the court, although often this may involve complicated and lengthy negotiations.

A further program in operation since October 1993 involves the grant of state interest subsidies on loans taken out by Hungarian citizens or by domestic companies (as defined in the Foreign Exchange Code) to support the purchase of the assets of companies, which are at least twenty-five per cent owned by the state and which are either bankrupt or in liquidation.

Privatization Act 1995

As in other Central and Eastern European countries, concern has been expressed both within the government and among the general public as to the percentage of the Hungarian economy that should be held by foreigners.

However, the government's program published in September 1994 acknowledged that at present there are not enough funds available within the Hungarian economy to fund the levels of investment required and, with this in mind, the government set about drafting a new Privatization Act designed to create the legal basis for further encouraging the introduction of new capital and the reduction of the state's influence in the economy over the following four years. The aim is for the privatization process to be completed by 1998.

Aims of the New Legislation

The principal hallmark of the new legislation is that it is designed to "reasonably" accelerate the transfer of assets from state hands into private ownership and thereby to reduce the economic role played by the state. A major criticism of the State Asset Holding Company and the State Property Agency under the previous government had been their tendency to perform slowly and inefficiently, an inefficiency which had been exacerbated throughout the period from 1990 to 1994 by virtue of a significant portion of state assets becoming subject to ownership by a diverse variety of state-controlled bodies. This occurred particularly through various credit reorganizations involving the exchange of debt for equity, particularly in the banking sector, but a significant amount of assets also ended up in the hands of state liquidation organizations as a result of liquidation and bankruptcy proceedings. The principal

changes, introduced by the Act, which are largely geared to improving the efficiency of the privatization process, are:
(1) To merge the State Asset Holding Company and the State Property Agency with a view to streamlining the privatization process under the control of a single body (called the State Privatization and Holding Company or APV Rt), thereby making it more efficient and less costly.
(2) To retain within state ownership a much reduced number of companies. Originally, the State Asset Holding Company was given responsibility for managing some 163 strategically important companies. Now, the number retained fully by the state is less than fifty and will be confined to such areas as MAV Rt, the state railway, the post office, prisons, forestry, research and transportation and the internationally famous Tokaj wine producer.
(3) To continue to prefer the sale of state-owned companies over their restructuring.
(4) To give preference to cash sales and place greater emphasis on sales through public offers, rather than sales involving compensation coupons, Existence or E-loans and other alternative payment methods.
(5) To encourage management-controlled "simplified" privatization for small and medium sized companies. However, the plan also states a preference for cash buyers and simplified privatization will only occur after a further round of attempts to secure cash sales have been made by the APV Rt. Management buy-outs and employee buy-outs will continue to be encouraged by offering preferential prices.
(6) To make sale procedures more transparent to the public and to Parliament to allay suspicions among both domestic and foreign investors that there has been corruption or undue influence.

Retention of a much reduced number of companies' state ownership represents a departure from the previous strategy which had focused on certain strategic assets and shares being retained by the state in the longer term; now the general principle is that of "temporary" state ownership and the categories of assets being retained are much reduced. Although the state ownership share among companies retained in long-term state ownership may generally not be below fifty per cent plus one vote, in exceptional cases, the minimum set may be at twenty-five per cent plus one vote or a share ensuring voting priority on particular issues, i.e., a "golden" share.

Typically, the "golden" share would give the APV Rt the right to call general meetings of the company and to be represented at board and supervisory board level, but more importantly would require the APV Rt to consent to matters such as: changes in the company's principal activities or a transfer of a substantial part of those activities; decrease in the registered capital; issue of any new shares or the amendment of rights attaching to shares to the detriment of the APV Rt; and the merger, de-merger, transformation or winding up of the company.

A significant number of companies in which the state formerly intended to retain a majority interest will now only be subject to the retention of a minimum shareholding of twenty-five per cent plus one vote, the minimum needed to block certain corporate decisions under the Companies Act (these relate principally to amendments to the Deed of Association, increases and decreases in the capital of the company, changes in class rights attaching to the capital and decisions on the termination, winding up, merger and consolidation of such companies).

Having reduced the percentage shareholdings that the state wishes to retain in key strategic industries, this will allow increased (and, correspondingly, more attractive) parts of such companies to be sold off to overseas strategic and trade investors. The immediate agenda is anticipated to include the partial privatization of the gas and electricity supply industries, the electricity generation sector and further bank privatizations. These privatizations, however, in addition to the privatizations of companies that produce military material will, according to the government's plan, need parliamentary approval. This could again prove to be a bureaucratic and slow process rather than being a measure that encourages the privatization process.

The desire for greater transparency arose because in the latter part of the term of office of the previous government, bids by the management had often seemed to be favored even where there was a competing higher bid from an overseas investor that might have introduced much-needed capital. As a result of the lack of reasoning given by the State Property Agency and the State Asset Holding Company as to the processes of their decision-making, this had created a strongly negative impression on such investors. Equally, sales prices were often not disclosed thereby preventing the market gauging the market value of similar assets.

The State Privatization and Holding Company

The APV Rt is a single member joint stock company originally founded by the Hungarian government as the State Asset Holding Company and which has assumed the rights and liabilities of the former State Property Agency and the Treasury Property Management Organization. The designated role of the APV Rt is the earliest possible sale to the private sector of the shares and assets that it holds, subject to the retention of a defined list of minimum shareholdings. Pending sale it is required to manage the assets in accordance with their designated purpose and to prepare them for privatization.

Decision-Making Process

During the preparations for privatization and the decision-making process, the APV Rt is required to cooperate with the various governmental ministries concerned and to enable professional considerations to be weighed appropriately. Privatization, employment policy, competition policy and environmental protection considerations are also required to be appropriately considered, together with financial performance of obligations.

The Privatization Act sets out the level of long-term state ownership as well as the state organizations or Minister exercising the state's shareholder rights. Defining the pace and ratio of the privatization of shares exceeding the minimum state share is the task of the relevant Minister, while the implementation of privatization is the task of the APV Rt, conducted in agreement with the Minister concerned. In relation to issues that the Companies Act places under the exclusive authority of the shareholders' meeting, the APV Rt is required to take into account the opinion of the Minister concerned.

The APV Rt's shareholder's rights meanwhile are exercised by the Minister without Portfolio responsible for privatization, except for rights conferred on the government by the Act. If the property transferred to the APV Rt includes a protected natural area or real estate protected as a historical or national monument or a historic relic or collection, the disposal, placing under management or encumbrance requires the consent of the Minister for Environmental Protection and Regional Development as well as that of the Minister of Culture and Education, pursuant to a separate law.

The government, however, is required to decide on the privatization concept of companies deemed to be significant to the viability of the national economy, which it may submit to Parliament for approval. The range of companies significant to the viability of the national economy was to be defined by Parliament by 15 August 1995. The trade and employee interest representation bodies are also entitled to express their opinion prior to decision-making on the issue of the privatization concept of these nationally significant companies. In addition, prior to the APV Rt taking a decision on privatization, the chairperson of the APV Rt's board of directors may propose, with the simultaneous suspension of the decision-making procedure that the Privatization Minister, as the person entitled as shareholder in the APV Rt, to turn to the government for an opinion in the case concerned. It remains to be seen whether this element of increased scope for governmental supervision will result in improvements in structuring the privatization of those key companies or whether it will be a potential source of bureaucratic delays.

Supervision of the APV Rt's Activities

While the APV Rt has an internal supervisory system which is responsible for the continuous monitoring of the handling of privatization transactions, this is supplemented by the State Audit Office to which the APV Rt's board is required to report every six months on changes in and utilization of the property assigned to it. As a measure of parliamentary control, the government — simultaneously with submitting the bill on implementing the state budget of the previous year — is required to report to Parliament on the activity of the APV Rt, on changes in the property owned by and that assigned to it, as well as the results of its utilization.

In addition, the competent parliamentary committee has the right to request the APV Rt's board of directors to report to it on any privatization case dealt with out of turn or to Parliament at the motion of at least twenty per cent of the members of Parliament.

Methods of Sale of Property in the APV Rt's Portfolio

Various options are open to the APV Rt for conducting the sale of state property. Sales may be effected directly, or indirectly through

the system of institutions of the capital market or through investment-purpose funds or companies, or through leading officials of companies themselves (simplified privatization). Whether or not the sale is to be effected directly or indirectly, the following procedures are available to effect the sale:
(1) Competitive sale through a public or exclusive tender or through a public auction or bid;
(2) Public offering;
(3) Private or exclusive placement whereby a company is offered to a selected party by inviting a bid; and
(4) Assignment to stock exchange sale/ commission for sale at the Stock Exchange.

In the case of competitive sales, the announcement of a public tender (i.e., where the sphere of bidders cannot be identified in advance) containing the important data of the company must be published in two national dailies or in one national daily and a local paper, according to the seat of the company, as well as in the public information brochure of the APV Rt at least thirty days preceding the initial date set for tender submission.

Exclusive tenders can be announced, but only in exceptional cases. For an exclusive tender, only the fact of bid invitation must be published or announced pursuant to rules prescribed for public tenders. Those concerned exclusively would be invited to bid directly. This option has more usually been adopted where the identity of future owners has been considered to be of significant importance to Hungary's long-term interests. Detailed rules on public auctions and the judgment of tenders are set out in the APV Rt's regulations on invitations to competition.

Public offers were originally viewed as the principal means of broadening and stimulating share ownership in Hungary as well as a means of strengthening newly developing capital markets. However, the limited liquidity of the Budapest Stock Exchange, the difficulty of meeting legal requirements and political indecision over which companies to float (and at what prices) have severely curtailed the number of public offerings. The government hopes to kick-start this initiative by requiring the forthcoming sales of part interests in the utilities sectors to be followed by flotations of those companies on the Stock Exchange by 1997–1998, so as to allow the substantial balance of the state's interest to be sold off.

In private placements, given the limited demand in the domestic capital markets, private placements, particularly to foreign institutional investors, seem likely to continue to play a significant role in Hungary's future privatization efforts; privatizations by way of placement have often involved an international placement of shares combined with a smaller domestic public offering.

In the course of the sale of securities, provisions defined in the securities legislation and associated legal regulations concerned must also be taken into account.

Competitive Bidding

The APV Rt has a general obligation to try to sell the property to be put on public sale or under property management through competitive bidding. Competitive bidding can, however, exceptionally be dispensed with in a limited number of cases:
(1) The public sale of shares of Rt companies limited by shares established for the management of portfolio packages;
(2) Exclusive placement and commissions for stock exchange sale;
(3) Share swaps;
(4) Transferring corporate shares as non-cash property contributions to investment funds promoting privatization;
(5) If the APV Rt sells state property to employees up to a preferential extent (*see* below); or
(6) If the APV Rt (or its legal predecessor) has granted an option for external investor(s).

Sale of Minority Shares

As a general principle, the Act aims to eliminate minority state ownership. state corporate interests below twenty-five per cent plus one vote and not included in the privatization portfolio must be offered for sale by the APV Rt proportionately to the other members of the company or to the company, in this order. If this fails, the share will be sold though public bidding.

Where minority shares remain after the sale of majority shares within the privatization portfolio, these must be sold through auction or public offering (trade) or through exclusive placement, unless a transfer is exceptionally justified without pecuniary compensation. There are two cases of "exceptional" justification for a transfer of state property free of charge. Firstly, if a buyer, by providing appropriate guarantees, assumes the performance of liabilities in respect of such matters as reorganization, capital increase, technical development, restructuring and employment policy, income and social provision for employees and limiting environmental damage. Secondly, if the transfer is to a public foundation, public purpose foundation, public body, or, to some other society of public purpose that takes over the performance of public duties.

Content and Evaluation of Tender

Tender invitations announced by the APV Rt, whether for a sale or for the management of property, must contain:
(1) The aim of the tender;
(2) An indication of the property to be sold and, if necessary, its value (nominal value, exchange rate, etc.);
(3) Conditions of sale, including the applicable payment method, any requirements concerning business policy, employment and development policy as well as the reduction of environmental damages and burdens, as appropriate, and the utilization of assets serving the company's welfare objectives;
(4) The preferential privatization techniques applicable in a particular case; and
(5) Place and deadline of tender submission.

The tender invitation may indicate that a detailed tender package is available for purchase that will be released to the investor on signature of a confidentiality undertaking. The detailed package is required to contain in addition:
(1) The presentation of the company, including basic corporate details as to its name, head office, date of foundation, sphere of activities, period of operation; capital; liabilities and receivables; number of staff; real estate owned or used by the company; and the important personal and professional data of the leading officials and higher-ranking employees;
(2) The description of the business activities of the company supported by analyses, enabling comprehensive evaluation, especially information on production, sales, research and development and investment;
(3) The latest financial data (balance sheet, profit and loss statement, etc.) authenticated by the auditor;
(4) The condition of environmental protection concerning the operation of the company; and

(5) Details of the sale including the planned amount of sales; type of rights of representing the assets (securities) and rights attached to them, the privileges due to founders and the nominal value and/or price.

The APV Rt also must ensure that information related to the property to be sold is made equally available to all parties interested in the sale or investment and ensure equal chances for investors.

Factors Relevant to Privatization Decisions

The new legislation sets out a fairly extensive list of matters to which the APV Rt is required to have particular regard in the course of effecting sales of the assets it holds. These criteria may be grouped into a number of categories: those which are likely to involve economic reorganization; those which are likely to involve a transfer of technology or know-how and those areas where there is a need for domestic sensibilities to be borne in mind.

Economic considerations include:
(1) Increasing economic efficiency and ensuring the provision of the capital required to reduce the deficit of capital in the economy;
(2) Encouraging economic restructuring, including preserving the viability of business organizations and promoting the renewal of corporate structures; and
(3) Reasonably decentralizing structures impeding competition, expanding the range of market participants; and maintaining and strengthening the privatization interest of foreign investors with special regard to strategic (trade) investors, using privatization revenues for financial stability.

The capital deficit will be reduced partly by the introduction of strategic investors, who will be required by the terms of the tenders in which they participate to include proposals for capital increases and partly by the development of the domestic capital market so as to attract both domestic and international capital through companies and investment funds.

Technological considerations include:
(1) Acquisition of internationally advanced techniques, management and marketing knowledge, with a view to stopping the loss of markets and assisting the acquisition of new markets;

(2) Development of product structure and technology; and
(3) Reduction of environmental damage and burdens and export expansion.

Domestic considerations include:
(1) The support of the acquisition of assets by domestic persons, including by employee and management buyouts and by suppliers and raw material producers with special regard to the agricultural and food industry;
(2) Ensuring the protection of domestic producers and industry in accordance with international treaties;
(3) The maintenance and creation of jobs and enforcement of employees' social considerations; and
(4) Allocation of appropriate property for compensation vouchers.

Of these considerations, the APV Rt is required to disclose in advance in the privatization tender those individual considerations whose realization it expects to achieve through the privatization transaction concerned and any principles of evaluation of these considerations in the judgment of the bids submitted.

The general principle of evaluation is that, after weighing every criterion, the APV Rt is required to conclude the sale agreement with the bidder making the best bid. In evaluating the tenders or the individual bids, special regard is also to be given to liabilities assumed by the bidder concerning reorganization, capital increase, technical development, restructuring and employment policy, income and social care of employees and the limitation of environmental damage and burdens. According to the tender announcement, the assumption of such liabilities by the bidder can be preferred to a better price offer in the course of evaluation.

However, the reason for granting any possible preference must be indicated in the information memorandum and to enforce the performance of such liabilities, additional obligations or, as the case may be, other collateral — including sanctions for breach of contract — will be stipulated in the sale contract to be concluded. This supplements the general requirement that the sale contract must stipulate how the APV Rt is to supervise the performance of the contract. The buyer may not exclude responsibility for violating the contract. Equally, where a purchase price is set at the tender, the APV Rt may not exclude its responsibility for breach of contract on sale of the property unless this option is expressly stipulated in the tender announcement.

In addition, in light of the diversity of different privatization techniques permitted by the Act, further guidance is given as to evaluating competing bids using different techniques. In evaluating cash bids and/or bids involving preferential privatization techniques submitted for the property to be sold through competitive bidding, the APV Rt must take the expected revenues into account at their real market value (present value). Bids involving preferential privatization techniques can, however, only be evaluated if no bid has been submitted which meets the tender conditions and meets or exceeds the limit price set by the APV Rt, with payment to be made in full in cash within sixty days after concluding the contract. If several bids have been submitted for the same property applying the preferential privatization techniques, price offers must be compared on the basis of the real market value expected on the basis of the selected privatization technique (i.e., payment method) at the time of evaluation.

If bids are of equal value and deal suitably with any special considerations specified in the tender invitation, priority among the bidders or offerers will be in the following order:
(1) The business organization or cooperative operating with the part- icipation of at least twenty-five per cent of the employees of the business organization concerned;
(2) Participants of the Employees Share Ownership Program of the business organization concerned; and
(3) The employee of the business organization concerned, as an individual entrepreneur.

In the event of equal bids as between a non-Hungarian and a Hungarian bidder, the bid of the domestic investor(s) will be preferred.

The APV Rt is required to publish the result of the tender for sale or for the placing under management, lease, sale or commission, together with the justification of the decision without delay in the same place as the publication of the original tender announcement. For an exclusive tender, this information must also be disclosed directly to bidders. A memorandum must also be prepared, setting out key aspects of the whole sale process. This includes a justification of the selected mode of sale and payment, together with a summary of the submitted bids and justification of the approval of the best bid, indicating the considerations of setting the purchase price (including assumed liabilities influencing the purchase price), the appropriateness of stipulated collateral and other circumstances deemed significant by the APV Rt. Where the employee interest group has expressed an opinion, the APV Rt's written response must be included in the memorandum.

Protection of Employee Interests

The APV Rt is required to give employee interest groups at least thirty days' written notice of any tender advertisement or announcement. In addition, prior to making the actual decision, it is required to provide all details which may affect the employment of employees, their earnings and wage relations, social care, work conditions and training and details of opportunities for employee ownership and which are expected to arise as a consequence of the sale of the property. The APV Rt must also give employee interest groups the opportunity to state their opinion with respect to the privatization decision to be made. This opinion must be included with the information memorandum issued to interested tenderers.

The APV Rt is also obliged to respond in writing to the employees' opinion within fifteen days of receipt and must provide the employee interest groups concerned with the provisions of the concluded sale or property management contracts and other contracts that relate to the matters specified above.

Employee interest groups, as such, have no right to veto a proposed privatization; only a right to be kept informed and to express their opinion. However, their consent is required for the utilization of assets serving welfare or social purposes such as the traditional provision by large Hungarian companies of kindergarten facilities to workers and subsidized accommodation at company-owned resorts.

Simplified Privatization

Certain corporate shares of small-sized and medium-sized business organizations are to be sold through a technique known as "simplified" privatization where the company's own capital did not exceed HUF 600-million (approximately US $4.5-million) and the annual average number of full-time staff did not exceed 500 in 1994.

The APV Rt is to publish two lists of companies subject to simplified privatization — together with a call seeking sale for cash — by 30 September 1995 and 31 December 1995, respectively. Simultaneously with such publication, the APV Rt must ensure that the standard corporate data prescribed by the Act is made available to investors. In "especially justified" cases, the APV Rt may order simplified privatization of companies not falling within these criteria or, before the publication of the afore-mentioned lists, may withdraw a company from the simplified privatization process. Simplified privatization cannot be applied to a financial institute or insurer.

Within ninety days of publication of the lists, cash offers can be submitted for the corporate shares included in the list. If cash offers above the limit price specified in the list are received, the APV Rt will evaluate such cash offers within sixty days after the expiration of the deadline for submission of bids and shall notify the company concerned of the success or otherwise of such offer. If no sufficient cash offer is submitted within the deadline, the APV Rt shall immediately notify the company involved to launch the simplified privatization procedure.

The simplified privatization procedure involves the company's board of directors in the case of an Rt company, or its managing directors in the case of a Kft company, being "entitled and/or required" to decide on the simplified privatization of the business and to take the measures necessary to prepare for privatization. Simplified privatization is generally required to be carried out according to the same provisions and considerations relating to direct privatization by the APV Rt. However, two methods of privatization may not be used, in privatizing a company limited by shares (i.e., an Rt Company) as part of the simplified privatization process: an exclusive placement or a sale without competition. Unlike other privatization methods, nor may state property be transferred free of charge under simplified privatization.

To prepare the privatization, the company may employ a consultant at its own cost. If the preparatory work establishes that the leading officials of the company or the employees of the company or a company majority-owned by the former intend to buy corporate shares up to a total of at least fifty per cent, the board of directors or managing director must inform the APV Rt and ask for its decision. If this is not the case, the company must in any event report its preliminary decision on privatization to the APV Rt and indicate what purchase offers have been received.

In case of several offers, the offer deemed the most favorable by the board of directors or the managing director of the company, by applying the same evaluation criteria as are applied by the APV Rt, shall be indicated. A memorandum on the reasoning for the decision shall be included with the report. The APV Rt must express its opinion on the report within sixty days of receipt and having taken into account the opinion of at least two external consultants on the company's report.

The APV Rt may block the sale or stipulate conditions for the sale and may define collateral for the performance of the contract, but must justify such a decision and notify the company thereof. Even if it does not make use of these rights, the APV Rt must hand over the consultants' opinions to help privatization. If the APV Rt does not exercise its right to prevent the sale or to attach conditions within sixty days after receiving the report, the company may proceed with the simplified privatization in accordance with the report. The APV Rt will sign the share sale contract and may only refuse signature if the contract deviates from the content of the report in its essential content or does not correspond to the Companies Act or other legal regulations. If, for reasons attributable to the company, the contract is not presented to the APV Rt for signature within ninety days after the announcement of the APV Rt's decision or the expiration of the relevant deadline, the APV Rt may terminate the simplified privatization procedure.

Two incentives, effectively a stick and a carrot, are included to ensure that simplified privatization, as far as possible, results in the completion of the disposal of the smaller and medium-sized companies in the APV Rt's portfolio. Leading officials of companies eligible for simplified privatization have an obligation to participate in the sale process and, if, for reasons attributable to them, a sale is not achieved by 31 December 1996, corporate law or labor law measures shall be taken against them, including their removal.

This provision is directed at avoiding managers acting in ways which prolong or disrupt the privatization process; for example, in the past there have been some complaints from the investment community that managers of state companies have withheld information during tender rounds so as to affect the results of the tenders for shares in their companies.

If, however, the sale contract is concluded by 15 June 1996 i.e., within one year after the Act comes into effect, ten per cent of the cash revenue is due to the company and will be applied to the company's assets exceeding the registered or prime capital for use, within a year, for a capital increase. The capital increase would then be issued on a fifty-fifty basis to the company's leading officials and to its employees free of charge.

Preferential Privatization Techniques

The Act prescribes a number of so-called preferential privatization techniques that are essentially refinements of existing privatization techniques. It must be noted, however, that bids involving preferential privatization techniques can only be evaluated if no bid reaching the limit price set by the APV Rt, aimed at paying the full counter-value in cash within sixty days after concluding the contract and meeting the relevant tender conditions, has been submitted.

Sale Through Payment in Installments

Property can be sold on a preferential installment basis over a period of up to fifteen years. Title to the property passes to the buyer on payment of the first installment. Following payment, installments are applied first towards the management fee due at the time of settlement, then on interest and finally on the principal debt. The buyer can also request a grace period of between one and three years with the exception that the first installment is due on the thirtieth day after the conclusion of the sale contract. During this grace period, only the interest and a service charge are payable. The interest rate may not be less than fifty per cent of the base interest rate of the National Bank of Hungary.

The buyer is entitled to perform his payment of the installments in one lump sum in cash at any time and to accelerate the payment of any individual installment at any time. The buyer's performance shall be ensured by stipulating auxiliary liabilities providing appropriate guarantee to the APV Rt as to the performance of the buyer's liabilities without unduly limiting the exercise of the buyer's shareholder's rights. If any installment is not promptly paid, the preference terminates and the balance becomes payable in full and default interest begins to accrue. The APV Rt is also entitled in such circumstances to withdraw from or terminate the contract unless it has been entered into with an ESOP organization.

Sale by Maintaining Ownership Right (Privatization Leasing)

This technique has tended to be used where other methods of privatization are not practicable. It involves the sale, through a public tender, of assets or shares in a transformed state enterprise on an installment basis, such that the ownership rights transfer on payment of the final installment. The leasing technique aims to develop those companies that currently operate inefficiently, but which may be brought into profit through effective financial and asset management and to widen the sphere of the privatization participants to include Hungarian investors without significant capital. The buyer must now be a natural person, whereas under the previous legislation the lessee could be any natural or legal person, Hungarian or otherwise, who was capable of entering into a civil contract. This would appear to be a major constraining factor on the degree to which this technique will be employed over the next phase of privatization.

During the "lease" period, which is effectively a period of deferred alienation of the property, the lessee provides management and organization services directed at the reorganization of the company, based on a separate contract for which it receives a management fee. In turn, the lessee also pays a fee that constitutes a partial price for the company's shares or assets; at the end of the period, the lessee obtains ownership of the company or assets in question.

Fees paid to the lessee must be applied towards amortization, but can be accounted for by the company as extraordinary expenditure. On settlement of the total amount of the fee, the shares of the leased company or the leased assets are transferred to the lessee's ownership without separate fee or agreement. If, however, the total amount is not settled, the APV Rt is entitled to terminate the contract and any installments made up to that point are irrecoverable. To reduce the APV Rt's risk, the lessee can also be required to provide a guarantee in relation to the payment of the fee.

The period of deferred alienation is set out in the contract and may be at most ten years, during which period the lessee has every membership right (for example, participation at the shareholders' meetings, a right to vote and a right to dividends) except the right of alienation, subject always to any limits or conditions placed by the APV Rt on the exercise of these rights in the contract.

Manager and Employee Buy-Out

Shares in state-owned business organizations can be acquired (with the assistance of loans available for this purpose) by their management or employees through a buy-out, i.e., an offer submitted by an economic or Civil Law association established by the management and employees together. One or more external members can also participate in the association, but their voting right may not reach fifty per cent before the date of transfer determined in the purchase contract.

In case of a management or employee buy-out, the offeror(s) must offer to buy at least twenty per cent of the state's ownership share for cash, with payment in cash to be made within sixty days after conclusion of the contract. The APV Rt will, however, relinquish its voting right over the whole state ownership share for the benefit of the offeror(s) for up to five years, according to the conditions set in the contract. During this period, the buyer is obliged to buy additional corporate shares in the manner, and at a price and under interest conditions as defined in the contract, so that a fifty per cent plus one vote majority must be achieved within five years. The acquisition of corporate shares can take place in each case only for cash and in a lump sum.

If the buyer seriously violates its contractual liabilities, especially its purchase obligations or if the company's financial position significantly deteriorates as a result of the buyer's activity, the APV Rt may immediately abandon the contract, although this does not affect the ownership right of the corporate shares already paid for. The APV Rt will also annually check and, if necessary, review, at the company's expense, the company's balance sheet.

Management or employee buy-outs have fluctuated in popularity. Initially they attracted little interest, but later became more popular during the latter period of the previous government and even seemed to be given preference in a number of cases to financially more favorable bids from non-Hungarians. However, the strong preference in the legislation towards cash sales would seem to mean that this may limit the previous trend towards more management buyouts.

Employee Share Ownership Program (ESOP)

Act Number XLIV of 1992 on employee share purchase programs was passed with the aim of enabling the employees of an already-transformed state enterprise to acquire shares within the framework of an ESOP.

Employees may finance the share buy-outs by E-loans (*see* below) or other loans. Employees, employed for at least half of the legal working time by the company and whose working relationship lasts for at least six months, are entitled to participate in the ESOP, although the statutes of the ESOP organization to be established for handling the acquisition of ownership of shares may establish a period of up to five years as a condition of entitlement. If the working relationship is terminated, the employee's participation right in the ESOP is also canceled. An employee may participate in only one ESOP organization at a time. This scheme has proved to be especially successful in small-sized to medium-sized companies.

Preference for Employee Ownership Acquisition

On the sale of corporate shares in a transformed business organization employees are entitled to acquire state property on a preferential basis, unless the majority share is acquired by an investor which has assumed contractual liability in a sales contract, supported by appropriate collateral, for the employment of employees and the improvement of their working conditions.

The forms of preference will be extended to employees individually and for the companies, co-operatives or ESOP organizations established by them in a uniform manner, and the preferences extended in various ways are taken into account together. If a buy-out is initiated by an employee group, or if not all the employees participated in the preferential purchase program, the possible extent (amount) of preferences is established in proportion to the number of employees. The preference can be granted at a later date to those who have not utilized it as well. The following preferences are available:

(1) A preference corresponding to 150 per cent of the annual minimum wage can be granted to each employee, but so that the aggregate amount of any corporate shares so acquired does not exceed fifteen per cent of the company's subscribed capital; and

(2) Price discounts and/or payment-in-installment options can be extended to employees up to fifty per cent of the sales price. If payment of the reduced purchase price is to be made in installments (with the exception of sale under the ESOP for which the provisions of the ESOP law are applicable), the period for payment in installment can be up to three years after payment of fifteen per cent of the reduced purchase price

in cash, and the prevailing interest rate payable on state debt can be charged as interest for the purchase price outstanding.

When the employees shares are sold, the projection base is the nominal value. During the sale, preference can be granted to a maximum of ninety per cent of the nominal value. In past privatizations the employees have generally been allowed to purchase their shares for between ten and fifty per cent of par value.

Privatization Loans (Existence Credit or E-Loans)

The E-loan program was established in 1993 as another scheme designed to help Hungarians purchase interests in state-owned companies. Typically such loans have been provided by commercial banks to state employees seeking to buy their companies on satisfying the relevant criteria as to creditworthiness. Maturities vary from ten to fifteen years, with a grace period of up to three years. By 1995, over HUF 120-billion had been borrowed in relation to over 450 companies. The shares or assets purchased with the credit can only be disposed of with the consent of the financial institution making available the credit for so long as the credit remains outstanding.

However, over the next one to two years, many of the initial E-loans will become due for repayment and the government is conscious of the risk of large-scale default. Many of the recipients of the loans could therefore fall into bankruptcy with a knock on effect on a banking system already burdened by high levels of bad debt. Against this background the Government decided in the Privatization Act 1995 to introduce a cap on the use of E-loans; previously there had been no limit on the amount of money a company could receive through the E-loan scheme. Now, E-loans can be used by individual domestic entrepreneurs to fund up to half of the purchase price, subject to a maximum of up to HUF 50-million. This limit applies irrespective of the numbers of buyers or contracts to be concluded with several buyers of the same property.

The curtailment of the E-loan program is likely to assist the drive to cash sales not only by virtue of the reduced availability of loans, but also in relation to purchasing companies that are struggling to repay E-loan debts, who may be anticipated to need financial assistance from external investors so as to repay the original E-Loans.

Temporary Utilization of Property

If the sale of the property fails, or it can be established that the conditions for its alienation are temporarily unfavorable, the APV Rt is entitled, following a public tender, to conclude property management contracts with a property manager either through an agency contract, an entrepreneurial contract or a portfolio property management contract to utilize the property in question, the object being the preservation or achievement of the property value set in the contract or the achievement of the growth of property through yield (whether as to dividends or share value). The parties are free to compose the content of the contract within the limits of the Privatization Act and other legal regulations as well as the terms of the tender conditions. There are several types of individual contract of property management:
(1) The agency contract, which is aimed at preserving the value and condition of the property, may provide that, in addition to the commission fee, a certain portion of the yield of the property is also due to the property manager.
(2) The entrepreneurial contract, in which the entrepreneur exercises ownership rights over the property, other than alienation and encumbrance rights, for the fee paid by him as defined in the contract and undertakes to guarantee the achievement of a previously defined yield on the property as well as being obliged to maintain or reach the level of the property value determined in the contract. The APV Rt may agree to cede a part of the yield to the entrepreneur. However, this must be indicated in the tender conditions and the contract.
(3) The portfolio property managing contract under which the property manager assumes liability for achieving a yield or property growth defined in the contract. In return it is paid a fee paid by the APV Rt and exercises ownership rights over the property, including the right of alienation. The contract may also be directed at paying a certain amount of cash or the acquisition of membership rights in other companies. The APV Rt and the property manager may agree on the division of the yield or the property value growth provided this was referred to in the tender conditions and the contract. The property management contract may also stipulate that payment is due to the manager only on the achievement of the result determined in the contract: this, however, does not affect

the refunding of costs emerging in connection with the property management. In the event of a serious breach of the contract, the APV Rt may terminate the contract with immediate effect.

The Act also lays down certain basic rules of property management, which require the property manager to perform its liabilities under the contract and take responsibility for them *vis-à-vis* the APV Rt with the appropriate increased expertise and diligence. To secure fulfillment of the obligations undertaken in the property management contract, the property manager will also be required to guarantee the contract and to charge its own property (e.g., by way of lien, security deposit or suretyship). The APV Rt is also required to monitor regularly the activity of a property manager to whom proprietary rights have been transferred.

Property management may also lead to privatization in two ways. Firstly, during the period of the property management contract, the property manager may propose to buy the corporate share managed by him from the APV Rt. Secondly, the contract may itself provide that, after at least two years, the property manager may either buy the property managed by him by way of a unilateral written statement or may be compelled to buy the property at the written call of the organization exercising the state's ownership right.

IMPLICATIONS FOR FOREIGN INVESTORS

The changes introduced by the Privatization Act are generally considered to be less radical than were expected or could have been introduced. Nevertheless, the consolidation of the legislation and of the bodies responsible for implementing the privatization process is to be welcomed, as is the fine-tuning of a number of existing privatization techniques. The changes on the procedural level should also serve to provide more comfort for would-be investors that there will be greater transparency as to the factors that will be relevant in the making of decisions on privatization and greater publicity as to the reasoning behind the decisions.

However, much will depend on the way that the Privatization Act is applied in practice. Investors will undoubtedly not have forgotten that, at the time this legislation was being prepared, there were a number of high profile instances of governmental intervention in the privatization process (for example, in relation to the abortive sale of the Hungar Hotel chain). Nor will they fail to note point that the Privatization Act potentially allows more governmental intervention than did the previous legislation.

The greater willingness to cede majority control in major companies is, however, a significant step and will alleviate the concerns of investors about their ultimate ability to be able to control the investments they make without suffering undue governmental influence. Although control will not normally be granted immediately, it should not be overlooked that inward investors who, in the past, have been allowed only to take a significant minority interest in a number of the higher profile privatizations, have in practice been able to exercise a significant degree of control. For example, in the case of MATAV, the Magyar Com consortium, although holding only thirty per cent of the shares was given half the seats and a tie-breaking vote on the operating committee of MATAV, as well as being entitled to nominate the chief financial and technical officers, albeit not the chief executive. The holding of a share interest of at least twenty-five per cent plus one vote also enabled it to delay the APV Rt's plans for a flotation of a tranche of its remaining shares in the company.

The state asset holding companies have, however, in the past not been immune to trying to use their presence as a continuing member in a company to try to secure the payment of dividends even though this may be inconsistent with the interests of the company in question; the state holding companies suffer from the dilemma that insofar as shares are not sold off, the shares must be regarded as a source of income in the form of dividends. As such, the dividend policy is a matter about which investors will continue to be well advised to clarify at the time of making their investment.

CONCESSIONS

Another device that has been used by Hungary to "privatize" the activities carried out by the public sector has been through the offering of concessions. Act Number XVI of 1991 on Concession (Concession Act) sets out the categories of assets of, and activities currently carried out by, the state, whether by the APV Rt or at the level of local municipalities, whose use or performance may only be delegated to the private sector through a concession. These include the following principal areas: infrastructure (roads, railways, ports, airports, canals and sewerage), utility services, mining, transport, gambling, and postal services.

The concession process involves the invitation of a tender for the utilization of certain assets or the undertaking of the specified activities. A concession agreement will be entered into with the winner of the tender. These activities can also be carried out by a majority state-owned company established or to be established by the state for such purpose. The concession agreement should regulate the terms and conditions of the concession, such as:

(1) The amount of concession fee, if any;
(2) The list of those ancillary or additional activities that could be carried out by the concession company;
(3) The term of the concession (the maximum is thirty-five years; this period may be extended without holding a new tender by up to half of the original concession period);
(4) The termination of the concession; and
(5) The right and obligation of the state to supervise compliance with the provisions of the Concession Agreement and any other relevant terms and conditions included in the relevant sectoral laws.

The winner of a concession tender must form a concession company within ninety days after the winning of the concession tender. Failure to do so should result in termination of the agreement. The concession company may not authorize any other business organization to provide the concession activity without the prior approval of the state or the municipality.

Winning a tender to operate a concession is, however, not the end of the matter. Thereafter it becomes necessary to finance the project and the financing of a number of concession projects has been affected by the deterioration in Hungary's macro-economic position during 1994 and 1995, which has correspondingly resulted in the government being drawn into making a greater contribution towards the projects than originally planned or even allowing concession contracts to be amended.

CONCLUSION

Hungary's approach to privatization can be characterized as having been of a much more piecemeal nature than those of its East European neighbors. Rather than mass privatization schemes it has tended to privatize individual enterprises, through a variety of sale techniques. The principal sale technique has been the trade sale owing to the general lack of domestic capital and the underdevelopment of the financial infrastructure, factors that have limited the scope for employing methods such as public offers and management buyouts.

Although this has meant that the privatization process is in some respects less complete than in, for example, the Czech Republic, it is anticipated that in the longer term this may result in better managed and more efficient companies. In particular, the policy in favor of direct trade sales seems to have had some success in introducing new capital and technological, marketing and management expertise, with the restructuring of the enterprises being left to the new owners rather than being carried out by the state before privatization. A criticism that, by contrast, has been increasingly leveled at the Czech model of privatization has been that privatization has only occurred at the legal level, in that the state has retained, directly or indirectly, major shareholdings in a significant number of corporations. Moreover, the investment funds that have become the principal shareholders in the "privatized" corporations have yet to develop the level of shareholder supervision that can be expected from a trade investor becoming a direct shareholder in a company.

Equally, not only do mass privatization schemes not attract external financing for the purposes of industrial restructuring, they provide less focus in relation to the allocation of environmental responsibilities as between the state and investors and, correspondingly, do not tend to promote environmental improvements. The device of the trade sale particularly allows the government and the trade investor to come to some kind of agreement as to how to allocate responsibility for past environmental damage. However, as against this, full-blown discussions over responsibility and/or the costs of clean-up may equally lead to purchases falling through.

This may be even more true with the introduction in the Hungarian Environmental Act 1995 of joint liability between the owners of property and the users of the same property. As against this, privatization officials with a remit to accelerate privatization and to secure revenues for the state budget may be likely to come under pressure to close deals quickly by making relatively *ad hoc* arrangements in relation to environmental liabilities. This is reflected by the fact that in the period 1990–1994, the State Property Agency provided over HUF 52-billion in guarantees to companies in its portfolio, including HUF 8-billion in relation to guarantees to cover the costs of repairing environmental damage whose existence was not known at the time of privatization.

However, despite these hopeful signs about the appropriateness of the privatization techniques which have been adopted and despite securing significant levels of inward investment over the last five years, Hungary's privatization progress in recent times has been generally disappointing, and there remain ahead many stiff challenges to the privatization program, particularly for a government keen to guarantee maximum proceeds so that such proceeds can be included in the budget income.

The Privatization Act has, however, introduced a number of measures to facilitate the privatization process, which have generally been positively received by the business community, both in Hungary and internationally. However, their nature is such that they will take time to bear fruit and much will depend on the development of the APV Rt's practice. It remains, in particular, to be seen whether governmental supervision will result in improvements in structuring the privatization of those key companies or whether it will be a potential source of bureaucratic delays. Moreover, as important as the content of the new legislation and the much-touted streamlining and transparency of the revised privatization process will be the fact that even if governmental interference is minimal and the practice of the APV Rt even-handed in its dealings with investors, there will still be numerous legal and practical issues left to be resolved with investors. Some of these are indicated below.

First, re-organization of the governmental agencies and the companies under their control and the re-allocation of their responsibilities has led in some cases to problems of identification of title to assets and, in particular, land and shares. This is confused still further by the statutory entitlements of municipalities and state social security funds to receive transfers of shares (in the latter case valued at some HUF 300-billion), all of which are capable of confusing the position as to whom is entitled to sell any particular packet of shares.

Second, having an efficient and open privatization procedure can still be undermined if investors are not provided with sufficient corporate information or if insufficient responses are given to queries arising out of the due diligence process. Equally, timetables to effect sales need to be realistically set rather than artificially dictated by the requirements of ensuring that some monies reach the state's coffers for this financial year.

Third, often, an investor will find that the rights of employees are fairly well entrenched, be it in the collective agreement entered with the relevant trade union or even in the articles of association adopted at the time of transformation.

Finally, the state can be expected to attempt so far as possible to require the trade purchasers to accept responsibility for past environmental liabilities and clean-up costs. With the entry into force in December 1995 of the new environmental legislation, it seems likely that buyers will increasingly want to agree an appropriate solution as to these matters and will not be prepared to make a purchase of potentially environmentally hazardous land or a company owning such land without some kind of protection.

Despite these problems, now that the Privatization Act is in place, the government will have fewer excuses if the privatization process continues to meander. Moreover, over the first half of 1995, there has been increasing recognition from the government that the prolongation of the privatization process has not only witnessed a significant decline in value of the assets in question, but the uncertainty as to the privatization timetable has had an impact on the long term development strategy of companies and has tended to result in companies focusing more on short-term interests. Accordingly, the need to proceed more quickly is acknowledged before the value of the portfolio held by the state declines still further.

Similarly the experience in relation to the privatization of the energy sector has been one of growing realization on the part of the government as to the need to be responsive to the requirements of investors and to put in place appropriate corporate structures and legislative framework so as to ensure that privatizations are done on a realistic basis; Hungary can no longer consider itself the only safe place in Central and Eastern Europe for the money of investors. The combination of the new legislation, together with these more progressive indicators, suggest that the privatization process in Hungary appears to be reverting to a steadier course and gives some cause to expect that the forthcoming privatizations in the energy sector will go some way to restoring Hungary's reputation as a stable home for investments in the Central and Eastern European region.

ITALY

Emanuele Turco
Studio Legale Emanuele Turco
Rome, Italy

INTRODUCTION

The Italian privatization process does not follow traditional rules. Privatization means the transfer of ownership of government-controlled state enterprises to the private sector.[1]

In eastern and western countries, privatization has been the product of a drastic change in the socio-economic regime or of a new political majority. However, privatization in Italy has been the result of neither of these traditional causes.

Political Background

Since the end of World War II, the Italian political scene has been dominated by two political forces: the Christian Democrat Party and the Communist Party. The *Democrazia Cristiana*, in coalition with minority parties, governed the country almost uninterruptedly for nearly fifty years and was in power when the privatization process began. Although the Italian Communist Party was the largest opposition party and the strongest communist party of the western world, it never governed the country nor did it collapse along with the Berlin wall and the regimes of Eastern Europe. In Italy, consequently, the privatization process was started by the same political forces which inherited, and later expanded, what was probably the most extensive state ownership system of the western world.

---

[1] Blommenstein, Geiger, and Hare, *Methods of Privatizing Large Enterprises* (Organization for Economic Cooperation and Development (1993)), p. 11.

The presence of the Italian state in the private sector dates to 1926. At that time, the Fascist government was forced to acquire the assets of the bankrupt *Banca Italiana di Sconto* which had gained control of financially troubled manufacturing companies and banks. Economic and social reasons forced the Mussolini government to acquire other banks with their portfolio of manufacturing companies. For instance, at the end of 1930, just before it was acquired by the Italian *State, Banca Commerciale Italiana* directly or indirectly controlled more than 320 companies out of a total of about 17,400 companies nationwide.[2]

State Acquisitions

Following World War II, acquisition by the state of financially troubled companies was also viewed as a way of containing the vast unemployment left by the war. Although economic reasons played a role in the expansion of the state-entrepreneur, social reasons were the dominant factor. In fact, social doctrines inspired the state's expansion in traditionally private economic areas and its investing in new sectors. The Christian Democrats, who governed the country, were heavily influenced by the social doctrines of the Catholic Church.

The opposition, the Italian Communist Party, was obviously influenced by Marxist social doctrines which favored full employment over profit realization. The policies of these two parties on unemployment often converged in the Italian Parliament in the law-making process. Social doctrines, filtered through political parties, explain in large part the significant involvement of the Italian State in the private sector. This made Italy a unique case among the seven most industrialized western countries.

Beginning of the Privatization Process

In 1991, the year before the privatization process took some of its most significant initial steps, *Istituto per la Ricostruzione Industriale*

---

[2] Di Stefano, *Privatizzazioni e Sistema delle Partecipazioni Statali*, (ETI–IL FISCO, 1994), p. 15.

(IRI), a state conglomerate holding, had more than 408,000 employees (2.3 per cent of the total Italian work force) and controlled 267 companies.[3] The same year, *Ente Nazionale Idrocarburi* (ENI), the state petrochemical holding, had a work force of 131,248 and "consolidate(d) a total of 321 companies and joint ventures" worldwide.[4]

The state deficit, however, had spiralled to 115 per cent of Italy's gross national product by this stage. This was considered intolerable by an increasingly large section of the population.[5] The sale of state holdings was perceived as a necessity for the budget. The proceeds could have been used to contain the public debt and the state would no longer have to constantly recapitalize distressed state enterprises with public funds.[6]

Some political forces used the deficit issue to advocate privatization. This was actually an indirect way to attack the political positions of the Christian Democrats and of the Socialist Party, the second largest member of the government coalition. The state deficit, public opinion pressure and the arguments of some opposition

---

3 IRI *Gruppo*, 1992–93 Yearbook, p. 19. IRI was established by Royal Decree Law Number 5 of 23 January 1933 on the "incorporation of Istituto per la Ricostruzione Industriale, with registered offices in Rome". IRI's legal nature and powers were redefined by Legislative Decree Number 51 of 12 February 1948 on the "approval of the new bylaws of Istituto per la Ricostruzione Industriale (IRI)" (LD 51/48). Under Article 1 of LD 51/48, IRI "is a financial entity of public law . . . (and) shall manage the (equity) participations and assets owned by it. In the public interest, the Council of Ministers shall establish the general trend of the Institution's activities". After the war, IRI was assigned a new task by Law Number 940 of 30 August 1951 on the "increase of the endowment fund of Istituto per la Ricostruzione Industriale" (Law 940/51). Article 4 of Law 940/51 provides that IRI "must invest part of its resources in Southern Italy for the reconstruction, creation and development of manufacturing industries, in order to reach at least the level of employment existing in the southern regions prior to the war destruction and relating to industries which were dependent, in any way, on the same Institution". (IRI was reorganized into a company in 1992).

4 ENI Group Consolidated Financial Statements, 31 December 1991, pp. 13 and 20.

5 Uckmar, "Problemi Giuridici delle Privatizzazioni", *Giuffr*, 1994, p. 38.

6 Cardia, "Profili Giuridici della Privatizzazione", *Il Sole 24 Ore*, 1994, p. 21.

politicians were the primary causes which forced an otherwise disinterested government and parliament to act on privatization in 1990.

The Impetus for Privatization

Starting in 1992, investigating judges in Milan proved that political corruption was more deeply rooted than expected. Their judicial investigations unveiled a pattern of bribes, corruption and patronage which characterized the connections between politics and the economy. An immediate result of these highly publicized investigations was the drastic decline in popularity of the Christian Democrats and of the Italian Socialist Party. As a result, privatization was perceived as a moralization factor in politics by reducing state involvement in the productive sectors of the economy. Further incentive to the privatization process came from European Union legislation discouraging any financial support to "public undertakings" which might effect or alter competition. This legislation provided additional pressure on the Italian government to act on privatization.[7]

Containing the public debt and moralizing the public sector became the main objectives of the Italian privatization process. One corollary objective was a debt-equity swap by the state to transform government bondholders into shareholders of privatized companies. Another related objective was the attainment of market efficiency by subjecting former state managers and companies to stock market and bankruptcy rules. A further objective of privatization was to implement the Constitution, aiming at a more balanced property-owning democracy. In fact, Article 47 of the Italian Constitution "favors the access of the people's savings . . . to direct and indirect investment in shares of the large productive undertakings of the country".

It was predictable that the objectives of privatization would meet strong political resistance. The Italian privatization process had started with an intrinsic contradiction: politicians were expected to sever their ties, through privatization, with the same state holdings

---

7 Treaty of Rome, Articles 92–94 on "aides granted by states" and Commission Directive 80/723/EEC of 25 June 1980 "on the transparency of financial relations between Member States and public undertakings", as amended.

they had nourished or created and utilised for half a century as sources of power, easy financing, votes and patronage.

Therefore, it is not surprising that the main legislative tool used to implement the privatization plan has been the *Decreto Legge*, or Decree Law (DL), which is a law activated by government rather than by parliament. Under Article 77 of the Constitution, the government "in extraordinary cases of necessity and urgency" can issue "provisional measures having the force of law". DL's can be amended by parliament and lose their "efficacy" if they are not "converted into law" by parliament within sixty-days.[8] Many DL's on privatization have never been converted into law. A few had to be presented several times before they were converted into law with the amendments requested by parliament. Despite the opposing forces involved, the privatization process is in motion and has already made significant progress.

REGULATION OF THE FIRST PRIVATIZATIONS

Between the middle of 1990 and the end of 1993, when the first major privatizations began, more than forty laws were enacted and implementing regulations issued by the authorities delegated to structure the legal framework of the program.

The most significant legislation and regulations are examined and discussed below.

The Law on Public Credit Institutions

The first major law on privatization was an ordinary law enacted by parliament: Law Number 218 of 30 July 1990 on "provisions regarding the restructuring and asset integration of public law credit institutions" (the Law on Public Credit Institutions). It indicates the corporate law solution to privatize public entities in

---

8 DLs are effective from the date of their publication in the *Official Gazette* of the Italian Republic. Parliament's amendments are effective the day after the law converting a DL is published in the *Official Gazette* (Article 15, Paragraph 5 of Law Number 400 of 23 August 1988 on "regulation of government activity and organization of the Presidency of the Council of Ministers" (the Government Organization Law)).

general and establishes the general tax regime of privatizations. The law authorizes the *enti creditizi pubblici* (public credit institutions) to reorganize into *società per azioni* (SpA), that is,[9] companies (Article 1). As a consequence, *Istituto Mobiliare Italiano* (IMI), a major medium-term credit institution and financial services group and *Banca Nazionale del Lavoro* (BNL), a large credit institution, were reorganized into SpA's in 1990 and 1991 respectively.

The Law on Public Credit Institutions provides that capital gains are not realized through the capital contributions (in cash, in kind or receivables) to the SpA's, resulting from the reorganization of the public credit instructions (Article 7.2).[10] "The registration, mortgage and cadastral taxes" applicable to "mergers, reorganizations and capital contributions" are due at the aggregate "rate of one per thousand and up to the maximum amount not exceeding 100-million Lire" (Article 7.1).

Registration Tax

The tax base of a capital contribution in kind is normally the market "value" of the immovable property or of the business concern contributed whereas for a merger of companies the tax base is the "capital and reserves of the merged companies".[11]

The standard tax rate for a capital contribution of immovable property is eight per cent while the standard rate for a merger is one per cent.[12]

---

9 SpA is are governed by Articles 2325–2461 of Royal Decree Number 262 of 16 March 1942 on the "approval of the text of the Civil Code".

10 Capital gains are governed by Article 81 of the Decree of the President of the Republic (DPR) Number 917 of 22 December 1986 on the "approval of the consolidated laws on income taxes". Two basic income taxes are normally applicable at the aggregate rate of 52.2 per cent: IRPEG or corporate income tax (36 per cent) and ILOR or local income tax (16.2 per cent).

11 Articles 50(3)(4) and 51(2) of DPR Number 131 of 26 April 1986 on the "approval of the consolidated text of the provisions concerning the registration tax" (Registration Tax Law).

12 Articles 1(1) and Article 4(1)(b) of the Tariff, first part, attached to the Registration Tax Law.

Mortgage and Cadastral Taxes

The tax base for the mortgage and cadastral taxes is normally the same as that for the registration tax.[13] The standard rates are 0.4 per cent for the cadastral tax and 1.6 per cent for the mortgage tax.[14]

The Economic Public Entities Law

Decree Law Number 386 of 5 December 1991 on the "reorganization of the economic public entities, disposal of state shares and sale of assets object of economic management", converted into Law Number 35 of 29 January 1992 (the Economic Public Entities Law), authorized the reorganization into SpA's of economic public entities (EPE's).[15]

The EPE Law provides that the companies resulting from the reorganization "succeed" the EPE's "in all legal relationships" and their "endowment fund becomes the company capital owned by the state".[16] Under this legislation, they are also "subject to the general company laws in force".[17] The EPE Law also provides[18] that the shares (participations) owned by the state in the companies resulting

---

13 Articles 2(1) and 10 of Legislative Decree Number 347 of 31 October 1990 on the "approval of the consolidated text of the provisions concerning the mortgage and cadastral taxes" (Mortgage and Cadastral Taxes Law).

14 Mortgage and Cadastral Law, Article 10(1) and Article 1 of the attached Tariff.

15 Although EPE's are normally established by law and have legal personality in public law, their activities are governed by private law but are not subject to bankruptcy under Article 2221 CC. EPE's business activities, however, are instrumental for the attainment of public interests. EPE's were defined as "public entities which operate in the production field and carry out an economic activity under the competition regime" by Article 1 of Law Number 1303 of 16 June 1938 on "revocation of the prohibition concerning the inclusion in trade unions of public entities, in any way named, operating in the production field and carrying out exclusively or mainly an economic activity". This law is no longer in force.

16 EPE Law, Article 3.

17 EPE Law, Article 5.

18 EPE Law, Article 9.

from the reorganization "can be sold in compliance with the directives" to be issued by resolution of the Interministerial Committee for Economic Planning (CIPE).[19] The CIPE directives regulated "the publicity, limits and conditions" of the "procedures of valuation, placement and sale of the (share) participations". Even partial placement operations are to be made:

> ". . . on the financial market and with institutional investors . . . on valuation . . . and establishing the sale conditions, prices, amounts, modalities and the forms of protection of the public shareholder's rights, even if a minority shareholder, as well as the assignment of controlling shares, considering the companies' efficiency needs".[20]

The sale must ensure that the shares are freely circulated and widely available to the public. It must also prevent, indirectly, concentrated accumulations of shares or dominant positions.[21] The reorganization of the EPE's into companies and the valuation and sale of the shares of the reorganized companies can be carried out with the assistance of intermediary institutions of proven experience. The professional fees for the valuation are to be established by Decree of the Minister of the Treasury having consulted with the Minister of Justice.[22]

The proceeds resulting from the sale are paid to the budget revenue with the modalities to be determined by the Minister of the

---

[19] The CIPE is a committee composed of the following Ministers: (1) President of the Council of Ministers (chairman); (2) Minister of Budget and Economic Planning (vice-chairman); (3) Minister of Foreign Affairs; (4) Minister of the Treasury; (5) Minister of Finance; (6) Minister of Industry, Commerce and Crafts; (7) Minister of Agricultural, Food and Forest Resources; (8) Minister of Foreign Commerce; (9) Minister of Public Works; (10) Minister of Labor and Social Security and; (11) Minister of Transportation and Navigation. CIPE was established by Law Number 48 of 27 February 1967 on "authority and organization of the Ministry of Budget and Economic Planning and establishment of the Committee of Ministers for Economic Planning".

[20] EPE Law, Article 10.

[21] EPE Law, Article 11.

[22] EPE Law, Article 12.

Treasury.[23] The tax benefits provided for by the Law on Public Credit Institutions are also applicable to the reorganization of EPE's into SpA's.[24]

The Economic Public Entities Reorganization Law

The first law to actually mandate the reorganization of certain EPE's into companies was Decree Law Number 333 of 11 July 1992 on "urgent measures for the recovery of public finance", converted into Law Number 359 of 8 August 1992 (the EPE Reorganization Law). This law reorganized IRI, the seventh largest conglomerate in the world, ENI, the petrochemical EPE, *Istituto Nazionale Assicurazioni* (INA), the insurance company, EPE, and *Ente Nazionale per l'Energia Elettrica* (ENEL), the electricity company EPE, into private companies. The shares of these companies, as well as those of IMI and BNL were transferred to the Ministry of the Treasury and the Minister was to exercise the "shareholder's rights". The Minister of the Treasury was directed:

> "... to prepare a reorganization program ... aimed at the increase in value of the (state) participations also by way of provisions for the transfer of assets and branches of businesses, participation swaps, mergers, consolidations and any other act necessary ... the listing of the companies resulting from the reorganization ... and the amount of the proceeds to be used for the reduction of the public debt".[25]

"The operations connected with the (company) reorganization ... shall be exempt from any tax and duty."[26] The reorganization program had to be prepared by the Minister of the Treasury in agreement with the Minister of Budget and Economic Planning and the Minister of Industry, Commerce and Crafts (the Privatization Ministers) and

---

23 EPE Law, Article 13.
24 EPE Law, Article 18.
25 EPE Reorganization Law, Article 16.
26 EPE Reorganization Law, Article 19.

the Minister of State Participations.[27] The Minister of the Treasury conveyed the program to the President of the Council of Ministers (Prime Minister) who, in turn, requested the opinion of the Chamber of Deputies and of the Senate (Italian Parliament). Finally, the program had to be submitted to the Council of Ministers (Cabinet) to become operative.[28] The program was approved on 30 December 1992 by resolution of the Council of Ministers.

The CIPE Resolution

Article 9 of the EPE Law provided that the CIPE had to issue "directives" to regulate "the publicity, limits and conditions" of the "procedures of valuation, placement and sale of the shares" owned by the state through the Minister of the Treasury. On 30 December 1992, the CIPE issued directives concerning the modalities and procedures for the transfer of state participations in companies resulting from the reorganization of economic public entities and autonomous agencies (CIPE Resolution).

Although this resolution does not have the force of law, it is a fundamental regulatory source of the Italian privatization program. It was aimed, in particular, at regulating the disposal of the companies resulting from the EPE Reorganization Law as well as their controlled companies.[29] As will be seen later, the influence of the CIPE resolution on the 1994 comprehensive privatization law has been quite pervasive.

Provisions of the Interministerial Committee Resolution

Prior to their sale, the companies to be privatized, in agreement with their owner, may be assisted by specialized consultants

---

27 The Ministry of State Participations was abolished as of 22 February 1993 by Decree Law Number 118 of 23 April 1993, converted into Law Number 202 of 23 June 1993, on urgent provisions for the abolition of the Ministry of State Participations and for the reorganization of IRI, ENI, ENEL, IMI, BNL and INA. The authority of the Ministry of State Participations was transferred to the Ministry of Industry, Commerce and Crafts.

28 EPE Reorganization Law, Article 16.

29 CIPE Resolution, Paragraphs 1 and 2.

(merchant banks, auditing firms, legal and tax experts) if corporate, industrial, financial and organizational restructuring is required.[30] Furthermore, recapitalization operations are to be favorably considered.[31] The next steps are valuation of the companies and selection of the underwriting group. For this purpose, at least three offers from "national and/or foreign specialists" must be obtained in order to valuate the company to be privatized and to select the manager of the underwriting group.[32]

The selection of the firm entrusted with the valuation is to be made by the "owner" of the company to be privatized. The owner is to consider the specialists' offers, also from the qualitative point of view.[33] The valuation of the companies which are being earmarked for privatization is to be made with the assistance of one or more national or international specialized intermediaries. The valuation must take into account the size of the company capital, its income capacity and the values determined for similar operations relating to businesses of the same sector concluded in Italy or abroad. Furthermore, the specific importance to the potential buyers of the participations offered as well as the market conditions and the appropriate price adjustments in order to favor widely dispersed share distribution must be taken into account.[34] The manager of the underwriting group cannot be entrusted with the valuation. This firm, however, must be part of the underwriting group.[35]

The privatization methods are limited to three:
(1) Public offering, whether at a fixed price or at a price determined with an auction system;
(2) Public auction, with possible preselection of participants also finalized to the formation of a stable nucleus of lead shareholders; and
(3) Private negotiations.[36]

---

30 CIPE Resolution, Paragraph 5.
31 CIPE Resolution, Paragraph 16.
32 CIPE Resolution, Paragraph 7.
33 CIPE Resolution, Paragraph 7.
34 CIPE Resolution, Paragraph 4.
35 CIPE Resolution, Paragraph 6.
36 CIPE Resolution, Paragraph 3.

Public Offering

Public offering can be selected when the objective is to create a widely dispersed shareholding or to limit it to a block of shares. Public offering can be utilized in conjunction with the other two sale methods if the privatization of a company is scheduled by tranches. The wide dispersion of stock capital is to be favored in particular in the sector of the public utility service companies.[37]

The bylaws of public utility companies to be privatized are to be amended before the public offering.[38] The bylaws should also include clauses:

> "... granting special rights to the state for the appointment of one or more directors and/or auditors, to prevent sales of business units, branches or parts thereof such as to entail substantial changes of the typical activity actually carried out at the time of the disposal".[39]

Special clauses should also:

> "... prevent the acquisition of substantial participations in the company as well as to prevent the adoption of amendments to the bylaws which directly or indirectly may alter or obstruct the exercise of said special rights".[40]

Specific forms of protection for minority shareholders are to be adopted[41] in the bylaws aimed at guaranteeing them an adequate representation in the management bodies through a particular voting system called *voto di lista*, which entails voting by lists of candidates.[42] If deemed appropriate, "the bylaws may provide for maximum individual ceilings of capital participation (also with respect to groups)".[43] In principle, no discrimination is to be made

---

37 CIPE Resolution, Paragraph 8.
38 CIPE Resolution, Paragraphs 10 and 11.
39 CIPE Resolution, Paragraph 11.
40 CIPE Resolution, Paragraph 11.
41 CIPE Resolution, Paragraph 10.
42 CIPE Resolution, Paragraph 17.
43 CIPE Resolution, Paragraph 18.

between national and foreign investors. If permitted by European Union legislation, the bylaws may provide that a share of the capital be held by the Italian state, Italian public entities or Italian nationals.[44] The public offering may provide for an upper limit to the quantity of shares obtainable by each individual buyer.[45]

Price reductions may be contemplated when the objective is the widest shareholding dispersion. In this case, however, the price reduction should be adequately advertised "in order to create an actual incentive and promotional factor".[46] In order to avoid resale of the shares in the secondary market, buyers may be given a voucher to obtain free shares of the same class if those bought are "not sold for at least three consecutive tax periods".[47]

The public offering may provide special terms for specific categories of buyers by allowing payment in instalments or "preferential criteria in the allocation".[48] Employees of the company to be privatized, and of the "owner" of such a company and of the companies controlled by it, can benefit from the special terms. Beneficiaries of the special terms of the public offering may also include "persons bound by a particular contractual relationship with the company" to be privatized. These beneficiaries may be insured persons, the clients of credit institutions or the customers of public utility service companies.[49]

Public Auction

The public auction method of privatization could be chosen when the objective is the selection of one buyer or of a *nucleo stabile di azionisti di riferimento* (stable nucleus of lead shareholders).[50] Although the goal of this sale method is to maximize the price, due consideration is to be given to the experience of the potential buyers in the area of the company to be privatized and to "possible synergies with it". As a rule, the stable nucleus of lead shareholders must be

---

44 CIPE Resolution, Paragraph 18.
45 CIPE Resolution, Paragraph 8.
46 CIPE Resolution, Paragraph 8.
47 CIPE Resolution, Paragraph 9.
48 CIPE Resolution, Paragraph 9.
49 CIPE Resolution, Paragraph 9.
50 CIPE Resolution, Paragraph 12.

composed of only a few members. A ceiling to individual share participation must be established and the nucleus, as a whole, should own "less than the absolute majority of the stock capital".

The potential purchasers are to be selected:

> "... on the basis of a preliminary offer worded according to criteria determined by the seller, containing in particular the indication of the terms of the price payment and of possible guarantees, as well as of the industrial and financial strategies".

The seller must have the flexibility to "interrupt the procedure" once the offers are received and to allow consecutive higher bids and "to proceed with private negotiations".[51] The stable nucleus of lead shareholders is to be achieved through shareholder agreements in order:

> "... to assure stability in the shareholding structure and unity of direction in the management of the company by way of the formation of syndicates".[52]

The duration of the shareholder agreement is between five and ten years.[53]

The shareholder agreement should provide two special rights to the Ministry of the Treasury or of a company controlled by it if they are members of the stable nucleus of lead shareholders.[54] The Ministry of the Treasury or its controlled company must have "the pre-emptive right in the event other parties to the agreement intend to transfer their syndicated shares". The Ministry must also have:

> "... the right of option to buy the syndicated shares held by parties to the agreement which, on termination, do not intend to renew it, at a price to be determined by mutual agreement or, in the absence of an agreement with the appointment of an arbitrator".

---

51 CIPE Resolution, Paragraph 12.
52 CIPE Resolution, Paragraph 13.
53 CIPE Resolution, Paragraph 14.
54 CIPE Resolution, Paragraph 14.

Moreover, when the Ministry of the Treasury is a member of the syndicate, "specific agreements of international significance or of particular strategic value" entered into by the state or by the companies controlled by it are to bind the parties to a shareholder agreement.[55]

Private Negotiations

Sale through private negotiations "may be utilized solely if public interests of particular relevance are involved".[56] In order to ensure "maximum transparency", the sale price is to be determined after a valuation of the company to be privatized is made by at least two national or foreign specialists. The price should "reflect the significance to the buyer of the portion of the company's capital object of the disposal operation".[57]

When public utility service companies are involved, appropriate authorities for the regulation and control of services produced and prices applied "may be established in the consumer's interest".[58]

The Privatization Directive

Another fundamental regulatory tool of the Italian privatization program is the Directive of the President of the Council of Ministers of 30 June 1993 on "acceleration of the sale procedures of the state participations in the companies resulting from the reorganization of the economic public entities".[59]

The Privatization Directive establishes a central institution of the privatization program. The President of the Council of Ministers, on the proposal of the Treasury Minister and in agreement with two

---

55 CIPE Resolution, Paragraph 14.
56 CIPE Resolution, Paragraph 15.
57 CIPE Resolution, Paragraph 15.
58 CIPE Resolution, Paragraph 10.
59 The President of the Council of Ministers has the power "to send Ministers political and administrative directives in implementation of resolutions of the Council of Ministers", Government Organization Law, Article 5(2)(a).

other Privatization Ministers, created a Permanent Committee of Global Consultating and Guarantee.[60] This Committee, chaired by the Director General of the Treasury, is composed of four independent experts with experience in the national and international markets. The functions of the Committee are to provide "technical assistance" to the authorities entrusted with the implementation of the program provided for by the EPE Reorganization Law.[61]

Technical assistance is also provided for the various operations of the program and for the time necessary to carry them out in order to encourage their success, transparency and assure coherence of the decisions and their timely co-ordination. The Committee has the power to request the interested companies to supply any information which may be necessary for their privatization and it has the duty to keep such information confidential. Furthermore, the Committee may avail itself of the technical support of the Directorate General of the Treasury as well as of the competent offices of the Presidency of the Council of Ministers, the Ministry of Industry, Commerce and Crafts and the Ministry of Budget and Economic Planning. Additional technical support outside public administrative authorities may also be availed of.

A calendar of the privatization operations is proposed by the Committee to the Minister of the Treasury, according to priorities set by the Committee. The Committee may also suggest proposals in the areas of taxation and law in that they are necessary for the success of the privatization program. With the assistance of the Committee, privatizations are to be completed by public offering whenever possible. Public offerings, however, must:

> "... favor wide dispersion of the securities among investors; avoid concentrations of significant blocks of capital with individual shareholders; and allow the establishment of a nucleus of shareholders that assures the stability of the shareholding structure".

The Committee has a role in the preparatory phase of the disposal operations.

---

60 Privatization Directive, Paragraph 2.
61 EPE Reorganization Law, Article 16.

In this phase, the titleholders controlling the companies to be privatized may be assisted by special consultants to elaborate possible proposals for restructuring the enterprise from the corporate, industrial, financial and organizational points of view. This phase may also be used for selecting the most adequate method of disposal among those indicated in the CIPE Resolution.[62] The use and selection of the special consultants must be agreed on with the Committee.

The Minister of the Treasury or the interested companies must be assisted by the Committee in selecting national and international institutions for the purpose of valuating companies to be privatized "according to the directions under the CIPE Resolution".[63] The institution selected for valuation of the company to be privatized must report only to the Committee. The Committee is to act as consultant in the selection of the manager of the underwriting group among "leading banking and financial institutions of consolidated experience in matters of public offerings of Italian securities".[64]

The "institution" selected for valuation of the company to be privatized must be a member of the underwriting group but it cannot act as manager. The "special consultants" selected for the reorganization of the company prior to the disposal and the "institution" selected for valuation must raise any conflict of interest they may have during the "assignments and, in particular, in the placement operations".[65] The remuneration of the special consultants, however, is to be "established in line with the current values in the international markets for operations of similar nature and size".[66]

The Amortization Fund Law

Law Number 432 of 27 October 1993 on the "establishment of the amortization fund for state securities" (Amortization Fund Law) allows shares or other property sold under the privatization program to be paid with state securities.

---

62 CIPE Resolution, Paragraph 3.
63 CIPE Resolution, Paragraph 4.
64 CIPE Resolution, Paragraph 4.
65 CIPE Resolution, Paragraph 5.
66 CIPE Resolution, Paragraph 6.

It also mandates that the proceeds from the privatization sales be deposited with a special fund and that they be used to purchase state securities which will then be cancelled in order to reduce the public debt.

INITIAL MAJOR PRIVATIZATIONS

The Privatization Directive listed seven companies whose privatization was to begin by July 1993:
(1) *Credito Italiano* SpA (CREDIT);
(2) IMI;
(3) *Banca Commerciale Italiana* SpA (COMIT);
(4) INA;
(5) ENEL;
(6) AGIP SpA (AGIP); and
(7) STET *Societa' Finanziaria Telefonica* p.a. (STET).

However, according to CONSOB, (National Commission for Companies and Stock Exchange), only the first four companies had been privatized, as of the end of September 1995.[67] These privatizations are discussed below.

Credito Italiano SpA

The first major company to be privatized was CREDIT, one of the forty-five banking institutions and financial companies directly or indirectly controlled by IRI.[68] In December 1993, IRI sold 840-million common shares (equal to sixty-four per cent of the bank's capital) together with 50,435,000 saving shares reserved for employees. Saving shares do not grant the holders the right to call or to attend the shareholders' meetings. They merely grant preference in the distribution of profits and repayment of capital.[69]

---

67 *Commissare Nazionale per le Societá e la Borsa, Mercato Azionario e Governo dell'impresa, Senato della Republica* (28 September 1994).
68 IRI *Gruppo*, 1992–93 Yearbook, p. 43.
69 Decree Law Number 95 of 8 April 1974, Article 14, on "provisions relating to the securities market and to the tax treatment of shares", converted into Law Number 216 of 7 June 1974 (CONSOB Law).

The public offering (62.8 per cent of the total offering) was five times oversubscribed. The private placement (37.2 per cent of the total offering) reserved for qualified investors was six times oversubscribed. Foreign investors subscribed 69.1 per cent of the private placement. The remaining 30.9 per cent was subscribed to by Italian investors (insurance companies, mutual funds, pension funds, intermediary financial companies, and others).

IRI received 1,743-billion Lire from the sale of the common shares alone. Morgan Guaranty Trust Company of New York was advisor/valuator to the bank while Goldman Sachs International Limited and CREDIT were global co-ordinators.

IMI

On 31 January and 1 February 1994, the Ministry of the Treasury sold a thirty-seven per cent interest in the capital of IMI. As mentioned above, IMI is a major medium-term credit institution and financial services group. The Ministry's total direct or indirect interest in IMI was 59.2 per cent prior to the sale. An amount of 57.1 per cent of the issue was sold to qualified investors through a private placement while the remaining 42.9 per cent was sold through a public offering. This privatization, like that of CREDIT, saw foreign investors acquiring the lion's share with eighty per cent of the private placement. The issue was ten times oversubscribed.

As part of the privatization, IMI became the first Italian bank listed on the New York Stock Exchange. IMI was also listed on the London Stock Exchange Automated Quotations International and the sale proceeds were 2,384-billion Lire.[70]

Banca Commerciale Italiana SpA

On 28 February and 1 March 1994, IRI sold its fifty-two per cent interest in COMIT, another bank of the IRI group. An amunt of 64.4 per cent of the issue was subscribed to through a public offering

---

70 Credit Suisse First Boston Limited were the advisors/valuators. SG Warburg Securities Limited and IMI were the global co-ordinators.

while the remaining 35.6 per cent was subscribe to by qualified investors through a private placement.

This privatization also had a positive reception outside of Italy. Foreign investors represented 73.7 per cent of the investors subscribing to the private placement. This issue was nine times oversubscribed, and IRI received 2,916-million Lire from this privatization.[71]

Istituto Nazionale Assicurazioni SpA

On 27 and 28 June 1994, the Ministry of the Treasury sold its fifty-four per cent interest in INA (*Istituto Nazionale Assicurazioni SpA*). An amount of 60.3 per cent of the issue was subscribed to through a public offering and the remaining 39.7 per cent by qualified investors through a private placement. Once again the private placement was successful abroad. Foreign investors represented 69.5 per cent of the investors who subscribed to the private placement were foreign. Italian investors subscribed to the remaining 30.5 per cent.

The issue was three times oversubscribed. INA shares were listed on the New York Stock Exchange[72] and the London Stock Exchange Automated Quotations International. The Ministry of the Treasury received 5,136-billion Lire from the privatization.[73] Excluding the proceeds from the sale of the CREDIT saving shares, IRI and the Ministry of the Treasury collected a total of 12,179-billion Lire out of the first four major privatizations.

ADDITIONAL PRIVATIZATIONS

It is important to note that, while the above companies were all sold through public offerings, other state-controlled companies were

---

[71] Morgan Guaranty Trust Company of New York was appointed as advisor/valuator while Lehman Brothers International Europe and *Banca Commerciale Italiano* were appointed as global coordinators.

[72] INA was only the second non-United States insurance company to be listed on the NYSE.

[73] J. Henry Schroder Wagg & Co. Limited and Fox-Pitt, Kelton Limited were appointed as advisors/valuators and IMI, CREDIT, COMIT, and Goldman Sachs as global coordinators.

sold through public auction or private negotiations, that is, the two alternative privatization methods provided for by the CIPE Resolution. Two major examples of these privatizations are discussed below.

Firstly, in December 1993, a group led by General Electric acquired from ENI, for 700-billion Lire, a 69.3 per cent controlling interest (subsequently increased to 78.3 per cent) in *Nuovo Pignone* SpA, a mechanical engineering company specializing in gas turbine production. The sale was completed by public auction, as directed by a Resolution of the Council of Ministers of 30 December 1992.[74]

Secondly, in 1993, IRI divided *Società Meridionale Finanziaria* SpA (SME), its holding company in the foodstuff sector, distribution networks and refreshment and catering services. Three new companies originated out of this split: SME SpA (SME), *Finanziaria Italgel* SpA (*Italgel*) and *Finanziaria Cirio-Bertolli-De Rica* SpA (CBD). Before autumn 1993, IRI sold its 62.12 per cent share participation in Italgel and CBD to Nestlé, SA and *Fi.Svi-Istituto Finanziario per la Cooperazione* SpA, respectively for a total of 748-billion Lire. The final unit of the restructured SME, which included the supermarket group GS and the Italian highway restaurant company, Autogrill, was sold at the end of October 1994 to an Italo-Swiss joint venture primarily composed of Benetton's Edizione Holding and the Swiss catering group, Mövenpick. The sale price for thirty-two per cent of SME was approximately 704-billion Lire. The sale was the result of private negotiations as directed by the Resolution of the Council of Ministers of 30 December 1992.[75]

---

[74] At a meeting held on 30 December 1992, the Council of Ministers resolved to dispose of the interest owned by ENI in *Nuovo Pignone* by using the method of public auction. The Council of Ministers also agreed on the disposal of the industrial activities of SME as well as the shares owned by IRI in the same company, according to the approval of IRI's board of directors. IRI aimed to increase its industrial and financial capacity in a company with widely dispersed shareholding with the objective of including a "stable nucleus" of institutional investors and of national and foreign entrepreneurs. Union Bank Switzerland Limited was appointed as valuator, and IMI was the advisor.

[75] Wasserstein, Perella & Co., Inc. was appointed as advisor/valuator.

THE PRIVATIZATION LAW

The 30 December 1992 Interministerial Committee for Economic Planning Resolution and the 30 June 1993 Privatization Directive were administrative regulatory tools, deprived of the force of a law enacted by parliament. The experience of the first privatizations provided the historical setting for a comprehensive law on privatization. The government issued Decree Law Number 332 of 31 May 1994 on provisions for the acceleration of the disposal procedures of state participations and of converting public entities into companies. This was ultimately amended and became Law Number 474 of 30 July 1994 (the Privatization Law). Four previous Decree Laws with similar contents had not been converted into law.

The laws regulating government accounting[76] are not applicable to the sale of participations by the state and by public entities. Nor are they applicable to the functions and operations complementary and instrumental to the same sales, including the granting of guarantees according to market practice. [77]

Provisions on Sales

The sale of participations held by the state or by public entities should normally be made by a public offering. Public offerings are governed by Law Number 149 of 18 February 1992 on the regulation of public offerings for the sale, underwriting, purchase and exchange of securities (Public Offering Law). The sale can also be made by direct negotiations with potential purchasers or by a combination of both procedures. The choice of the sale method must be made by Decree of the President of the Council of Ministers, on the proposal of the three Privatization Ministers.[78]

As already explained, the CIPE Resolution provides for three methods of privatization: public offering, public auction and private

---

[76] Royal Decree Number 2440 of 18 November 1923, on new provisions for the administration of property and on general state accounting, and Royal Decree Number 827 of 23 May 1924 on regulating the administration of property and for general state accounting.

[77] Privatization Law, Article 1.1.

[78] Privatization Law, Article 1.2.

negotiations. The Privatization Law limits the sale methods to public offering and direct negotiations and establishes that the ultimate decision on the sale method be taken at the highest governmental level by decree. Particular rules are established when the sale is to be made by direct negotiations in order to establish a stable nucleus of lead shareholders.[79] In this case, the potential buyers must have the "requisites of adequate entrepreneurial capacity". In their "offer" they should undertake certain "financial, economic and managerial" obligations to be included in the share purchase agreement. Clauses prohibiting the sale of the shares or of the business of the privatized company for a certain time period and providing for liquidated damages and a penalty (as provided for by Article 1382 of the Civil Code) may be imposed on buyers in the share purchase agreement.

In order to assure maximum transparency, the share purchase agreement and the shareholder agreement are to be deposited with the Tribunal where the registered office of the company to be privatized is located and an extract is to be published in two national newspapers.[80] If the Treasury is a party to the stable nucleus of lead shareholders, the Minister of the Treasury can reserve a pre-emptive right of purchase in the event that the other parties to the shareholder agreement intend to sell their syndicated shares. This pre-emptive right must be limited in time and contemplated by the share purchase agreement.[81]

Preparing and Executing Sale

For the preparation and execution of the sale operations, the Minister oxf the Treasury, in agreement with the two other Privatization Ministers, may be assisted by national and foreign companies of proven experience and operating capacity, as well as by professionals who have been listed in the registers provided by law for at least five years.[82] The professionals and the selected

---

79 Privatization Law, Article 1.3.
80 Privatization Law, Article 1.3.
81 Privatization Law, Article 1.4.
82 Privatization Law, Article 1.5.

companies[83] are charged with studying, consulting, valuing, operating assistance and managing the securities owned by the state. They are also responsible for managing placement operations with powers to execute instrumental and complementary operations on behalf of the state.

Auditing firms which acted as consultants of the company to be privatized in the two years prior to the Privatization Law are not eligible for valuation. Compensation and payment terms for the assignments are agreed on by the parties in advance.[84] Furthermore, the proceeds from the sale of shares held by public entities are used to reduce the size of their indebtedness.[85]

Public Interest Companies

The Prime Minister will list by Decree a group of companies:

> "... in the sectors of defense, transportation, telecommunications, energy sources and of other public services ... taking into account national objectives of economic and industrial policy".

(Public Interest Companies).[86] The list of the public interest companies is to be proposed to the Prime Minister by the three Privatization Ministers as well as by the Ministers responsible for the particular industrial sector, "on communication to the competent parliamentary commissions".[87] The privatization of the Public Interest Companies must follow the establishment of "independent authorities for tariff regulation and quality control of services of significant public interest".[88]

Before the Italian State loses its controlling interest in them, the Public Interest Companies must adopt a special "clause" in their bylaws as "defined" in a decree to be issued by the privatization

---

83 Article 1.5 of the Privatization Law provides that the selection is to be made in compliance with Council Directive 92/50/EEC of 18 June 1992 relating to the coordination of procedures for the award of public service contracts.
84 Privatization Law, Article 1.5.
85 Privatization Law, Article 1.6.
86 Privatization Law, Article 2.1.
87 Privatization Law, Article 2.1.
88 Privatization Law, Article 1 bis.

ministers.[89] This special clause will grant the Minister of the Treasury and the other two privatization ministers "one or more" of the following four groups of powers:

(1) The Minister of the Treasury has the power to grant approval of any "acquisition" of a significant participation, defined as a block of at least five per cent of all the common shares of the Public Interest Company, or a lesser percentage set by Decree of the same minister.[90] The directors of the Public Interest Company must send a "communication" to the Minister of the Treasury requesting permission to register a share transfer exceeding the five per cent limit.[91] The approval by the Minister of the Treasury must be "expressed" within sixty-days. During the sixty-day period, or until the approval is granted, the "transferee" cannot vote the "shares representing the significant participation". The shares are to be sold within one year if the Minister of the Treasury denies the approval or is inactive during the sixty-day period. In case the shares are not sold, the Minister of the Treasury may request the Tribunal to order the sale through a stockbroker, a bank or other credit institution.[92]

(2) The Minister of the Treasury must also grant approval of any shareholder agreement subject to communication to CONSOB[93] when the parties to the agreement hold title to at least five per cent of all the common shares of the Public Interest Company or the lesser percentage set by decree of the Minister.[94]

---

[89] Privatization Law, Article 2.1 *bis*.

[90] Privatization Law, Article 2.1 a.

[91] The directors of an Italian company have a role in the registration of a share transfer. In fact, Article 2 of Royal Decree Number 239 of 29 March 1942 on "provisions regarding the mandatory registration of securities" provides that "the transfer of shares shall be made, under the responsibility of the (directors of the) issuing company, by an entry of the new title-holder on the share certificate and in the shareholder book, or through an endorsement on the share certificate . . . entered in the shareholder book".

[92] Privatization Law, Article 2.1(a).

[93] Any agreement regulating voting or the transfer or purchase of shares of listed companies must be "communicated" to CONSOB (Article 10.4 of the Public Offering Law). Any agreement which is not communicated to CONSOB is valid but not "effective".

[94] Privatization Law, Article 2.1b.

The approval is "a condition of validity" of the shareholder agreement. CONSOB must inform the Minister of the Treasury of the shareholder agreements communicated to it. The approval is to be "expressly" granted within sixty-days from CONSOB's communication to the Minister of the Treasury. Until the approval is granted or if the sixty-day period expires without action by the minister, the parties to the agreement cannot vote the syndicated shares. Shareholder agreements are not effective in case of refusal of approval or of inaction by the Minister during the sixty-day period. In these two cases, the resolutions adopted with the "determining vote" of the shareholders, parties to the agreement, may be attacked if such shareholders acted at the shareholders' meeting as if they were fulfilling contractual obligations.

(3) The Minister of the Treasury has the power to "veto the adoption of resolutions on the dissolution of the company, transfer of the business, merger, division, transfer of registered office abroad, change of corporate purposes and amendment of the bylaws which suppress or modify the powers" of the same Minister.[95]

(4) The final "special power" of the Minister of the Treasury is the ability to "appoint at least one director or a number of directors not greater than one fourth of the members of the board as well as one auditor".[96] The shareholders of the Public Interest Companies who dissent from the resolutions granting the special powers to the Minister of the Treasury can withdraw from the company.[97] The dissenting shareholders can "obtain reimbursement of their shares on the basis of the average price during the last semester", as provided for by Article 2437 of the Civil Code.

Limits on Share Ownership

Public Interest Companies, state-controlled banks and insurance companies or public entities "may insert in their bylaws a maximum limit of share ownership". This limit, however, cannot exceed five

---

[95] Privatization Law, Article 2.1.c.

[96] Privatization Law, Article 2.1.d.

[97] Privatization Law, Article 2.2.

per cent for the Public Interest Companies.[98] The shares exceeding the limit cannot be voted.[99] The clauses of the bylaws providing for the share ownership limit and "those introduced for the purpose of assuring the protection of minority shareholders" cannot be amended for three years.[100] The clause, however, providing for the share ownership limit is no longer in force if a "majority of the voting rights" is acquired under the Public Offering Law.

The public interest companies, state controlled banks and insurance companies or public entities which have adopted the share ownership limit must "introduce in their bylaws a special clause... for the election of directors" through the so-called "vote by lists of candidates".[101] The clause, intended to protect minority shareholders, cannot be modified as long as the bylaws include the share ownership limit clause. In order to assure transparency and protect minorities, a shareholder meeting is to be called with at least thirty days' notice. The agenda cannot be changed during the meeting and it must list all the items to be discussed. The lists of candidates for the board of directors may be submitted by outgoing directors or by shareholders representing at least one per cent of the common shares.

The lists are to be made public by depositing them at the registered office of the company twenty days before the meeting and by publishing an announcement in three national newspapers (two of which must be financial) ten days before the shareholder meeting. Minority shareholders are "reserved as a whole at least one-fifth of the directors", other than those appointed by the Minister of the Treasury and one auditor.[102] The Privatization Law allows voting by mail at shareholder meetings of Public Interest Companies, state-controlled banks, insurance companies or public entities.[103]

---

98 Privatization Law, Article 3.1.
99 Privatization Law, Article 3.2.
100 Privatization Law, Article 3.3.
101 Privatization Law, Article 4.
102 Privatization Law, Article 4.
103 Privatization Law, Article 5.5 provides that the implementing regulation has to be "adopted" within thirty days by the Bank of Italy, CONSOB: Institute for the Supervision of Private Insurance Companies and of Collective Interest (ISVAP). The regulation concerning the conditions and modalities for the exercise of voting rights by mail was issued on 30 December 1994 and published in the *Official Gazette* of 5 January 1995.

The Privatization Law provides for a special measure to preserve the wide dispersion of shareholding of privatized companies and to prevent privatizations from being used to gain control of a company sold at a reduced price.[104] The parties to a shareholder agreement must buy the same quantity of shares through a tender offer if: the shares are bought within two years from the public offering privatizing the company; and such shares allow the parties to a shareholder agreement to gain a "majority of voting rights" or a "dominant influence" at the shareholder meetings of the privatized company.

The price, however, is established by CONSOB taking into account, in particular, the "weighted average of the prices of shares contributed to the shareholder agreement", purchased after the public offering of the privatized company and the "average of the five highest prices quoted on the stock exchange" after such public offering. The shares of the companies to be privatized and governed by the Privatization Law can be paid in instalments over a three-year period.[105] If one instalment goes unpaid, the share certificate is retransferred to the seller company which does not need to refund the instalments already paid by the defaulted buyer.[106]

FORTHCOMING MAJOR PRIVATIZATIONS

Of the seven companies listed in the Privatization Directive, as of the end of September 1995, only ENEL, AGIP and STET are still to be privatized.

The privatization of these three companies, however, will follow the enactment of legislation establishing the "authorities for tariff regulation and quality control of services" provided for by Article 1-*bis* of the Privatization Law.[107]

---

104 Privatization Law, Article 8.
105 Privatization Law, Article 9.1.
106 Privatization Law, Article 9.6.
107 On 15 March 1995, the Senate approved the Bill on "provisions on competition and regulation of public utility services". Article 2(1) of the bill provides for the establishment of three authorities, "the first of which shall be competent for electricity and gas, the second for communications and the third for transportation". It was expected that the Bill would be enacted by the end of 1995.

ENEL

ENEL's privatization will not only be a major financial event, it will also drastically restructure the entire Italian electricity system. ENEL was established as an EPE following the nationalization of the Italian electricity industry in 1962.[108]

As a result of the nationalization, more than 1,200 electric industries were transferred to ENEL, which acquired a virtual monopoly over the Italian electricity industry. ENEL was reorganized into a company by the EPE's Reorganization Law in 1992. Since its incorporation, ENEL has connected 99.7 per cent of the Italian population to the national electric grid.[109] It increased its net maximum production capacity from about 12,963 MW to 52,053 MW. ENEL is the third largest electric power company in the world (after EdF in France and the Japanese TEPCO) with regard to electricity sales, and the second in terms of the number of customers served and installed capacity. Presently, ENEL is responsible for 79.7 per cent of the national production of electric energy while auto producers (15.7 per cent), local public utilities (4.1 per cent) and other utilities (0.5 per cent) provide the residual market supply. Italy, however, still imports about 18.3 per cent of the electricity it consumes.

The privatization plan for ENEL has been inspired by two theories: one separatist and the other unitary. The Berlusconi Government, in power until December 1994, supported the separatist theory. On 11 November 1994, the three Privatization Ministers

---

[108] Nationalization was enacted by the Italian Parliament with Law Number 1643 of 6 December 1962 on the "establishment of Ente Nazionale per l'Energia Elettrica and transfer to it of the enterprises operating electric industries" (the Nationalization Law). ENEL was given the task of exercising its activities in the national territory, such as production, importation and exportation, transmission, transformation, distribution and sale of electric energy produced from any source. ENEL also received a public law personality and was subject to the supervision of the Minister of Industry. ENEL, in the public interest, had to "provide the coordinated utilization and the expansion of plants with the aim of ensuring, with minimum management costs, availability of electric energy adequate, as to quantity and price, to the needs of a balanced development of the country. The ownership of the enterprises that exercised said activities shall be transferred to ENEL" (Nationalization Law, Article 1).

[109] *ENEL in Italy and Abroad*, 1994, ENEL, Rome, pp. 15,18, and 20.

translated their theory into a press release. If market conditions permitted, ENEL was to be sold by June 1995, after drastic reorganization. The "activities of transmission and distribution" had to be kept "distinct" from "the accounting and the corporate structure". The "production activity" was to be reorganized "in one or more appropriate companies to be incorporated before the placement". A non-exclusive concession was to be granted by the state to ENEL to produce electricity. The concession agreement should have provided for the sale "within three years from the placement of an adequate portion of the existing production plants". The National Control Center (the so-called 'Dispatcher"), coordinating production, transmission and distribution of electricity, was to be separated from ENEL "in an autonomous and independent manner".

The Dispatcher was to have the power to grant concessions to third parties to produce electricity on a competitive basis. "One tariff in the entire national territory" had to be applied. The Minister of Industry was to present a bill to the parliament delegating to the government "the reform of the legislation on concessions and to liberalize the production of electric energy". The Dini government, which followed the Berlusconi administration in December 1994, supported the unitary theory for ENEL's privatization. ENEL is to be sold as a unit in its present vertically integrated structure. This solution should allow the immediate sale of the company and assure larger proceeds.[110]

ENI

The plan to privatize the petrochemical sector has gone through three phases; Agip, Super Agip and ENI:

AGIP

The 30 June 1993 Privatization Directive listed Agip, an oil and gas exploration and production subsidiary of ENI, as the company to be

---

[110] Kleinwort, Benson Limited was chosen as the international advisor/valuator and *Mediobanca-Banca di Credito Finanziario* SpA Mediobanca and Merrill Lynch International Limited as global coordinators.

privatized. It soon became clear, however, that the sale of Agip alone would not have been sufficiently attractive to the financial markets. A group of companies was then considered for privatization.

Super AGIP

The Super Agip plan acknowledged the negative trend of the ENI chemical sector and assumed that it could not be considered for immediate privatization. A group of ENI's most profitable hydrocarbons holdings had to be separated and considered as a unit to be privatized. In addition to Agip, the group would have included *Agip Petroli* SpA (oil refining and distribution), *Saipem* SpA (construction and drilling), *Snam* SpA (gas distribution) and *Snamprogetti* SpA (project engineering). The value of the group was estimated at approximately US $30-billion to US $40-billion which would have involved "five tranche sales", according to experts.[111]

ENI

In the autumn of 1994, it was clear that the negative trend of the chemical sector had ended. At a hearing before the Tenth Commission of the Chamber of Deputies on 20 October 1994, the chairman of the board of directors and the managing director of ENI[112] reported on the progress of the reorganization of the group of companies and of the privatization program. ENI has been reorganized into three business units: energy (about eighty per cent of total business activities), chemical and "non strategic activities". This

---

111 Barnett, "Privatising European Energy; Issues and Lessons", *Financial Times Business Information* (1994), p. 105.

112 ENI was incorporated by Law Number 136 of 10 February 1953 on the "establishment of Ente Nazionale Idrocarburi" (the ENI Law). The then EPE was granted legal "personality of public law" with the authority to promote and carry out initiatives of national interest in the fields of hydrocarbons, steam and the chemical sector. It was also granted exclusive rights in the Po Valley for the exploration and exploitation of hydrocarbons reservoirs, the construction and operation of pipelines for transportation of national mineral hydrocarbons and the authority to carry out processing, transformation, utilization and trade of hydrocarbons.

last unit "is being disposed of" and seventy-six sales were completed between 1992 and 1994 for which ENI received 3,368-billion Lire. ENI expects about fifty additional sales and to receive "about 7 to 8,000-billion Lire" from these new sales. The value of the "reorganized ENI" exceeds 50,000-billion Lire. ENI is the second largest Italian industrial group after FIAT SpA and ranks among the top ten oil and gas groups in the world.

ENI's ideal objective is to privatizate its energy and chemical units ("which represent ninety to ninety-five per cent of total turnover") as a whole. In February 1995, the plan to privatize the entire ENI organization became official.[113] The timetable of the plan, however, will be affected by the regulatory action Italy must take to comply with European Union legislation. In fact, ENI was granted by law the exclusive right to explore and exploit hydrocarbons in the Po Valley. These rights are to be abolished by Italy before 1 January 1997.[114] The loss of the exclusive rights in the Po Valley will affect ENI's valuation.[115]

STET

The privatization of STET will essentially constitute the privatization of Italian telecommunications. In order to properly focus on the size and role of STET, it is necessary to go through the main stages of the program to reorganize Italian telecommunications. Law Number 58 of 29 January 1992 on "provisions for the reform of the telecommunications sector" (Telecommunications Reform Law) is the origin of the program.

Prior to the Telecommunications Reform Law, formal title to the "telecommunication services for public use" was held by the State

---

[113] On 9 February 1995, in an interview with the *International Herald Tribune*, the Prime Minister, Lamberto Dini, stated that "ENI's total market value has been estimated at as much as US $30-billion" and that "a tranche of ENI might go on the market" in the 1995.

[114] Articles 7 and 14 of Directive 94/22/EEC of the European Parliament and of the Council of 30 May 1994 "on the conditions for granting and using authorizations for the prospection, exploration and production of hydrocarbons".

[115] NN Rothschild & Sons Limited was appointed as advisor/valuator and IMI and Credit Suisse First Boston Limited were appointed global coordinators.

Agency for Telephone Services (ASST) and by the Post and Telecommunication Administration. The Telecommunication Reform Law mandated the Minister of Post and Telecommunications to grant a concession to operate the telecommunications services for public use to a company to be incorporated by IRI; telegrams, electronic mail, radio shipping safety communications and telematic services rendered through post offices were not to be included in the concession.[116] ASST was suppressed[117] and CIPE was mandated to implement the Telecommunications Reform Law.[118]

In May 1992, IRI incorporated IRITEL SpA (IRITEL) which became the concession holder for the operation of the telecommunication services for public use. On 2 April 1993, CIPE passed a resolution on the "determination of general criteria for the reorganization of the telecommunication sector".[119]

CIPE acknowledged that the "unification in one operator of the companies of the IRI group, presently concession holders of telecommunications services is an indispensable step". CIPE mandated "the Minister of the Treasury, as sole shareholder of IRI SpA, to have the pertinent reorganization plan presented by 30 June 1993". In 1994, IRITEL, Italcable SpA, (operating telecommunications between Italy and non-European countries), *Telespazio* SpA, (operating satellite communications), *SIRM Società Italiana Radio Marittima* p.a, (operating radio and shipping safety communications) were merged through absorption by *SIP Società Italiana per l'Esercizio delle Telecomunicazioni* p.a (SIP), (operating domestic telecommunications) SIP changed its name to Telecom Italia SpA (Telecom) which, on 18 August 1994, became the operator of the sixth largest telecommunication system in the world. In 1995, Telecom spun off its satellite and cellular assets to two newly incorporated companies. Telecom is a subsidiary of STET.[120]

---

116 Telecommunications Reform Law, Article 1.
117 Telecommunications Reform Law, Article 3.
118 Telecommunications Reform Law, Article 4.
119 CIPE Telecommunications Resolution.
120 Morgan Stanley & Co. Limited and Euromobiliare SpA have been appointed as advisor/valuator for STETs privatization and Mediobanca as global coordinator.

PROSPECTS FOR PRIVATIZATION

The short-term prospects for privatization in Italy are clear. Successful sales can reasonably be expected of ENEL, ENI and STET, the three major companies scheduled for privatization. In the long term, however, the success of the privatization program is uncertain. Once all the "crown jewels" have been sold, the government will be left with less profitable and more unprofitable companies to be privatized. Unions and political forces may oppose the continuation of the program for the same social reasons which justified nearly seventy years of acquisitions and state expansion in traditionally private economic areas. Trade unions could take an activist position if faced with severe unemployment caused by the sale of unprofitable companies.

The possibility of new parliamentary elections in 1996 renders the progress of privatization even more unpredictable. This will be the second time the new majority electoral system is tested. Two political groups will confront each other: a coalition group formed of center-left parties and a coalition group formed of center-right parties.[121]

If the center-left coalition group wins the elections, it is reasonable to expect that the privatization program may slow down or even stop if it creates vast unemployment. If the center-right group wins the elections, it is also reasonable to expect that the privatization process may slow down or even stop if it creates unemployment and affects companies located in southern Italy. Moreover, AN's presence in the coalition may force the government to maintain control of at least the defense sector. The European Union may express a dissenting opinion but its influence on the Italian government, however, could be minimal if unemployment continues to grow.

A new role might have to be found for IRI if the privatization process slows down or stops. IRI could act as an agent-manager,

---

[121] The leader of the center-left group will most likely be Mr. Romano Prodi, former chairman of the board of directors of IRI. The largest party of this coalition group will be the Democratic Party of the Left (PDS), successor to the Communist Party. PDS had 20.3 per cent of the votes at the last general election in March 1994. The splinter leftist wing of the Italian People's Party (PPI), successor to the Christina Democrats will most likely join the center-left coalition group. PPI had 11.1 per cent of the votes at the last general election.

exercising the special powers of the Minister of the Treasury with the Public Interest Companies. This stage of the process may trigger a heated debate on the nature and extent of "privatization".

Questions may be raised on the dimension of the state's "natural monopoly" of social services as to whether privatization should be extended to railways, postal services, schools, hospitals and prisons. This debate may continue into the next century and at that time it may be the European Union which proposes solutions.

Note: This article was prepared with the assistance of Gregory Valenti, an associate of Studio Legale Emanuele Turco, Rome.

THE SLOVAK REPUBLIC

Kevin T. Connor and Julian Juhasz
Squire, Sanders & Dempsey
Bratislava, Slovak Republic

INTRODUCTION

Privatization in the Slovak Republic, as in the other transitioning countries of Central and Eastern Europe, has been the most heated and complex transformation issue. Importantly, the methodology of privatization, not the concept, has been the focal point for debate. The Slovak Republic has irreversibly committed itself to transfer a substantial portion of the means of production into private hands. This article traces the development of privatization in Slovakia from 1989 to mid-November 1995 with an emphasis on the economic, political, and social affects of recent changes to the privatization process.

Privatization in the Slovak Republic can be divided into two general periods: the period after the "Velvet Revolution" when the Slovak Republic was still part of the Czech and Slovak Federative Republic (1990–1992), and the period starting in January 1993 when the Slovak Republic became an independent nation. Although these two periods are useful for structuring a discussion of Slovak privatization, they cannot be examined as distinct periods because privatization in Slovakia today is inextricably bound with decisions made and laws adopted by the former federal parliament. In short, an understanding of privatization in Slovakia today necessarily requires an understanding of the privatization process initiated by the Czech and Slovak Republic.

PRIVATIZATION IN THE CZECH AND SLOVAK REPUBLIC

In the two years following the "Velvet Revolution" of November 1989 and free general elections of June 1990, the federal parliament of the Czech and Slovak Republic implemented a variety of market-oriented measures including changes in taxation, liberalization of pricing and foreign trade, internal convertibility of the Czechoslovak crown and the adoption a new commercial code. The government also committed itself to transferring property seized by the state under the communist regime back into private hands (restitution) and to move state-owned enterprises from government control to private sector control (privatization).

RESTITUTION AND SMALL-SCALE PRIVATIZATION

The first step of privatization was the restitution to the original owners of property seized by the communists. Through a variety of legislative measures, property was returned to persons who had lost it through nationalization following the communist party's ascension in Czechoslovakia in 1948. When physical return was impractical or impossible, financial compensation was provided.

Enactment of the Small-Scale Privatization Act[1] was the next step the Czech and Slovak Republic took on the road to privatization. Small-scale privatization focused on state-owned enterprises that could quickly be transferred into private ownership, such as small shops, restaurants, and hotels. The primary method used was public auctions. By the end of 1993, over 9,500 businesses were transferred to Slovak citizens, mainly through auction, with a total value in excess of SKK 14-billion. Small-scale privatization was a quick, positive and highly effective method of transferring state property into private hands. In addition to economic efficiency, small-scale privatization was also psychologically important because the citizenry could see tangible beneficial results of privatization.

LARGE-SCALE PRIVATIZATION

The Czech and Slovak Republic system of mass privatization and vouchers was established by the Act on the Conditions of Transfer of State-Owned Property to Other Persons,[2] commonly referred to as the Large-Scale Privatization Act. Under the Large-Scale Privatization Act, each state-owned enterprise to be privatized was required, by a

---

1 Act Number 427/1990 Zb.

2 Act Number 92/1991 Zb.

certain date, to file a proposal, a "privatization project", for its privatization to the ministry governing its industry. The Czech and Slovak Republic contemplated a two-wave privatization process. The state-owned enterprise could be privatized in a number of ways including public tender, public auction, direct sale to a predetermined buyer (foreign or domestic), distribution of vouchers or any combination of these methods.

Competing proposals could be filed and citizens had the opportunity to participate in the process by obtaining shares in companies for a nominal price through the use of investment vouchers. The government and the relevant ministries decided which state-owned enterprises would be subject to voucher privatization and to what extent. The enterprises were then transformed into joint-stock companies with registered capital representing the difference between total assets and liabilities.

To implement voucher privatization, the Center of Voucher Privatization was created under the auspices of the Czech and Slovak Republic Ministry of Finance. Any Czech and Slovak Republic citizen over the age of eighteen could participate in the voucher program by purchasing a voucher book for 35 Crowns (approximately one United States dollar at the time) and paying a 1,000 Crown registration fee. The booklets contained vouchers with 1000 points, the maximum any citizen could use in any privatization wave. Citizens were entitled to invest their points directly for shares in former state enterprises or in privatization investment funds. Nearly two-thirds of eligible Slovaks registered to participate in the first wave.

During the initial stage of the bidding process, share prices in each former state-owned enterprise involved were published. In the first round of the first wave, these prices were based on the state-owned enterprises' book values. Citizens and investment funds then ordered shares. If the shares of a particular state-owned enterprise were oversubscribed by more than twenty-five per cent, the shares in that state-owned enterprise were not sold at that price, the points bid returned, and the state-owned enterprise's shares offered at a higher price in a subsequent round of bidding. Shares that were undersubscribed were offered at a lower price in the next round. Five rounds were held in the first wave.

The first privatization wave was completed in October 1993 and included more than 700 Slovak companies with a total book value in excess of SKK 175-billion. The Czech Republic completed its second wave of privatization in 1994. As discussed below, the second wave of voucher privatization in Slovakia was started in 1993, variously postponed until 1995 and canceled in July 1995.

PRIVATIZATION IN THE SLOVAK REPUBLIC

The Slovak Republic became an independent nation on 1 January 1993. As of that date, the legal structure of the Slovak and Czech Republics was the same, including privatization. As to be expected of countries with distinct cultural and historical legacies, the Slovak and Czech Republics have moved on different paths towards the goal of creating a market economy.

The Czech Republic moved forward with the second wave of privatization, completing the process in 1994. Privatization has moved forward differently in Slovakia, primarily as a result of political debate on the methodology of privatization.

Privatization Changes Course

Following its electoral victory in the 1992 elections, the Movement for Democratic Slovakia (HZDS) headed by Vladimír Meciar began moving away from voucher privatization. In September 1992, the government postponed coupon privatization and instead focused on direct sales. For a variety of reasons, mostly political, the volume of privatization decreased significantly in 1993. Responding to renewed calls to quicken the pace of privatization, the government announced in July 1993 that the second wave was being readied and that it would begin in 1994. The second wave never materialized and was instead replaced by heated political debate over the appropriateness of certain direct sales approved by the Meciar government.

Following a noconfidence vote in the National Council of the Slovak Republic (Parliament) in the spring of 1994, caused in part by dissatisfaction with the pace and method of privatization, Jozef Moravcik replaced Mr. Meciar as prime minister. The Moravcik government reintroduced voucher privatization as the preferred privatization method, and the program was scheduled to begin in September 1994 with a total value of approximately SKK 70-billion (US $2.3-billion).

Despite considerable political wrangling, the Ministry of Finance issued voucher books for the second wave of privatization and registration began in early September 1994. Interest in the second wave was high and by the time registration was complete, nearly 3.5-million voucher books had been registered, representing over 90 per cent of eligible citizens. Preparations for the second wave continued, new investment funds were organized, and the first round was slated to begin in December 1994. In the interim, elections were held in late September 1994. The HZDS, headed by Vladimír Meciar, won the most seats in Parliament and he was installed as Prime Minister of a coalition government.

In one of its first acts, the new Meciar government postponed voucher privatization, rescheduling it for the summer of 1995. The value of assets slated for coupon privatization, originally set at approximately SKK 70-billion, was, by June 1995, reduced to approximately SKK 20-billion. Importantly several companies slated for voucher privatization were sold by direct sale and other highly rated companies were removed from the list altogether. In July 1995, the government announced that coupon privatization was being canceled. The government introduced a series of important amendments that have changed the direction of privatization in Slovakia.

National Property Fund Bonds

On 12 July 1995, Parliament passed a highly controversial amendment to the Large-Scale Privatization Act terminating voucher privatization as a method of privatization. Pursuant to the amendment, the National Property Fund of the Slovak Republic will instead issue bonds with a face value of SKK 10,000 (US $330) to every citizen registered for voucher privatization (bonds). The bonds mature in 2001 and should bear interest at the discount rate of the National Bank of Slovakia (9.75 per cent as of 15 November 1995). The bonds can be used for a variety of purposes including the purchase of apartments, payment for extra health and pension benefits and for the purchase of National Property Fund shares traded in the public securities market. The bonds may also be sold to persons who acquired companies from the National Property Fund by direct sale. Such purchasers may use the bonds to fulfill their obligations to the National Property Fund or banks. The bonds will not be traded on the open market.

Strategic Enterprises Act

On 13 July 1995, the Act on the Protection of the State's Interests in the Privatization of Key Strategic State Enterprises and Joint Stock Companies (Strategic Enterprises Act)[3] was enacted. The Strategic Enterprise Act, which took effect on 7 September 1995, lists certain state companies that are to be excluded from privatization and enumerates others that are to be privatized pursuant to certain rules. Section 2 of the Strategic Enterprises Act specifies a variety of companies from several sectors that are considered strategically important state enterprises and cannot (at least for the time being) be privatized. Among them are *Slovensky plynárensky priemysel*, š.p. (gas), *Slovenské telekomunikácie*, š.p. (telecommunications), *Slovenské elektrárne*, a.s. (electricity), and Imuna, š.p. (pharmaceutical).

Numerous other companies listed in the Act that are wholly or partially owned by the State now face new management because the National Property Fund had to transfer its rights and obligations as a shareholder in those companies to the "relevant central authority", that is, the companies' founding ministry.

Impact and Analysis of Recent Changes

The newly enacted provisions fundamentally alter the privatization landscape in the Slovak Republic and represent the largest shift from the methodologies adopted by the Czech and Slovak Republic.

This section briefly analyzes some of the reasons behind the changes and the practical effects for privatization and the Slovak economy in general.

Politics of Privatization

Although ostensibly passed to increase the transparency of the privatization process and regulate the relationships between the National Property Fund, the Ministry of Privatization and the founding

---

[3] Act Number 192/1995 Zz.

ministries, few would question that the new provisions are politically motivated. Indeed, many have claimed that the new program is a well thought out plan to concentrate economic and political power with the government coalition headed by Mr. Meciar.

These people claim that through direct sales to domestic investors (typically the existing management of the state-owned enterprise) at reduced prices and with favorable repayment terms the coalition party is using the redistribution of wealth and power to strengthen its position. These critics further argue that this is being accomplished at the expense of ordinary Slovaks.

Constitutional Challenge

Adopted hastily in the summer of 1995, the amendment to the Large Scale Privatization Act was not signed by President Kovác and was returned to Parliament for further consideration. The President asserted that the amendment violated various provisions of the Slovak constitution. The amendment became law in September 1995 despite the President's veto when Parliament again approved it by a simple majority vote. Shortly after the amendment became law, opposition members of Parliament filed a constitutional challenge with the Slovak Constitutional Court. As of the date of this chapter, the Constitutional Court had not decided on the validity of the amendment.

Despite the constitutional challenge, the government, through the National Property Fund, has quickened the pace of direct sales. The potential impact on the privatization process of a decision declaring the amendment unconstitutional is unclear. Theoretically, if the amendment was found unconstitutional, the Large-Scale Privatization Act, including voucher privatization, would again be valid. The second wave of voucher privatization could also go forward, but since coupon privatization is not a required method of privatization, exactly what would happen is unclear. At least one group believes a public referendum should be held and has sought to force such a vote.

An important issue would be what companies would be involved because several originally slated for coupon privatization have since been sold by direct sale. It is difficult to imagine a scenario where companies privatized through direct sale would be "taken back". Such a result would certainly create a disturbing precedent for an already skeptical foreign investment community. Possibly, the government would increase the amount available for coupon privatization from other sources, potentially some of those currently considered strategic under the Strategic Enterprises Act. As a practical matter, substantially all of the state-owned enterprises could be sold before any constitutional decision is reached and there would be no further voucher privatization.

Practical Impact of Bonds

One of the stated purposes of voucher privatization was to enable all citizens to acquire an interest in state-owned property, compensate them and generally encourage a positive attitude toward privatization. However, instead of becoming shareholders, those citizens who choose to do so (approximately 32,000 Slovaks obtained a refund on their coupon books) will become owners of bonds, the value of which is less than clear. Assuming an inflation rate of approximately 10 per cent over the next five years, the real value of the bonds will certainly be less than today. Also, the apartment purchasing benefit is difficult to quantify because some municipalities have threatened not to accept the bonds. The benefit of purchasing shares on the exchange is illusory because few National Property Fund shares are traded. Finally, the benefit of obtaining additional pension and health benefits is also unclear because no extra benefits are currently available.

Because of concerns with the ability of the National Property Fund to repay the bonds, most experts believe that the supply of available bonds will exceed demand. As a result, most of the bonds will probably be bought at a steep discount by direct sale purchasers of National Property Fund property who will use them to cover their obligations to the National Property Fund.

Affect on Investment Funds

Investment funds, which flourished during the first wave of privatization, and anxiously awaited the second, have been hard hit by the termination of voucher privatization. Investment funds acquired nearly two-thirds of the shares during the first wave and, as a result, control most of the first wave companies privatized. Over 150 new investment funds registered with the Ministry of Finance in anticipation of the second privatization wave.

Under the new amendments to the Large-Scale Privatization Act, investment funds are entitled to receive a one-time payment of SKK 500,000 (approximately US $16,500) as compensation. The offered compensation is not sufficient to cover the costs of registration.

Direct Sales

While the political debate on the end of coupon privatization continues, the National Property Fund has quickened the pace of direct sales. In the first six months of 1995 alone, direct sales with an approximate value of SKK 15-billion have been approved by the National Property Fund.

The sales are typically made to the existing management of the company sold. Payment is spread over a ten-year period with a small percentage required as a down payment. Given the long repayment period, the National Property Fund typically retains considerable control over the company sold.

CONCLUSION

As the recent shift in privatization in Slovakia demonstrates, privatization and the methods of implementation can be extremely controversial and complex. Slovakia, and in particular the Meciar government, has come under heavy criticism from both domestic and international circles for abandoning voucher privatization. These critics argue that privatization is now being used as a tool of political largess to extend the influence of the governing coalition. While one cannot deny that political intrigue has helped shape the privatization landscape in Slovakia, one must not lose site of the fact that privatization not only continues but has quickened throughout 1995.

From a macro-economic standpoint, it is difficult to claim that voucher privatization is "better" than direct sales. The most important objective is to move property from state control to private ownership. Direct sales accomplish this objective. So long as the government remains committed to free market principles, the market should ensure that the owners of newly privatized companies work to increase productivity and efficiency. The true test of whether privatization will be a "success" in Slovakia is whether market economics will prevail over political interests.

SLOVENIA

Peter Grilc and Miha Juhart
University of Ljubljana
Ljubljana, Slovenia

TRANSFORMATION OF SOCIAL PROPERTY — INTRODUCTION

The abolition of socially owned property in Slovenia is dealt with by a complex set of legislation, which covers several aspects of property ownership. The main regulations are:
(1) Law on Denationalization;[1]
(2) Law on Co-operatives;[2]
(3) Law on Apartments;[3] and
(4) Law on Ownership Transformation of Socially Owned Companies.[4]

Law on Denationalization

The Law on Denationalization deals with denationalization of property that has been nationalized. It regulates agrarian reform, nationalisation, confiscation and implementation regulations. The theoretical background for the Law on Denationalization is the abolition of collectivization.

The beneficiaries of denationalization are natural persons whose property was nationalized following the regulations after the World War II, property nationalized until 1963, and property transformed into state property. The beneficiaries are the former owners or their heirs. Present citizenship is irrelevant for having status as a beneficiary for denationalization, but citizenship is relevant at the

---

1 *Official Gazette* 27/91.
2 *Official Gazette* 13/92, 7/93.
3 *Official Gazette* 18/91.
4 *Official Gazette* 55/92, 7/93, 31/93, 43/93.

time when the property was nationalized in the above forms. The person obliged to return property is the legal person owning the goods and property that should be returned to the former owners.

The rule is that the property may be claimed to be returned *in naturam*. If the ownership right has been acquired in the meantime, the beneficiaries may not claim return of property *in naturam* but only compensation. The compensation must be paid by the Compensation Fund of the Republic of Slovenia. Another exception to the *in naturam* principle is that the real estate property cannot be returned *in naturam* if it is a part of property intended for the functions of state administration or an indivisible part of a system of objects or devices or other resources of public undertakings.

Real estate cannot be returned *in naturam* if the economic and technological functionality of entrepreneurial complexes may be disturbed or if there is a danger of bankruptcy or dismissal of a great number of employees. The return of property does not influence the existing leases, tenancy and similar agreements, which stay in force for up to ten years. The beneficiary acquires the property right after the property is returned to him. If the property to be returned is a company, it may be returned to the former owners as a company. Otherwise, a proportional part of shares may be returned.

Law on Co-Operatives

The Law on Co-operatives essentially affected the area of co-operatives. This area has not been developed and understood in the classical sense during the last five decades. The Law enables denationalization of the former property of co-operatives that was nationalized or transferred to other legal entities without any compensation after 1945. By enabling the property to be returned to the former owners, the law re-establishes the former ownership structures. Existing co-operatives must transform themselves into classic co-operatives or establish new entities.

If the former property of co-operatives cannot be returned to the former co-operatives, the property goes to the Association of Co-operatives of Slovenia. The Association of Co-operatives of Slovenia then allocates it to another co-operative, which must be established within one year within the area of operations of the former co-operative.

The existing co-operatives or members of co-operatives that used to operate with socially owned companies in the field of agriculture are specifically enumerated by the Law. They are transferred into new co-operatives and may acquire forty-five per cent of existing socially owned companies that were their business partners in the past. Some socially owned companies that were also enumerated by the law itself had to transform themselves into stock companies and deliver to the co-operatives forty-five per cent of shares.

LAW ON APARTMENTS

The Law on Apartments originally dealt with property relationships, operation of apartments and contractual and tenancy relationships. Again, classic property and obligation tenancy relationships have been reinstituted. The former holders of the dwelling right acquired the right to purchase their apartments at a discount of up to seventy per cent. The buyer became the proprietor immediately after concluding the contract.

The Law also privatized companies dealing in apartments. These companies have been established for the purposes of operating with socially owned apartments. The companies became the property of communes, which must change their organizational status into stock companies and privatize them by selling their shares.

LAW ON OWNERSHIP TRANSFORMATION OF SOCIALLY OWNED COMPANIES

Privatization

The ownership transformation of companies formerly constituting social property means the transformation of a company with social capital into a company with known owners of the total fixed assets of the transformed company.

Under the former Company Law, most companies exist in the form of a special legal entity. Only few of the companies were transformed into incorporated or limited companies with social capital, which was allowed under amendments to the former

Company Law. Therefore, ownership transformation also entails the transformation of the legal status and form of the legal entity.

Procedure

The procedure for ownership transformation leads the managing board of the company, which appoints the privatization commission. The basis for the ownership transformation is the opening balance in which the value of the social capital of the company is set. A Governmental Order prescribes the procedure for preparing the opening balance in accordance to accounting standards. The opening balance should be made as from 31 December 1992.

If the value in the opening balance is not in accordance with the market value of the company, some other methods of fixing the value are allowed. The company may be evaluated by an authorized person holding an agency permit for privatization in accordance with the international standards. The company can opt for such valuation if the market value is lower than the value in the opening balance.

Forms

The company transforms itself into a limited company or stock corporation and issues shares on the basis of the value derived from the opening balance or authorized valuation. Most companies have chosen the legal form of stock corporation, because of a provision in the Company Law that limited companies should not have more than fifty shareholders. For this reason, only the procedure of transforming into a stock corporation will be described. The Law prescribes seven ways of privatizing social capital.

Transformation of company ownership is performed by:
(1) Transfer of ordinary shares to the Funds;
(2) An internal distribution of shares;
(3) An internal sale of shares;
(4) Sale of company shares;
(5) The sale of the total assets of the company;
(6) A transfer of shares to the Development Fund of Republic Slovenia; and
(7) A combination of the above methods.

Procedure and Methods

The managing board of the company must accept the transformation program. The program must include especially a description of the chosen ways of transformation and preliminary financial and management structural modifications. All employees must be informed of the program by the written report, especially about the possibilities and conditions of their participation in the transformation process.

The transformation program must be submitted to the Agency for privatization, which must approve it (first approval of Agency). The Agency may reject the program within thirty days after its receipt. If the Agency does not reject the program in this term, it is deemed confirmed.

The company must publish its program in the *Official Gazette* within thirty days from the receipt of the Agency's approval.

The transformation procedure is carried out in accordance with the approved program. All activities must be accomplished according to the terms appointed by the program. On termination of the transformation process, the company must report to the Agency, which controls performance of the approved program. The company must adopt all of the Agency's necessary decisions relating to its ownership and legal transformation. After these decisions are adopted, the company must apply for registration at the court register. The main condition for registration of ownership transformation is the second approval of the Agency.

The companies had to adopt the program by the end of 1994. The companies to be privatized who failed to fulfil this obligation were taken over by the Agency, which will prepare transformation programs and carry them out.

Foreign citizens and legal entities could participate in the process, but their possibilities are restricted. Most of the social capital will be transformed through the internal methods of transformation. Therefore, foreign persons can only buy the company as a whole or its ordinary shares issued. Purchases by foreigners that exceed a value of ECU 10-million require government approval.

The majority of companies that adopted their privatization programs in time decided for a very similar combination of privatization methods. First, the company issues ordinary shares for forty per cent of its social capital and transfers them to the Public Funds (ten per cent to the Slovenian Pension and Invalid's Fund, ten per cent to the Slovenian Compensation Fund and twenty per cent to the Development Fund).[5] This transformation step is obligatory because of public interest and the company cannot skip it. The only exemption is the sale of the total assets of the company, where the Funds do not get the shares, but a proportional part of purchase money.

The second step is internal distribution of ordinary shares, which may include no more than twenty per cent of the social capital of the company. The shares in internal distribution may only be acquired by employees, former employees and retired employees in exchange for their ownership certificates. All these persons have equal rights to participate in internal distribution. The company must inform them by announcement in the newspapers. The term for exchanging the certificate should not be shorter than thirty days. After this term expires, the company's commission for privatization establishes the amount and value of the collected certificates.

Obviously, the value of collected certificates will not correspond to exactly twenty per cent of the social capital or any other value noted in the transformation program. Where the value of collected certificates is lower, the remaining shares may be distributed in exchange for certificates of employees' family members or they may be transferred to the Development Fund. Where the collected value exceeds twenty per cent, each investor receives a proportionate number of shares and the remaining value of these persons' certificates is returned.

Internal distribution is not an obligatory method, but it is the condition for undertaking internal purchases of shares, which is the most attractive way of transformation for the employees. The shares from internal distribution are not transferable for a period of two years, except by inheritance. An exemption exists for shares transferred to the Fund.

The third step is internal purchase of shares, which may include the rest of social capital after transfer of shares to the Funds and internal distribution of shares (that means forty per cent) or any lesser value. Employees, former employees and retired workers of the company may participate in the internal purchase of shares. The fundamental condition for internal purchase is that more than

---

5 These Funds were established by a law, which also prescribes what the Funds may do with transferred stocks. The most important is the Development Fund, which sells its stocks to the Authorized Investments Companies.

one-third of the employees co-operate. Each participant must decide the amount of shares he intends to buy in the internal purchase. The total amount must be indicated in the privatization program.

The company issues ordinary shares for the capital that will be the object of internal purchases and transfers all shares to the Development Fund. Then, the company purchases the transferred shares back from the Fund in favor of rightful claimants (participants) on the basis of a special contract. The company must immediately purchase from the Fund twenty per cent of the transferred shares. The rest of the shares must be purchased by the company in the following four years.

The participants can pay for the shares with cash and obtain a fifty per cent of discount on the price of shares, which rises with the retail prices index. Only where employees' owner certificates have remained after the phase of the internal distribution may a part of the purchase price be paid with those certificates.

During the course of the internal purchase procedure, the Development Fund may exercise only some of its voting rights deriving from the shares it holds. The voting right may only be exercised in decisions on distribution, attachment, unification, cessation of the company, increase or decrease of the capital and sale, and on investment or leasing of a substantial part of assets. Special provisions provide for the Fund's right to a dividend. All participants may form a special representative body for exercising their rights in the company.

Small and middle enterprises with social capital can transform themselves in the combination of the above-mentioned methods. However, in large companies the shares distributed through internal distribution and internal purchase do not the reach the optimal value. In these companies, the transformation program must combine another method for the remaining value. The favored method is the sale of ordinary shares.

The company determines the price of shares on the basis of estimated value, revalued by the index of retail prices. The shares may be sold in different ways. The whole amount of shares or only part of it may be offered in the public auction. The shares may also be sold by collecting offers. Most of the companies opt for a public offer of shares.

Public offers are subject to the rules of the Securities Market Law. The basis for a public offer of shares is a prospect and a license from the Agency for the Securities Market. The shares offered to the public may be sold to domestic and foreign persons and legal entities. Domestic persons and entities have pre-emption rights. The shares are sold for cash and the purchase money is transferred to the Development Fund.

A part of shares may be offered to domestic persons in exchange for their ownership certificates. In this way, people employed in the public sector can directly acquire the shares of a company. Special and complicated rules regulate cases where the value of collected certificates exceeds the offer of shares.

Other methods of transformation were only rarely used. The company may be sold with all its assets on the basis of a decision by the managing board and a contract between the buyer and the Development Fund, to whom any purchase money is transferred.

The buyer takes over the company and its assets without former liabilities. These are assumed by the Fund. Then, the company ceases and is expunged from the court register. The legal consequences of bankruptcy come into effect for the employees.

In the transformation procedure, the company may also increase its capital by increments of at least for ten per cent of the existing capital. The company issues shares for its social capital and shares for the new capital. The shares for the social capital are the object of the mentioned transformation methods. The new shares may be sold for different types of payment, and the purchase money or its equivalent belongs to the company. The company may use this money only for the purposes set out in the transformation program.

A subsidiary method of transformation is transfer of shares to the Development Fund. The company transfers the remaining shares that are issued for the value of social capital. The transferred shares may be in the form of ordinary or preferred shares in accordance with the decision of the managing body of the company. The proffered stock gives the right to a fixed dividend at two per cent annual rate before any payment of a dividend on ordinary shares or the right of the same dividend as ordinary stock, when the dividend exceeds the two per cent annual rate.

Ownership Certificates

The mechanism of privatization involves ownership certificates issued by the state. The value of the issued ownership certificates corresponds to the value of socially owned capital in companies that are intended to be privatized. Therefore, every single company should allot a part of shares for internal distribution or for the purposes of distribution via appointed investment companies (the twenty per cent plus twenty per cent principle). This model enables the distribution of the total value of forty per cent of socially owned capital either within the concept of internal distribution or via the appointed investment companies.

The ownership certificates are issued by the Republic of Slovenia to the citizens of Slovenia according to the age of the entitled person (all persons with Slovenian citizenship on 5 December 1992). In this way, the entitled persons know the exact value of their ownership certificates.[6] The legislature did not accept the criteria of working age. This was mainly for practical reasons and because the criteria of the age simplified the distribution.

The ownership certificate by its nature has no paper value. Rather, it represents the ownership right enabling the citizens of the Republic of Slovenia to acquire shares in the companies being privatized. It is a specific right, whose value is limited and can be classified among claims against the state.

The value, already issued via ownership certificates, will be at the disposal of citizens only until the expiration of the single ownership certificate is reached. The ownership certificate is similar to a voucher, but there are no papers and no certificates in the physical sense because the concept of full dematerialization of the paper has been employed. Ownership certificates are not transferable; they are strictly personal and may be inherited.

The technique of realizing of ownership certificates, that is, exchanging them for shares, is executed through ownership orders. These in fact are the documents used by the entitled persons. Using the ownership order, the entitled person allows the drawing of credit from his or her certificate evidence account within the above limits. Control, exclusion of fraud and the right to participation within the privatization of an entitled certificate owner are completely and strictly decentralized. Therefore, the conversion of the certificate (partly or in whole) for shares in the company is executed only after the identity of the holder, his status and his right to the use of certificate itself have been checked.

---

6 Up to 400,000 Slovenian tolars, which corresponded to the value of DM 5,000 as of September 1995.

The ownership certificates may also be issued — following the consent of the Compensation Fund — to compensation beneficiaries according to the denationalization legislation. Every denationalization beneficiary may demand his property to be returned to him *in naturam*, that is, he may demand the return of the share of property or of a company. Alternatively, he may claim compensation. In this case, the Compensation Fund issues six per cent interest long-term bonds, which can also be used by the holder in the privatization procedures. The Republic of Slovenia has not issued a guarantee for the claims of owners of bonds (principal debt and interests) against the Compensation Fund.

Additional ownership certificates will be distributed to the employees of public institutions, to civil servants and to employees being mainly financed from state budgetary sources.

The purpose of ownership certificates is strictly designated. They enable their owners only to convert them for shares of companies being privatized or for use in authorized investment companies. Their use is limited in time and they are not transferable for money. The owners of certificates freely choose among possibilities for their investments. The value of shares of an individual company is formed according to the price of the transaction within the particular method of privatization. Only while investing the certificate in the authorized investment company for its shares does the nominal value of investment correspond to the nominal value of the certificate.

Authorized Investment Companies

Authorized investment companies are stock companies, as defined by a special law.[7] They are allowed to accumulate the ownership certificates of the citizens of Slovenia through the procedure of public accumulation of the ownership certificates.

To buy such certificates, through the procedure of the ownership transformation of the companies complying with the rules of the Law on Ownership Transformation of Socially Owned Companies, the authorized investment companies issue their respective shares to the investors of certificates in return for their ownership

---

7 *Official Gazette* 6/94.

certificates. The face value of shares corresponds to the value of the certificate (deduction of value is the provision of to the authorized investment company of a maximum 0.05 per cent).

UNITED KINGDOM

Robin Brooks
Norton Rose
London, England

HISTORICAL BACKGROUND

The United Kingdom privatization program, implemented by the Conservative Government in 1979, has been followed by governments all over the world and can be seen as starting one of the most radical trends in recent times. Most significantly, in October 1994 the new Labor Party leader, Tony Blair, publicly accepted the role of privatization in the modern economic world by radically calling for the abandonment of the clause in the Party's seventy-six-year-old constitution which had hitherto advocated state ownership of the means of production.

The term "privatization" covers a variety of transactions, from sales of governmental interests in industry to contracting out the provision of services to private contractors. The key factor, common to all privatization transactions, is the presence of a government or quasi-governmental entity and reduction of state ownership or control, including sales of assets or interests in assets by the state or arrangements whereby government interest in the provision of particular services is reduced. To appreciate the impact of privatization, it is important to first understand the reasons for the introduction of the program. The nationalized sector in the United Kingdom was largely created forty to fifty years ago by the Labor Government which came into power after the end of World War II, in line with the socialist philosophy of state ownership. In 1979, the nationalized industries in the United Kingdom accounted for approximately one-tenth of the Gross Domestic Product, one-seventh of total investments in the economy, around one-tenth of the Retail Price Index and employed about 1-million people.

In practice, the performance of these nationalized industries was generally perceived as disappointing, not only in terms of their total return on capital employed but also in terms of their record on prices, productivity, manpower costs and customer satisfaction in respect of services delivered by state-owned utilities. The reasons for these failings are complex but the fact that the industries were continually open to political interference as a result of state ownership meant that social and commercial objectives often became confused. In addition, the underwriting of the industries' borrowing by the government invariably led to the needs of individual state industries on occasion being subordinated to macro-economic or wider political requirements. On coming to power in 1979, the Thatcher government took the view that the only long-term solution for improving the efficiency of these industries would be to subject them to the harsh conditions of the marketplace which implied privatization, deregulation, reduction of monopolies and increased competition.

THE UNITED KINGDOM PROGRAM

By October 1993, forty-seven major companies and many smaller ones had been sold. About two-thirds of nationalized industries in the 1979 state sector, a number of civil service functions and about 940,000 jobs had been transferred to the private sector. The number of individuals owning shares had also dramatically risen threefold from 3-million in 1979 to 10-million. During the course of the fifteen year program, United Kingdom advisers have developed techniques which are now conventional features of privatizations all over the world, and which have also influenced the way in which purely non-state business is conducted. In particular, many of the techniques for the mass marketing of shares, developed in connection with privatization, are now being used to market other listed shares.

The United Kingdom Government's objectives today are still largely economic but are stated to be:
(1) To promote efficiency by exposing businesses and services to the greatest possible competition, to the benefit of the consumer;
(2) To widen and deepen share ownership; and
(3) To obtain the best value for each industry or service the government sells.

Forms and Methods

A number of key issues need to be considered in preparing a business for privatization. The method chosen will be greatly influenced by the policy objectives of the government or state entity involved, the nature of the enterprise or service concerned and the legislative, financial and economic context. Disposal may be achieved by a private or trade sale, or by some form of public offer for sale which may be accompanied by single or multiple stock market listings. A third form of privatization involves the contracting out of local government services, which will be considered later in this chapter.

Public Offer/Trade Sale

Factors Influencing the Method of Privatization

A private sale to a single purchaser may be the most efficient way of selling a small enterprise. On the other hand, there may be significant advantages in selling a substantial enterprise by a public offering on local and/or international stock markets. A sale of a substantial enterprise by public offering may be accomplished in stages over many years. For example, British Telecom has had three public offerings, in 1984, 1991 and 1993. Tables 1 and 2 provide a summary of the British Telecom and Electricity Industry Sales.

The need to establish a workable regulatory regime may dictate that the enterprise be divided into separate businesses rather than being sold as one entity. For example, the need to introduce competition into an industry may require its division into separately viable components; similarly, a vertically integrated set of businesses may need to be separated before privatization to avoid prejudicing other businesses in both the private and public sectors. The type of industry, that is, whether it is a public utility, such as water or gas, or whether it is a manufacturing industry, such as Rolls-Royce, will often have considerable bearing on the approach taken. Restructuring is considered further in this chapter. There have been a variety of approaches in the United Kingdom. With the British Gas privatization, the industry was left more or less intact. At the other extreme, the electricity industry was substantially restructured to create a semi-competitive market for electricity suppliers in the United Kingdom. British Telecom's business was not restructured, but a new competitor, Mercury, was licensed to introduce an element of competition. National interest will also dictate the approach. Sensitivity and controls, for example, through special shares and through the limitation of foreign investment, may be required for the denationalization of industries involved with defense, such as British Aerospace, BAA and Rolls-Royce. The need to balance the interests of consumers and shareholders in the longer term has become apparent with recent events in the electricity industry. The sale of a controlling interest in a business may command a greater price but may not be acceptable either politically or to the management of the business.

Interest in the relevant enterprise will determine whether a public offer is feasible or whether a trade sale will be more commercially advantageous. It will also determine whether a public offer is limited to the local stock market or whether it is extended to international stock markets. This in turn will depend to a large extent on the nature of the business of the enterprise concerned. The nature of the markets in which the enterprise trades may affect its suitability for a public offering. Its history may raise questions about its ability to trade successfully in the future; for example, a history of state subsidies may raise questions about the viability of the business in the longer term and may also give rise to dumping and countervailing duty problems in the USA and the European Community.

The raising of significant funds through a privatization may affect the liquidity available for other forms of government finance, such as government bonds. Where there is a significant retail offering to private investors, other forms of savings such as building societies may also be affected. Overseas listings may be necessary. Even if there is sufficient liquidity in the domestic market(s), additional demand from overseas might enable the government to secure a better price. Furthermore, legal difficulties connected with the assets being sold may make a public sale inappropriate. For example, concern about decommissioning costs and liabilities led to the withdrawal of the nuclear power plants from the privatization of the electricity industry in the United Kingdom.

Restructuring the Business for Privatization

An important initial consideration must invariably involve deciding whether the relevant enterprise should be sold in its present state or whether it would be prudent to restructure it and sell it in its constituent parts, thereby introducing an element of competition into the industry and consequently improving efficiency. Wider regulatory issues are also relevant. For example, the privatization of the electricity industry in England and Wales in 1990, which created three generating companies and transferred twelve electricity distribution companies to the private sector, resulted in greater competition within the market place and subsequently led to reduction of domestic prices. It also involved the establishment of a sophisticated regulatory structure which included price controls and the creation of a market mechanism (the pool), whereby electricity is bought and sold.

However, in many cases, restructuring may mean no more than identifying that part of a public corporation or service that is suitable for privatization and then constituting it as a company defined under the Companies Act, with its own commercial accounts and formal contractual arrangements with its customers (e.g., sale of the Insurance Services Group). Other sales, however, have required a greater degree of restructuring to achieve a commercially viable organization for sale.

Examples of privatizations involving an element of restructuring include:
(1) Britoil Flotation, 1992 (the exploration and production assets of British National Oil Corporation were stripped out and sold); and
(2) British Telecommunications plc (BT), 1984 (the telecommunications functions of the former General Post Office were separated out and sold). The privatization of the remaining parts of the former General Post Office continues to be a difficult political issue.

In some cases, an industry has been transformed from a loss-making business to a profitable business while still under state control. There are many examples, notably British Steel (which had an entry in the *Guinness Book of Records* as a loss maker) and British Airways. Two current examples include the coal industry, where a national industry is being sold in parcels, and British

Rail, both of which are considered in greater detail later in this chapter under "Future Outlook". The process of fixing the stock market capitalization or sale price of an enterprise to be privatized, whether by public offer or trade sale, will almost always involve a consideration of the value of its major assets. Where there has been a substantial restructuring of a business, this can be difficult to determine.

As a result of criticism which arose when a purchaser of a business which included certain property interests subsequently sold these interests at a very significant profit, special "clawback" provisions were included in trade sales. The sale in question involved Royal Ordnance, originally a Trading Fund within the Ministry of Defense, which was transformed into a public limited company in 1984. The Leeds tank factory was sold to Vickers in October 1986, with the remainder being sold to British Aerospace in April 1987 for £190-million. In August of the same year, British Aerospace was accused of "naked asset-stripping" when the company announced the closing of its Enfield small arms factory. This led to the view by the National Audit Office that the purchase price was "significantly less than the net asset value of Royal Ordnance", considering the extensive property interests. In the interests of maximizing the proceeds of sale, special terms can sometimes be included to cover assets which have a latent value. These provide for clawback by the government of profit realized after privatization on a sale of real property which is subsequently developed and sold off at an enhanced price. Similar provisions can be applied to other assets, such as intellectual property.

Legislation and Liabilities

While it would theoretically be possible to have a general "Privatization Act" to govern the transfer of all state-owned industries to the private sector, the United Kingdom has no such Act. Instead, each significant individual privatization had specific legislation covering, where appropriate, the restructuring of the entity, the introduction of a regulatory framework and, often, aspects of the mechanics of the privatization process itself. Whichever form a privatization takes, the relevant government body will generally be concerned to ensure that all the assets relating to the enterprise are disposed of and that the liabilities left with the government are kept to a minimum. This objective is generally achieved through legislation. For example, the British Steel Act 1988:

> "... transfers the assets and liabilities of the British Steel Corporation (BSC) to a company nominated by the Secretary of State (providing also for shares in the successor company to be issued to the government), and for the dissolution of the corporation."

Where particular liabilities (such as historic occupational risks) cannot be disposed of as part of the privatization, legislation may be needed to vest them in a continuing body which will handle claims and which may require separate government funding.

Ongoing Liabilities Resulting from Sale

The government will generally be concerned not to incur contingent liabilities by giving warranties relating to the assets or enterprise being privatized or, on a public flotation by failing to satisfy the disclosure requirements under the Financial Services Act (FSA)[1] or of any jurisdiction in which public share offerings take place.

Public Offerings

In the United Kingdom, obligations are imposed under the FSA and the Listing Rules of the London Stock Exchange (*Yellow Book*) on the directors and any person who takes responsibility for part of the listing particulars. Under Section 146 of the Financial Services Act, the persons responsible for the listing particulars are under a general duty of disclosure which provides that listing particulars must:

> "... contain all such information as investors and their professional advisers would reasonably require, and

---

[1] Financial Services Act 1986, Section 146.

reasonably expect to find there, for the purpose of making an informed assessment of:

"(1) The assets and liabilities, financial position, profits and losses, and prospects of the issuer of the securities; and
"(2) The rights attaching to those securities."

This general duty of disclosure applies only to information:

"... which is within the knowledge of any person responsible for the listing particulars or which it would be reasonable for him to obtain by making enquiries."

It should be noted that it is not sufficient that each statement in the listing particulars is factually correct, since liability arises not only for untrue information but also for misleading information and omissions.

From the government's perspective, it is the directors who have the real knowledge of the business on which the investor is relying. From the company's perspective, if it is the government which is raising money from the privatization and not the company, there is clearly a view which says that responsibility should be shared. The division of responsibility between the company and the government will be a matter for discussion on each offer. In practice the government has taken responsibility for the following areas:

(1) Statements about the government's past actions or intentions;
(2) Descriptions of any regulatory structure and its effects; and
(3) The implications of legislation.

The company and its directors have been responsible for all statements to do with the business, its prospects and financial information.

In the United Kingdom, a public offering may be accompanied by a marketing campaign involving press and television advertising, distribution of corporate brochures and publication to City institutions and journalists of detailed research on the company in the form of brokers' circulars. These documents are capable of affecting the contents of the formal listing particulars and great care must be taken to ensure that they are consistent. In the United Kingdom, the procedure by which the contents of the listing particulars is checked is called "verification". This is a thorough process in which evidence and justification for each statement in the listing particulars is collated and responsibility for checking the statement is allocated to an individual. Other jurisdictions, such as the United States, have different procedures, and these are followed cumulatively. The procedures are followed to some extent with regard to all documents used in the marketing campaign.

Private Sales

Warranties may be requested by private commercial purchasers, but are often reduced or avoided by requiring the prospective purchaser to undertake a thorough "due diligence" investigation. A commercial purchaser acquiring a business will normally request that the vendor give warranties and indemnities in relation to that business. In the context of a privatization, this approach would mean that the government becomes subject to ongoing contingent liabilities which could reduce the sale proceeds. For policy reasons, this is not attractive to a government. Claims in relation to warranties in the courts following a sale could cause significant political embarrassment. As a result, although certain warranties and indemnities are given, it is unusual for the government to give significant warranties relating to the business being privatized.

It has been the practice for the purchaser to undertake a significant due diligence investigation and to rely on this investigation. As a consequence, a purchaser would have no claim in respect of matters which subsequently emerged and which were damaging to the business. Even where a substantial due diligence exercise is conducted, a prudent purchaser will seek to support its conclusions with warranties and indemnities and this can give rise to complex negotiations. Where a purchaser is dependent on banks or financial institutions to raise finance for the purchase price, these lenders will have certain minimum requirements as regards warranties and indemnities to enable them to lend. To permit a purchaser, who may be an actual or potential competitor, access to the business secrets of a company being privatized raises other issues. In order to overcome, at least partially, these issues, reliance has been placed on confidentiality agreements. Even so, in some industries it may not be appropriate to give a purchaser access to all of a company's affairs.

Policy Considerations

In a privatization, the government is usually subject to constraints which do not apply to commercial vendors, such as open debate in parliament and scrutiny by the National Audit Office, which provides independent information to parliament and the public concerning the financial operations of government departments and other bodies which receive public funds. Thus, the need to avoid embarrassment will be a major concern. The government will wish to dispose of the enterprise concerned cleanly, without a need to have subsequent recourse to purchasers (other than for installments of the sale price). Furthermore, due to the politically sensitive nature of the transaction, the government will wish to avoid either pursuing or defending litigation following a privatization since the ensuing adverse publicity could detrimentally affect the whole program.

The minimization of these risks will often involve lengthy negotiations and delicate judgments in relation to, for example, the extent to which the actions or knowledge of one government department may be attributed to another, thereby jeopardizing compliance by the government as a whole with its statutory or contractual disclosure obligations. Such a delicate judgment was recently faced by the government in the Power Gen/National Power sale. The price of the electricity generator's shares fell below their issue price on the announcement of a planned review of electricity price controls by the electricity regulator. The announcement came only one day after the commencement of trading in the shares and resulted in criticism of the government. The government had been forewarned of the regulator's intentions but, following consultation with its legal and financial advisers, had decided not to disclose the information and to proceed with the sale on the basis that the announcement had been aimed at the distribution companies and not the generators.

Public Offering and Flotation

Privatizations effected by way of public offerings, coupled with flotation on the domestic and/or overseas stock exchanges, have proved to be highly successful where substantial amounts of capital have been required and there has been a willingness to invest. However, this method has also been used for the disposal of relatively small undertakings. A major public offering of securities is usually accompanied by a listing of the securities on appropriate stock markets, although it is not essential for a listing to be obtained in each jurisdiction in which a public offering is made. However, any such offer will be subject to the local securities laws in each jurisdiction where it is made, whether or not a listing is obtained. In the United Kingdom, the FSA and the *Yellow Book*, which protect investors in public share offerings, require the preparation of a prospectus, detailing the trading and financial history, the principal commercial arrangements and the future prospects of the enterprise. The information provided must be verified. Further protection is given by Section 154 of the Financial Services Act, which requires the approval and authorization of advertisements published in connection with Listing Particulars by the competent authority, which will usually be the Stock Exchange.

Methods of Sale

To date, the main methods of sale have been: a fixed price offer of shares; a tender offer at a striking price; or a combination of the two. In early privatizations, fixed price offers were greatly oversubscribed. Two practices grew up, which changes to structure sought to avoid:
(1) Multiple applications: the government included a representation on each application form that multiple applications were not being made and set up an elaborate policing structure to catch multiple applicants; and
(2) Stagging: the practice of stagging, where an applicant immediately sells shares, was tackled in two ways: by the grant of incentives (such as bonus shares or discounts from bills) to investors who held their shares and by delaying the announcement of allocation to private investors until after dealings had commenced. This effectively prevented private investors from selling when dealings first commenced in the shares.

Typically, the first major flotations comprised a fixed-price, United Kingdom public offer aimed at the retail investor and an institutional offer. In some sales (for example BT in 1984, British Gas in 1986 and Water in 1989) the international offer was at the fixed price available in the United Kingdom public offer. In others (for example the Scottish Electricity Companies in 1991), sale has been by way of international tender offer aimed to raise additional proceeds where trading was expected to open at a premium to the issue price. Techniques have become increasingly sophisticated and innovative, having to continually adapt to fluctuating market conditions to maximize return. In later sales, such as the BT flotations in 1991 and 1993, shares were not offered at a fixed price to the public or institutions. Instead, the price of shares sold in the United Kingdom public offer was set at a discount to the strike price secured in an international tender offer at the end of the offer period. These international offers were wholly competitive tenders, with allocations being made solely on the basis of the quality of bids. The two flotations were not underwritten because it was felt that the use of book-building removed the risk of failing to dispose of the shares.

International Offers

The earlier international offers, for example, BT in 1991, typically involved regional syndicates, led by a bank from the region concerned, which followed the traditional view that only United States banks could adequately access the United States market. However, United Kingdom banks, based in London, often with a strong presence in other major financial centers and a notably enhanced position in the United States, are increasingly being viewed as syndicate leaders. This approach was adopted in the BT sale in 1993, where United Kingdom advisers developed a global structure in which an eleven bank syndicate competed worldwide for demand from the 500 largest institutions. From the government's perspective, the outcome demonstrated that United Kingdom banks could access the key investors, crucial to the success of any large international offer. It thus created a precedent. To access the United States and subsequently the international market, shares in privatized entities became packaged as American Depository Receipts (ADR's) or Global Depository Receipts (GDR's). This enabled trading to take place in such instruments in dematerialized form.

Clawback

In the early sales, a specified share of the offer for sale or tender was allocated to the general public, to employees, to qualifying pensioners and to institutions (both in the United Kingdom and overseas). Any oversubscription by the general public led to cutting back its subscriptions, so that consequently its aggregated allocations matched the number of shares reserved. In later sales, the Treasury decided to deal with this oversubscription by the general public through a clawback mechanism which provided that if the public oversubscribed their allocation by more than a specified number of times, a proportion of the shares initially reserved for domestic and overseas institutions would be clawed back and made available to the public.

Book-Building

The system of book-building was introduced to induce competition among the institutions. Institutional and overseas investors were asked to indicate, through brokers, the amount which they would be prepared to invest at a range of yields/prices specified by the sponsoring governmental department. The technique was first used in the National Power/Power Gen flotation, where information was requested twice prior to the fixing of the price. Allocations were then made to the highest bidders on the basis of the second set of offers. In 1991, British Telecom bids were revised and updated periodically during the tender period with the final bids being specified by the end of the offer period. These final bids were further used for the British Telecom sale of 1993.

Back-End Tender

The procedure, first introduced in the National Power/Power Gen flotation, operates on the principle that where there is a sufficient demand, a proportion of the shares provisionally set aside for allocation to institutional and overseas investors is withdrawn. After the close of the fixed price offer to the general public, the shares which had been temporarily withdrawn are re-offered to the institutional and overseas investors by way of a tender. Allocation is subsequently made to the highest bidders.

Private or Trade Sales

Generally, sales of the smaller state-owned businesses and services have been by way of private contract which has the advantage of a greater flexibility due to the removal of constraints applicable to public offerings. The sales may be to existing companies or consortia in related industrial sectors. Alternatively, they may be made to existing management, supported by institutional investors. These latter management and/or employee buy-outs have been particularly encouraged by the government since they are consistent with its objective of promoting employee share ownership (*see* below). Enthusiasm and support from both management and employees is obviously of crucial importance to the success of a privatization.

Management Buy-Outs

Management buy-outs of state-owned industries present special problems. Often, management will have interests which may conflict with those of the government in its role as vendor; and yet the government will be dependent on management for its commercial information relating to the business. These issues may become critical where the government, for wider reasons of policy, is seeking to restructure the enterprise as part of the privatization process. As a result, management may be in a position to negotiate an advantageous price and also dictate the board's composition and structure, although the co-operation of the workforce will undoubtedly be of significant importance. However, a sale to management will also have advantages, which may include less pressure on the government as vendor to give warranties and fewer potential problems with the workforce. Where a sale is made to management and employees, restrictions are usually imposed preventing the sale of shares to non-employees and requiring the sale of such shares if a person ceases to be an employee. In these circumstances, an auditor's valuation of the company would normally be obtained.

Employee Participation

The United Kingdom Government has actively encouraged employee participation in both trade sales and public offers of shares, whereby workers are given a direct stake in their future. This program has been seen to be very successful. In fact, the privatizations of BT and the gas, water and electricity industries all involved long-term employee share ownership schemes. The offer made to employees is usually accompanied by special documentation. Such documentation will include special application forms and documents explaining the offer. Furthermore, these documents will often be accompanied by a brochure giving details of the company's business. The use of such documentation, in part, helps ensure that it is employees who benefit from such offers and not others.

Employees are typically offered incentives which include:
(1) Priority in the allocation of shares;
(2) An offer of free shares;
(3) An offer of free shares in proportion to the number of shares purchased by the employee; and
(4) A discount on the offer price of shares.

On a number of occasions, management has joined forces with employees in management and employee buy-outs (MEBOs) which have proved to be particularly successful in, for example, a significant number of National Bus sales.

The Small Investor

Flotations of privatized industries have been used as an opportunity to promote wider share ownership. The government's consistent policy has been to encourage private individuals to invest in privatized industries and this has led to the development of major retail offer structures from the privatization of BT in 1984 (the largest public offer in the world at that time) to the 1993 sale of virtually all the United Kingdom Government's residual holding in BT, which further developed the Share Shops scheme (discussed in greater detail below). Not all public offers of privatized shares have targeted the small investor. Where it is felt that a company is not necessarily the most appropriate for small investors, a retail marketing campaign is not mounted and the minimum investment and allocation policy is used to discourage such investors.

Incentives

The United Kingdom Government has introduced incentives and facilitated investment by the private individual by:
(1) Setting up special dealing arrangements to give private investors the benefit of lower commission rates;
(2) Facilitating the cost-effective holding and transfer of shares by intermediaries, such as banks, on behalf of large numbers of investors;
(3) Permitting simplified marketing documents to be sent to such investors, for example, "mini prospectuses" and corporate brochures;
(4) Creating special discounts on goods or services provided by the undertaking if the private shareholders concerned are also customers of the relevant undertaking;
(5) Issuing bonus shares to encourage long-term investment in the undertaking and avoid investment for speculative short-term gain;
(6) Encouraging employees and/or customers to hold shares through schemes offering free or discounted shares (*see* below);
(7) Enabling undertakings to issue simplified financial statements;
(8) Ensuring that the relevant company laws allow the logistical problems of large shareholder meetings to be overcome; and
(9) Using share information offices to provide information to retail customers.

Share Shops

The Share Shop initiative was introduced by the United Kingdom Government in 1991 during the sale of part of its residual shareholding in BT. Its function was to promote wider publicity on share dealing services and arrangements. By appointing eight financial service providers to act as Share Shops, mostly with a high street presence, the government provided cheap and accessible buying and selling arrangements for a range of shares and consequently raised public awareness in private sector share dealing services. The initiative was developed further in 1993 during the third BT offer. Individuals could choose to apply directly to the government as in previous offers or they could apply to one of some 150 private sector Share Shops, who would then apply to the government on their behalf. The impact of the Share Shops' initiative on share dealing in the private sector is perceived by the government as being "tremendous". Share Shops are now being used by the public, outside the scope of government share offers. In the sale of shares to the public in the electricity generators Power Gen PLC and National Power PLC, the government has used the existence of Share Shops to dispense with a Share Information Office which had previously been used to coordinate offers to the retail public.

Marketing

Major public offerings are typically accompanied by a marketing campaign, involving advertisements in the media and the issue of brochures. The brokers to the issue and the company may be commissioned to assist in the sale process and to research and produce further material. The marketing of a privatization issue passes through different phases and will differ according to the extent to which there is a significant effort to market shares to the general public in the United Kingdom. The privatization of British Gas inaugurated an era of mass marketing of shares to the retail public with the launch of a television campaign using marketing techniques only hitherto applied to normal retail products. The "Tell Sid" slogan was the cornerstone of this campaign. This approach was refined in subsequent campaigns and was a significant contributor to the widening of share ownership among the retail public in the United Kingdom.

There are typically a number of distinct areas in a privatization campaign. The first is the deliberate increase of awareness of the relevant company and its products by a campaign of corporate image advertising. Under English law, the extent to which such advertisements should be regarded as investment advertisements regulated under the Financial Services Act is not always clear. In practice, a number of factors, such as the passing of relevant legislation, the establishment of a date and public perception lead these advertisements to be treated as investment advertisements in due course. Generally, any document or other material inviting persons to enter into an agreement to acquire or dispose of securities or to exercise acquisition/disposal rights conferred by an investment, or containing information calculated to lead directly or indirectly to persons doing so, is likely to constitute an "investment advertisement".

The Financial Services Act provides that an investment advertisement may only be lawfully distributed in the United Kingdom if:
(1) It is issued by a person authorized to conduct investment business in the United Kingdom; or
(2) It is approved by such an authorized person; or
(3) It is issued only to certain categories of exempt persons to whom an unapproved investment advertisement can be issued (for example, brokers' circulars); or
(4) It is a category of document to which Section 57 does not apply (for example, a prospectus may constitute listing particulars and will then become subject to the Listing Rules).

Investment advertisements are required to contain certain warnings (commonly called a rubric) which state that it is an investment advertisement and has been issued or approved by an authorized person. In addition, they would commonly state that the price of shares may go down as well as up. A general concern in respect of all the marketing is to ensure that it is consistent with any prospectus or listing particulars and, from an early stage, the marketing materials will be carefully checked, and all statements by the company itself carefully controlled, to ensure that they are accurate and consistent. Controls may even be introduced covering all public statements made by senior employees of the relevant company.

In addition to material which is generally released, professional investors may be targeted with specific research prepared by brokers connected with the company and/or the government. This research is circulated only to professional investors and under the Financial Services Act regime is not treated as an investment advertisement. Since it may have a significant impact on those professional investors who chose to invest in the company, care still needs to be taken to ensure that it is consistent with the prospectus. Indeed, to distance the contents of such research from the prospectus or listing particulars, a "sanitation period" is usually imposed both before and after the publication of the listing particulars and any pathfinder prospectus. The purpose of this sanitation period is to prevent the contents of these circulars being used to question either the completeness or the contents of any listing particulars. The extent to which the company and/or vendor of the shares is responsible for the contents of these circulars will depend on a number of factors. These documents will themselves carry significant health warnings which try to limit the responsibility of the company/vendor. Brokers' circulars will frequently be supported by "road shows" or presentations made to investors. In addition to the brokers' circulars, corporate brochures which give a brief description of the company with no accounting information may be circulated to the public. These documents will contain basic, factual information about the company concerned and will usually be treated as investment advertisements, the circulation of which requires the approval of an authorized person.

One concern in respect of all of the marketing material is to ensure that any application for shares is made on the basis of the information contained in the prospectus alone. The application for shares will normally contain a declaration to this effect. Currently, even the television advertisements for the electricity generators contain this wording. One reform which the mass marketing of shares to the public introduced was the use of mini-prospectuses. This is specifically authorized under the Financial Services Act, which requires them to be approved by the Stock Exchange together with any other advertisements publicizing the availability of the prospectus or listing particulars. The extent to which it is permissible to use these additional marketing documents differs from country to country and means that the marketing process needs to be strictly controlled.

Control and Regulation

Control: the Golden Share

One of the stated purposes of privatization is to enable the government to make a "clean break" with each privatized industry at the point of sale. Consequently, management and employees are at liberty to follow the most desirable commercial strategy for the business, subject to free market pressures or, where appropriate, independent regulation, but free from interference by government for purely political motives. However, in a number of privatizations it has been clearly prudent to protect a newly privatized business from an unwelcome takeover or, as a temporary measure, to provide an opportunity for management to adjust to the private sector. Thus, where appropriate, the government has retained or has held a special "golden" share in a number of privatized companies.

This special share requires that certain provisions in the articles of association of the company may not be changed without the specific consent of the special shareholder, namely the state. Various restrictions have been utilized to date:

(1) Special voting rights or provisions (for example, both National Power and British Gas use a restriction on the variation of any voting rights attached to any shares);

(2) Restrictions preventing any holder of shares from exercising more than fifteen per cent of the votes (for example, in Jaguar cars);

(3) Foreign ownership restrictions requiring the mandatory sale of shares owned by an overseas investor if the percentage held exceeds the specified level, which is usually fifteen per cent but will be 29.5 per cent where national security is an issue (for example, Rolls-Royce uses such a restriction set at the upper limit of 29.5 per cent due to the defense-related nature of its business);

(4) Restrictions on issue of certain types of new voting shares (for example, the Regional Electricity Companies, BT and Amersham all used such restrictions);

(5) Restrictions on disposal of assets (for example, Jaguar and Rolls-Royce);

(6) Restrictions on dissolution or winding up (for example, Enterprise Oil);

(7) Requirements that there be a British chief executive (for example BT (1984) and BT (1991). In some cases, for example, British Aerospace (1985), there is a requirement that all directors be British); and

(8) Requirements that the directors be government-appointed (for example, British Petroleum has two government-appointed directors).

The most frequently used among these has been a restriction on the issue of new voting shares (other than ordinary shares) and also a restriction on any one person, or group of persons acting in concert, from controlling more than fifteen per cent of the company's equity. If this percentage is exceeded, the acquirer will be obliged to sell off the surplus holding. Generally, this limit has made no distinction between overseas and United Kingdom investment except where there was an element of national security, for example, that the nature of the industries' services was defense-related (for example, British Aerospace and Rolls Royce). In such a case, a limit of fifteen per cent on the proportion of the company held by overseas investors was initially imposed and was later increased to 29.5 per cent, as a result of pressure exerted on the United Kingdom Government by the European Commission. It is a principle of European Community law that discrimination between nationalities within the European Community is prohibited, and this has exerted pressure on the Government in relation to such provisions.

The provisions may be amended or waived where the government has deemed such action appropriate. For example, the special share in Jaguar was waived at the end of October 1988, subsequent to the takeover bid by Ford, whereas in the case of Britoil, the special share was retained after BP's bid for the company and then later redeemed in 1990. In the case of the Regional Electricity Companies, the government's special share is redeemable on 31 March 1995, whereas the restrictions on ownership continue for a further five years. There is likely to be significant pressure from institutional shareholders for the Regional Electricity Companies to alter their articles to remove the restriction on holdings of more than fifteen per cent. The special share may be either non-time limited but with a right to redeem at any time, or time limited (often where there is a need to allow a company a period of transition to the private sector). For example, special shares in the ten water companies, privatized in 1989, will expire in December 1994. The use of a special share is an important device because it gives the government an element of negative control, but is not designed to be a burden to the management. In practice, it is the management who are generally responsible for ensuring observation of the provisions and management may welcome such provisions since they give an element of protection from an unwelcome takeover bid.

Regulation

In addition to negative control through the "golden" share mechanism, the government will often need to exercise a degree of regulatory control after privatization. Regulation is particularly desirable where the privatized undertakings are public utilities which in the past operated as near monopolies, for example, the gas, water, electricity and communications industries. Particular controls are necessary to protect the consumer where the enterprise is a monopoly supplier of services. Consequently, a regulatory body, independent of government, has been established for each of the newly privatized utility sectors. Each is overseen by a Director General who typically assumes his or her post for several years before moving on. The bodies have a wide range of powers and duties to promote the interests of consumers as well as ensuring that there are adequate returns on capital for investors. The most important of these is price regulation. Duties also include the consideration of all complaints relating to the company's services.

Control of prices is exercised through a formula which generally limits the annual price increases to no more than, and usually less than, the rate of inflation. This capping mechanism operates by fixing the rate at which the regulated industry is permitted to raise the prices of its products or services for a limited period of time. The original formula[2] devised for BT worked on the basis that the regulator made an estimate of the efficiency gains which the business would be likely to achieve over the coming period (the so-called "X" factor). This figure would then be subtracted from the United Kingdom's retail price index ("RPI" — the conventional measure of inflation) to produce the individual utility price cap formula. This formula has been utilized subsequently, with various modifications, for the other utilities. For example, the water privatization introduced a "K" factor instead of an "X" factor, which was to be added to the RPI. The price formulae aim to force a company to pass on to its customers some of the efficiency gains accruing from privatization while also providing it with an incentive to reduce its costs. If a company achieves a cost reduction, in excess of the pre-set "X" factor, it may retain the difference for itself. The regulator will exercise its powers, as regards competition law matters, subject to the supervision of the Monopolies and Mergers Commission.

Compulsory Competitive Tendering

The government's privatization program includes Compulsory Competitive Tendering (CCT), that is, the contracting out of local government services, defined in legislation. Local authorities wishing to carry out a specific activity in-house through its own Direct Services Organization (DSO) or Direct Labor Organization

---

2 This formula is the brainchild of Professor Littlechild, currently Director General of the Office of Electricity Regulation (OFFER).

(DLO) are required to first consider private sector bids to provide the service. This is intended to promote competition and hence improvement in the quality of services. CCT was first introduced for construction, maintenance and highways work by the Local Government, Planning and Land Act (1980). It was extended by the Local Government Act (1988) to other "blue collar services", such as ground maintenance and refuse collection. This also introduced the concept of anti-competitive behavior, where an authority unfairly favors its own in-house bid. Further extension to sport and leisure management was achieved through secondary legislation in 1989. Future plans involve the extension of CCT to "white-collar services" such as legal, corporate and administration services, "housing management" and further "blue-collar services" such as on-street parking and security.

The Transfer of Undertakings (Protection of Employment) Regulations 1981 (TUPE) was introduced to implement into United Kingdom law the European Union Acquired Rights Directive.[3] There has recently been much debate regarding the extent to which TUPE operates so as to protect employees' terms and conditions when services are contracted out. Recently, the European Court of Justice held that the decisive criterion in assessing whether or not the Directive was applicable was whether the operation in question retained its identity after the transfer. Thus, the Directive will apply, provided that the activities of the undertaking before and after the alleged transfer are similar or the same, and that the transferee assumes the obligations of an employer towards the employees of the undertaking. The fact that there is no transfer of tangible assets or that the service in question is merely an ancillary activity would appear to be immaterial to the operation of the Directive.[4]

Future Outlook

The United Kingdom Government's stated policy is to continue to privatize state-controlled industries, where appropriate. The following is a brief analysis of privatizations which are under way.

---

[3] European Union Directive Number 77/187.

[4] *Schmidt* vs. *Spar und Leihkasse der früheren Ämter Bordesholm*, Kiel und Cronshagen, ECJ, 14 April 1994 (C–392/92). This case could have a significant effect on such privatizations in the future.

British Rail

The initial steps in the reorganization and privatization of the railway industry were set out in the government's White Paper, "New Opportunities for the Railways" and the Railways Act 1993 and provided the legal authority for such privatization to take place. British Rail has been split into eighty separate businesses, each of which it is anticipated will eventually be privatized. Each of these businesses will be required to put legal contracts in place to govern their various relationships.

On 1 April 1994, Railtrack was transferred from the British Railways Board to the government. Railtrack owns and operates all the tracks and associated infrastructure. It is intended that Railtrack will be floated on the London Stock Exchange by the middle of 1997. Furthermore, on 1 April 1994 all passenger rolling stock was transferred to three wholly-owned subsidiaries of British Railways Board collectively known as the "Roscos". It is intended that the Roscos will be sold by the end of 1995. The Roscos lease the rolling stock to train operating companies (the "Tocs") such as Gatwick Express. It is anticipated that the twenty-five train operating companies will be let as franchises as part of the privatization program. The Tocs will receive government revenue support which will be allocated by the head of the Office of Passenger Rail Franchising (OPRAF), the Franchising Director. The Rail Regulator was appointed under the Railways Act and is responsible for granting licenses, regulating certain agreements such as those between Railtrack and the Tocs in relation to track access and for enforcing domestic competition law in relation to railway services.

British Coal

The privatization of the coal industry after forty-eight years in the public sector will be completed in 1995 when British Coal offers its entire 150,000-acre property portfolio in packages, targeted at investors and property developers. Clawback clauses are likely to be included in some sales agreements to ensure that the Treasury can benefit from any subsequent re-development profits. The collieries and opencast pits, together with miners and support staff, were transferred to the private sector in the closing days of 1994.

National Power/Power Gen

The 1995 sale of the government's remaining forty per cent stake in the two power generators, National Power and Power Gen, was structured in two parts. It involved a United Kingdom public offer aimed at United Kingdom retail investors who were offered incentives (installment discounts or bonus shares), provided they had registered with a Share Shop before a specified date. In addition, there were two separate international tender offers for shares in National Power and Power Gen respectively, which were targeted at institutional investors, both in the United Kingdom and overseas.

Retail investors could also apply for shares under the tender offer. The offers were marketed through a syndicate of seventeen investment banks, with two banks acting as book runners and joint co-ordinators. Book-building was employed to enable the Treasury to monitor bids and arrive at an offer price. The use of incentives, together with an aggressive advertising program, attracted a large number of private investors. This resulted in an oversubscription of the public offer and consequently a clawback of the institution's share. Payment for the shares is in three installments, spread over eighteen months, with the last payment being due on 17 September 1996.

Post Office

The privatization of the Post Office was aborted by the government in November 1994 for political reasons. This action may be significant as a forecast of future policy on privatizations. Although privatization has not been completely ruled out, the future of the Post Office in the public sector is uncertain and the government will no doubt be looking at other possible options to increase efficiency and introduce private sector skills.

Feasibility Studies

In addition, feasibility studies have been commissioned, with respect to the privatization of the Docklands Light Railway and the air-traffic control activities of the Civil Aviation Authority.

Table 1

BRITISH TELECOM

METHOD OF SALE	RESIDUAL GOVERNMENT SHAREHOLDING	REMARKS
11 November 1984 Fixed price offer of 50.2 per cent of company at 130p/share. *12 December 1991* Offer of up to 21.9 per cent (subject to increase) of company in a combined Public Offer and International Tender Offer. The outcome was the sale of 25.9 per cent of company at a strike price of 350p per share (335p per share for those sold in Public Offer). *13 July 1993* Offer of up to 19.7 per cent of company in a combined Public Offer and International Offer. The outcome was the sale of 20.7 per cent of company at a strike price of 420p per share (410p per share for those sold in Public Offer).	1.1 per cent of ordinary shares, plus a holding of £1,344-million of loan stock. The government also retains one special share.	Leading United Kingdom Telecommunications Company, 1993 turnover of £13.2-billion.

Crown copyright is reproduced with the permission of the Controller of HMSO.

Table 2

THE ELECTRICITY INDUSTRY— ENGLAND & WALES

COMPANY	METHOD OF SALE	RESIDUAL GOVERNMENT SHAREHOLDING	REMARKS
Regional Electricity Companies	*December 1990* Fixed price offer of 100 per cent of all companies at 240p per share.	About three per cent of companies retained to meet bonus issue (and government retains one special share in each company).	Formerly the twelve electricity boards in England and Wales distributing electricity to customers. Combined 1993 turnover of £15,431-million.
National Grid	*December 1990* No shares in the company were offered for sale (all the shares in the grid's holding company were owned by the regional electricity companies).	Nil (but the government retains one special share in each of the grid company and its holding company).	The national grid owns and operates the electricity system in England and Wales and the interconnection assets linking the grid with the transmission systems in Scotland and France. 1993 turnover (from continuing operations) of £1,391-million.
Generating Companies	*March 1991* Fixed price offer of sixty per cent of each company at 175p per share combined with a "back-end" tender.	About forty per cent of each company (and the government retains one special share in each company).	Two companies, National Power and Power Gen, were formed to take over the non-nuclear generation of electricity from the CEGB (Central Electricity Generating Board). Combined 1993 turnover of £7,536-million.

Crown copyright is reproduced with the permission of the Controller of HMSO.

EUROPEAN COMMUNITY

Andrzej Kmiecik and Laurence Gourley
Van Bael & Bellis
Brussels, Belgium

INTRODUCTION

For the purposes of this chapter, privatization is understood to mean the process by which enterprises are transferred from state to private ownership. This chapter will first consider to what extent the European Community (EC) Treaty requires, or at least encourages, privatization. Next, the application of various aspects of EC law to the privatization process will be analyzed, including the rules on share ownership, state aid and merger control. Finally, the extent to which privatization frees companies from the obligation to comply with those EC rules which are binding on state-owned enterprises will also be reviewed.

DOES THE EC TREATY REQUIRE PRIVATIZATION?

The attitude of the EC Treaty to privatization is neutral. According to Article 222 of the EC Treaty, the rules of the Treaty "in no way prejudice the rules in Member States governing the system of property ownership". Consequently, both state and private ownership of enterprises is equally compatible with the EC Treaty. Although state ownership is compatible with the EC Treaty, the granting by a state of monopoly or privileged rights to enterprises, whether under state or private ownership, will often be contrary to the rules of the EC Treaty as interpreted by the EC Commission and the EC Courts. In particular, the granting by a state of exclusive import, export or distribution rights is liable to violate Articles 30, 34 and 37 of the EC Treaty. Furthermore, the case law concerning the application of Article 90, in combination with other Treaty provisions, places very significant limits on the ability of the state to grant special or exclusive rights to an enterprise to carry on any commercial activity.[1]

---

1 For example, the judgment of the EC Court of Justice of 19 May 1993 in *Procureur du Roi* vs. *Corbeau* [1993] ECR I–2533 and *crespelle* of 5 October 1994, not yet published.

In view of the above, the process of market liberalization (i.e., the abolition of monopolies and of preferential rights granted by the state) may be required by the EC Treaty. As state-owned enterprises have frequently enjoyed legally protected monopoly or preferential rights granted by the state, the process of liberalization and privatization are sometimes seen as two sides of the same coin. However, as far as the application of EC law is concerned, it is incorrect to assume that the obligation imposed on the state to introduce competition into a sector previously reserved for a state-owned monopoly in any way requires the state to give up ownership of the enterprise which benefited from the monopoly.

However, it must be conceded that although the EC Treaty does not require privatization, it may indirectly encourage it, especially with regard to state enterprises which have previously benefited from legal monopolies or privileged rights. One interest of the state in owning enterprises with these rights may be to increase its revenue with the monopoly profits earned. Once deprived of these monopoly profits as a consequence of the liberalization of the market imposed by the EC Treaty, the state may no longer find it attractive to retain ownership. Furthermore, the use of state ownership to protect employment and the standard of living of workers may be restricted by other rules of EC law, which may be enforced more vigorously once the process of market liberalization required by the EC Treaty has started. In a competitive market, for example, private enterprises are liable to press the EC Commission to enforce the rules on state aid against state-owned enterprises to prevent them from obtaining an unfair competitive advantage. The on-going legal conflict between privatized British Airways and the French Government over the operation of state-owned Air France is an example of the pressure which a government faces in trying to protect a state-owned company and its workforce in a market (in this case the air transport market) which has been liberalized pursuant to the EC Treaty. Most recently, British Airways, together with a number of other carriers, has filed an appeal with the EC Court against state aid granted to Air France.[2] A similar action has been brought by the United Kingdom Government before the EC Court

---

2 OJ 1994 C386/21.

of Justice.[3] In circumstances such as these, the constraints imposed by EC law may serve to undermine the rationale for state ownership without going so far as to bring into question its legality.

Finally, for economic reasons the EC Commission has itself come out in favor of privatization.[4] The Commission sees privatization as a means of improving the competitiveness of EC industry, which is now defined as one of the activities of the Community by Article 3(1) of the EC Treaty.

APPLICATION OF EC LAW TO PRIVATIZATION

Although the rules of the EC Treaty do not require the transfer of ownership of enterprises from the public to the private sector, they may nonetheless significantly affect the manner in which a privatization program is implemented. The current analysis will be limited to the application of the more important aspects of EC law to privatization programs. The topics covered are state aid, restrictions on shareholdings and merger control.

State Aid

A successful privatization often entails the "fattening up" of the relevant enterprise for the purpose of selling it. This may be achieved by various means such as the writing off of debts, cash injection or, in the case of private sales, cash inducements paid directly to the buyer. Such use of public funds may, however, give rise to conflict with EC state aid provisions.

EC State Aid Provisions

The general scheme of EC state aid rules is to prohibit any aid granted through state resources which distorts or threatens to distort competition by favoring certain undertakings or the production of

---

3 OJ 1994 C351/4.

4 Commission White Paper: "Growth, Competitiveness, Employment: The Challenges and Ways Forward into the 21st Century" com/93/700 final.

certain goods in so far as it affects trade between the Member States.[5] The term "undertaking" is a broad concept under EC law which embraces a company, partnership, sole trader or an association, whether or not dealing with its members. The Commission should be informed of any plans to grant or alter aid so that it can submit its comments and, if necessary, initiate proceedings if such aid is not compatible with the Common Market.[6] The Commission has adopted a very wide interpretation as to what may constitute an aid within the terms of Article 92(1). Financial transfers from state resources in any form are prohibited where they are not made in the ordinary course of business. These would include, *inter alia*, capital grants, capital injections, compensation for government-imposed financial burdens, debt conversion, direct subsidies, disposal of publicly owned assets on preferential terms, preferential tariffs, state guarantees, tax concessions and direct as well as indirect state participation in share capital.

Certain exemptions are, however, made to this general prohibition. These exemptions fall into two categories:

(1) Aid which is automatically deemed to be compatible with the Common Market;[7] and
(2) Aid which the Commission has a discretion to approve.[8]

The applicability of these exemptions in the context of privatization is discussed below.

Market Economy Investor Principle

The policy of the Commission has been to ensure that public undertakings are placed on an equal footing with privately owned undertakings from a competitive point of view. Member States are required by virtue of the so-called "Transparency Directive"[9] to ensure transparency in the financial relations between public

---

5 EC Treaty, Article 92(1).
6 EC Treaty, Article 93(3).
7 EC Treaty, Article 92(2).
8 EC Treaty, Article 92(3).
9 Commission Directive 80/723/EEC OJ 1980 L193/35, amended by Directives 85/413/EEC OJ 1985 L229/20 and 93/84/EEC OJ 1993 L254/16.

authorities and public undertakings. This Directive is intended to assist the Commission in its monitoring of the granting of state aid to such undertakings.

While the Commission has demonstrated itself to be favorably disposed to the principle of privatization, it has not hesitated to use its powers under Article 92 to either strike down or attach conditions to privatization arrangements which it feels involve public funding to an excessive extent. When examining the compatibility of funding from state resources with the Community state aid provisions, the Commission has applied the "market economy investor principle" by which the amount of state aid granted is quantified as the difference between the funds actually invested and those which a private investor would find it prudent to invest. The lawfulness of this test was upheld by the EC Court in *Commission vs. Belgium*.[10]

Financing by public resources will therefore fall outside the scope of the prohibition in Article 92(1) if similar financing could have been obtained on the private capital markets. A capital injection would not constitute an unlawful state aid if it could be shown that a private shareholder would have acted in a similar manner. For example, such an injection might be permissible if it could be shown that it was necessary to secure the survival of an undertaking which is experiencing temporary difficulties but which is capable of becoming profitable again, possibly after a reorganization.[11]

Furthermore, it has been indicated by the EC Court that a public shareholder may be compared to a large private investor so that long-term rather than short-term profitability considerations may be taken into account.[12]

In its twenty-third Competition Report, the European Commission summarized the criteria it applies in examining possible aid elements in the context of privatization.[13] When the privatization is effected by the sale of shares on the stock exchange, it is generally assumed to be on market conditions and not to involve aid. Before

---

10 [1986] ECR 2263.
11 *Belgium* vs. *Commission* [1986] ECR 2286.
12 *Italy* vs. *Commission (Alfa Romeo* case) [1991] ECR I–1603, at 640, Paragraph 20.
13 Twenty-third EC Competition Report 1994, point 402–404.

flotation, debt may be written off or reduced without this giving rise to a presumption of aid as long as the proceeds of the flotation exceed the reduction in debt. If the company is privatized by a trade sale, i.e., by sale of the company as a whole or in parts to other companies, a number of conditions must be observed if it is to be assumed that no aid is involved. These conditions include a requirement that the company be sold to the highest bidder. In other cases, trade sales must be examined for possible aid implications and therefore must be notified.

Furthermore, to be compatible with Community provisions, there may be no discrimination based on the nationality of prospective buyers of the shares or assets concerned.[14] Any sales on terms that cannot be considered normal commercial terms must be preceded by a valuation carried out by independent consultants. Privatization in sensitive sectors such as synthetic fibers, textiles and the motor industry must all be notified to the Commission beforehand. In practice, the Commission has interpreted the general prohibition in Article 92(1) very widely and many privatizations therefore involve elements which will require exemption.

Automatic Exemptions

Under Article 92(2) of the EC Treaty, certain aid is exempted *per se* from the general prohibition on state aid. In particular, the following forms of aid are exempted:
(1) Aid having a social character, granted to individual consumers, provided that such aid is granted without discrimination related to the origin of the products concerned;
(2) Aid making good the damage caused by natural disasters or exceptional occurrences; and
(3) Aid granted to the economy of certain areas of the Federal Republic of Germany affected by the division of Germany, insofar as such aid is required to compensate for the economic disadvantages caused by that division.[15]

---

14 EC Treaty, Article 221.

15 EC Treaty, Article 92(2).

In practice, these automatic exemptions are of limited application. The German Government has, however, invoked Article 92(2)(c) in the context of state aid granted to companies in the former East Germany in the course of privatization. The Commission has not stated definitively whether or not it accepts that this provision is applicable. In general, any aid element which has the effect of compensating for the disadvantages which the company to be privatized has experienced due to the division of Germany might be justified under Article 92(2)(c). In particular, the writing off of old debts or the indemnification for costs connected with environmental problems caused during the period of the state-controlled system in East Germany could be classified as indemnifiable disadvantages which can be linked directly to the economic effects of the former Communist regime. In the context of privatization, such aid should be compatible per se with EC provisions under Article 92(2)(c). The main proviso is that it should not exceed the amounts necessary to compensate the enterprise to be privatized for the economic disadvantages experienced by it as a result of the division of Germany. The Commission will, however, have a large margin of discretion in making such an assessment.

Discretionary Exemptions

Outside the context of the privatization of companies in the former East Germany, a Member State government must usually rely on one of the five discretionary exemptions contained in Article 92(3) to justify any input of state resources in the course of a privatization which contravenes the market economy investor principle. The most commonly invoked of these discretionary exemptions are Article 92(3)(a) and Article 92(3)(c). These provide that the following may be deemed compatible with the principles of the EC:
(1) Aid to promote the economic development of areas where the standard of living is abnormally low or where there is serious unemployment; and
(2) Aid to facilitate the development of certain economic activities or of certain economic areas, where such aid does not adversely affect trading conditions to an extent contrary to the public interest. Special provision is made for the shipbuilding sector.

Article 92(3)(a) permits aid, subject to the approval of the Commission, to certain severely depressed regions. For this exemption to apply, the standard of living and level of unemployment of the region in question is to be compared with the Community average. This provision will, therefore, usually only be invoked in areas such as those which have been designated as being of Objective One status for the purpose of EC structural funds.[16] In the context of privatization, aid can only be approved under this provision if the enterprise to be privatized is located in a region which suffers from abnormally low living standards or high levels of unemployment measured against a Community-wide standard.

Article 92(3)(c) is of more general application as it permits both regional aid for the development of regions which are disadvantaged in relation to the national average and sectorial aid which might assist in the restoration of long-term viability of specific industrial sectors. Aid to enterprises in the poorer areas of the European Community or to enterprises engaged in a sector of industry which is experiencing particular difficulties can be exempted under this provision. In the context of privatization, the relevant provision will, therefore, depend on the location of the enterprise to be privatized and the industrial sector in which it is involved.

Where state aid has been approved under either Article 92(3)(a) or 92(3)(c), the Commission has tended to impose a restructuring plan while also attaching strict conditions, such as an undertaking not to increase capacity in areas where overcapacity already exists. These conditions are evident in the numerous privatizations carried out by the *Treuhandanstalt* (THA), i.e., the public law entity entrusted with restructuring and privatizing enterprises in the former East Germany.[17] The Commission has also laid down guidelines on state aid for rescuing and restructuring firms in difficulty.[18] These guidelines are indicative of the type of conditions which may be attached to aid in the course of privatization where the enterprise to be privatized is considered to be in difficulty. In the *Sabena*

---

16 Article 8 and Annex 1, Council Regulation 2081/93 OJ 1993 L193/5 for Objective One status regions.
17 Twenty-third EC Competition Report 1994, point 405–415.
18 OJ 1994 No C368/15.

case,[19] aid was only approved under Article 92(3)(c) on the condition that the role of the state would be restricted to that of a normal shareholder.

To ensure compliance with any attached conditions, the Commission requires the submission of periodic reports giving details of the commercial results of the enterprise concerned, pricing policies and all other information which is useful for judging the evolution of the enterprise for which the aid is destined. The Commission will order repayment if there is a breach of any such condition. For example, in the *Renault* case,[20] where aid was also authorized in accordance with Article 92(3)(c), the Commission required Renault to repay some FF 3,500-million to the state and to re-enter on its debit sheet some FF 2,500-million of supplementary debt. The most vivid demonstration, however, of the Commission's determination to ensure that privatizations comply with the state aid rules was provided by the *Rover* case.

The Rover Case

In the *Rover* case, the United Kingdom Government wished to write off £800-million of debt of Rover Group Holdings as part of its sale to British Aerospace. The Commission deemed that this constituted a state aid as it exceeded the proposed purchase price by British Aerospace by £150-million. In a 1988 Decision,[21] the Commission decided that the debt of the Group had been overstated. A maximum state aid of £469-million was, however, authorized under Article 92(3)(c) on the basis that the privatization included a restructuring plan which foresaw a substantial reduction in car assembly and component capacities in the order of thirty per cent. The Commission also took into consideration the fact that the plan's central medium-term objective was to transform the Rover Group's production into the niche market for up-market models with higher value added and higher profit margins. The

---

19 Commission Decision 91/555/EEC OJ 1991 L300/48.
20 Commission Decision 88/454/EEC OJ 1988 L220/30.
21 Commission Decision 89/58/EEC OJ L25/92.

Commission, however, attached a series of strict conditions to the sale, which included, *inter alia*, that:
(1) There be no alteration in the proposed terms of sale of the Rover Group to British Aerospace as notified;
(2) The aid be used exclusively for the repayment of financial debts of the Rover Group; and
(3) No further aid be granted to the Rover Group before the end of 1992, with the exception of a maximum regional grant of £78-million.

It subsequently transpired, however, that the United Kingdom Government had made financial concessions amounting to £44.4-million, the so-called "sweeteners", directly to British Aerospace in the form of:
(1) A grant of £9.5-million to cover part of the £13.6-million cost to British Aerospace of purchasing the Rover Group's minority shares;
(2) A payment of £1.5-million to the Rover Group to cover consulting costs incurred by the company as a result of the sale; and
(3) The deferment of the purchase price from British Aerospace for a period of approximately twenty months resulting in a gross benefit for British Aerospace of £33.4-million.

After an original Commission Decision ordering repayment was quashed by the EC Court on procedural grounds,[22] the Commission opened fresh proceedings and again ordered British Aerospace to repay the money,[23] which they ultimately did.

Restrictions on Shareholdings

A Member State may attempt to retain an element of control over privatized undertakings or attempt to ensure that foreign nationals or companies do not acquire too great a degree of control in those undertakings. The rationale behind such a retention of control is that it enables the public interest to be defended in such areas as

---

[22] *British Aerospace and Rover Group Holdings Plc* vs. *Commission* [1992] ECR I-493.

[23] Commission Decision 89/58/EEC OJ 1989 L143/7.

continuity of provision, cost control and adequate and impartial service. This can be achieved in many different ways such as utilizing "golden shares", which will be discussed later. Article 6 of the EC Treaty, however, contains a general prohibition on any discrimination on grounds of nationality. Such arrangements should, in particular, be considered in the light of EC provisions on the right of establishment and on the free movement of capital.

Freedom of Establishment

Article 52 of the EC Treaty provides that restrictions on freedom of establishment of nationals of other Member States should be abolished. By virtue of Article 58, this provision also applies to companies or firms formed in accordance with the law of a Member State and having their registered office, central administration or principal place of business within the European Community. Similarly, Article 221 of the EC Treaty provides that:

> ". . . Member States shall accord nationals of the other Member States the same treatment as their own nationals as regards participation in the capital of companies or firms . . . ".

Furthermore, the jurisprudence of the EC Court has further emphasized the fact that the right of establishment in a Member State includes the right to acquire shares in a private limited company.[24]

Despite these provisions, the legislation of the various Member States has often placed restrictions on the rights of foreign nationals to acquire shares in privatized companies. For example, the *Conseil Constitutionnel* in France stipulated in 1986 that the unfettered ability of French citizens to purchase shares in French companies must be protected: "l'indépendence nationale devra etre préservé".[25] However, a provision limiting the amount of shares held by foreign investors to twenty per cent has since been amended and no longer applies to nationals of Member States.

---

24 *Commission* vs. *France* [1986] ECR 273.
25 Decision of *Conseil Constitutionnel* Number 86–207 of 25 and 26 June 1986.

In the United Kingdom, Part II of the Industry Act 1975 gives the Secretary of State power to limit, on grounds of national interest, investment by non-residents in important manufacturing undertakings. Such discriminatory clauses would appear, in general, to be in breach of Article 52. It should be noted, however, that provisions relating to industries which are connected with the production of, or trade in, arms, munitions and war material may legitimately be excluded from the scope of EC provisions by virtue of Article 223(1)(b) of the EC Treaty. Also excludable are those industries perceived as being of relevance to public policy, public security or public health within the terms of Article 56 of the EC Treaty.

Given that Article 52 is directly effective, i.e., it grants individuals rights which must be upheld by national courts, and in the light of the *Francovich* judgment,[26] individuals or companies who can demonstrate that they have suffered losses as a result of a Member State's failure to fully implement Article 52 might initiate an action for damages against the Member State concerned. The outcome of such an action is, however, unpredictable given the unknown scope of *Francovich*.

Clauses which impose direct or indirect restrictions on nationals or companies of other Member States due to nationality are, therefore, *prima facie* contrary to the provisions of EC law on freedom of establishment. However, in practice the Commission has not been overzealous in initiating proceedings against such national provisions and it appears to have tacitly accepted limits on foreign shareholdings as long as the limits are fairly generous. In any case, EC nationals do not appear to have difficulty in acquiring shares in privatized companies.

Golden Shares

Clauses which are applicable without distinction on the basis of nationality do not in principle conflict with EC provisions. Governments may therefore legitimately retain a certain amount of control in newly privatized companies. The device of the "golden share" or "action specifique" refers to the procedure by which the state or its

---

[26] *Francovich* vs. *Italy* [1991] ECR I–5357.

nominee retains a share in the private company enjoying special rights. The rights granted by the golden share may vary from one company to another. Such rights would, however, usually cover the right to oppose the crossing of a fifteen per cent capital threshold by one person acting solely or in concert, the right to participate in shareholders' meetings without having voting rights, the right to appoint a member of the board of directors, a veto over any transfer of the company's assets and a veto over voluntary liquidation. Such an arrangement is not *per se* incompatible with EC provisions as long as it is not based on discriminatory provisions. Similarly, overall limitations on shareholdings which do not discriminate on grounds of nationality should ordinarily fall outside the scope of Articles 52 and 221.

Delegation

Another method sometimes adopted by governments, rather than retaining shares in a privatized company, is to maintain some control over the sectors but delegate certain activities to a third party, preferably contracting out to a private company. This is often referred to as "delegation". Such quasi-privatization is a contractual procedure which entrusts the management of a public service to a private enterprise. One particular form of delegation commonly used in France is that of "concession". In a concession, the management of public services and public facilities is privatized, with the state retaining ownership of the majority of the assets. Furthermore, the state controls the conditions under which management is conducted. This arrangement has certain advantages in that it is a more flexible arrangement which may allow for a genuine defense of the public interest. At present, the concept of concessions does not exist in all Member States and has not been addressed by EC law. The concept may, however, lead to the application of public procurement Directives.

Merger Control

The effect of the privatization of an enterprise on the structure of competition in the market will be subject to review under the applicable competition and merger rules. Certain privatizations will fall within the scope of the EC Merger Regulation[27] and will have to be reviewed by the Commission before they can be put into effect.

Applicability of the EC Merger Regulation

A notification under the EC Merger Regulation will be required if a privatization gives rise to, firstly, a concentration and secondly, a Community dimension.

The Concentration Test

Except in the case of a legal merger, a concentration by definition requires an acquisition of control over all or part of an undertaking.[28] Thus, the sale by the state of the entire share capital of a state-owned company to a third party, whereby the state relinquishes control over the company in favor of the third party, will be a concentration. On the other hand, an offer of shares by the state to the general public in a state-owned company is unlikely to give rise to a concentration because no one party (or group of parties) will acquire control over the privatized company within the meaning of the EC Merger Regulation. In the case of a partial privatization, it will be necessary to assess whether the rights retained by the state as shareholder or through legislation are sufficiently important to prevent a transfer of sole or joint control to a third party.

The Community Dimension Test

Whether or not a concentration in the context of a privatization has a Community dimension will depend on whether the turnover thresholds set down in Article 1.2 of the EC Merger Regulation are met. A concentration has a Community dimension where, firstly, the combined worldwide group turnover of all the undertakings

---

27 Council Regulation Number 4064/89/EEC on the control of concentrations between undertakings OJ 1990 L257/14.
28 Article 3 of Council Regulation 4064/89/EEC.

concerned by the concentration is more than ECU 5,000-million, and, secondly, the Community-wide group turnover of at least two of the undertakings concerned by the concentration is more than ECU 250-million. This is unless each of the undertakings concerned by the concentration achieves more than two-thirds of its Community-wide group turnover in one and the same Member State.[29] For example, in a situation where the state sells 100 per cent of the shares in a company (X Co.) to a third party, the group turnover of the third party and of X Co., the undertakings concerned, would be taken into account to calculate whether the transaction has a Community dimension. Concentrations which do not meet the Community dimension turnover thresholds are not subject to review under the EC Merger Regulation, but may instead be subject to national merger control rules. These rules vary considerably from Member State to Member State.

Substantive Review of Privatization under the EC Merger Regulation

A number of total or partial privatizations have been reviewed by the European Commission under the EC Merger Regulation.[30] The EC Commission is obliged to prohibit a concentration if it creates or strengthens a dominant position as a result of which effective competition would be significantly impeded in the Common Market or a substantial part of it.[31] At the time of writing, the Commission has only prohibited three concentrations under the EC Merger Regulation: *Aerospatiale-Alenia / de Havilland*[32] and *MSG Media Service*[33] and Nordic Satellite Distribution.[34] Neither of these cases were concerned with privatization.

---

29 Article 2.1 of Council Regulation 4064/89/EEC.

30 *See*, e.g., *Air France / Sabena*, M157, 1992; *Elf Aquitaine-Thyssen / Minol*, M235, 1992; *Nestlé / Italgel*, M362, 1993; *Pilkington Techint / SIV*, M358, OJ 1994 L158/24; *Kali + Salz / MdK / Treuhand*, M308, OJ 1994 L186/38; *Tractebel / Synatom*, M466, 1994; *Tractebel / Distrigaz I*, M418, 1994 (notification withdrawn); and *Tractebel / Distrigaz II*, M493, 1994.

31 Article 2.3 of Council Regulation 4064/89/EEC.

32 M053, OJ 1991 L334/42.

33 M469, OJ 1994 L364/1.

34 M490, decision not yet published.

In a number of the privatization cases reviewed by the Commission, the proposed acquisition of a state-owned enterprise by a competitor would give rise to very high market shares in the markets on which they operated. In each case this resulted from the fact that the state-owned enterprise itself had a very strong market position at the time of the privatization owing to the protection from competition that it had enjoyed by virtue of its connection with the state. Although the Commission did not prohibit any of these privatizations, it did on a number of occasions persuade the parties involved to make changes to the original privatization plan to remedy the Commission's concerns about the effect of the transaction on the structure of competition.[35]

Air France/Sabena

The *Air France/Sabena* case concerned the purchase by Air France of a minority stake in the Belgian state airline (Sabena) from the Belgian Government. The parties agreed to surrender to third-party competitors certain routes on which they would have a dominant position following the transaction. In addition, they agreed to limit the number of take-off and landing slots which Sabena would use at Brussels National Airport in implementing the expansion program which was planned following the partial privatization. As a result of these and other undertakings, the Commission was able to clear the concentration.

Elf Aquitaine-Thyssen/Minol

The *Elf Aquitaine-Thyssen/Minol* case concerned the purchase, primarily by Elf Aquitaine, of the former East Germany's state-owned oil company (Minol) from the *Treuhandanstalt* (THA). Following the privatization, Elf Aquitaine would have been the market leader in the distribution of petroleum products through service stations in the eastern part of Germany. It would also have controlled two-thirds of petroleum depots in that area which had

---

35 *See* Air *France/Sabena*; *Elf Aquitaine-Thyssen/Minol*; *Kali and Salz/MdK /Treuhand*; and *Tractebel/Distrigaz I and II*.

previously been in the hands of Minol. Elf Aquitaine's competitors on the distribution market showed that there would be insufficient depot capacity which would not be owned by Elf Aquitaine to meet their needs. Elf Aquitaine agreed to issue binding offers to these competitors to grant them access to depot facilities on a cost-plus basis. In this case, the European Commission was evidently concerned that Elf Aquitaine could obstruct its competitors on the distribution market by denying them access to essential depot capacity. Taking into account these changes, the European Commission was able to conclude that competition from third parties would be sufficiently strong to prevent Elf Aquitaine from acquiring a dominant position on the affected markets.

Privatization of the Belgian Energy Sector

Certain recent privatization projects reviewed by the Commission have concerned the energy sector in Belgium. This sector is highly regulated by the state and competition is very limited. One case (*Tractebel / Synatom*) concerned the sale by the Belgian State of its fifty per cent stake in Synatom, the only supplier of enriched uranium to nuclear power producers in Belgium. The purchaser was Tractebel, the only other shareholder in Synatom prior to the privatization. Tractebel was also the dominant producer and supplier of electricity in Belgium. The second case (*Tractebel / Distrigaz I and II*) concerned the sale by the Belgian State of its fifty per cent stake in Distrigaz, the only supplier of gas in Belgium. The purchaser of a part of this stake was again Tractebel, which already owned 33.25 per cent of the shares in Distrigaz. In both cases, the Commission decided that the privatization gave Tractebel sole control over companies which previously it had only controlled jointly with the Belgian State. The European Commission decided that the rights which the Belgian State retained by virtue of its golden share (primarily intended to ensure that neither company acted in a manner contrary to the national energy policy) were not sufficient to give it joint control over Synatom or Distrigaz.

The Commission cleared the *Synatom* case without any modifications or undertakings being made by the parties. This was despite the fact that the dominant producer of electricity (Tractebel) was acquiring the dominant supplier of enriched uranium in a country in which sixty per cent of electricity is generated by atomic power stations. Furthermore, although Synatom did not have the exclusive right by law to purchase, convert and enrich uranium, it had concluded an exclusive supply arrangement with the state and with the Belgian electricity producers which would presumably be a significant barrier to entry. In clearing the transaction, the Commission stressed that the other companies involved in the production of nuclear power in Belgium, together with Tractebel, had not expressed concerns about the transaction and that new producers of nuclear power were unlikely in the foreseeable future.

In contrast, in the *Distrigaz* case, the Belgian State appears to have been obliged to abandon part of the privatization after a hostile reaction by the Commission to the notification. The principal problem appears to have been that the supply of gas to electricity producers in Belgium, which was the responsibility of Distrigaz, would fall under the sole control of Tractebel, the dominant producer of electricity in Belgium. The ability of Tractebel's competitors in the production of electricity to compete could be hindered by Tractebel's control over a crucial raw material, thereby strengthening the dominance of Tractebel in the production of electricity. This could be particularly important since the use of gas in the production of electricity was increasingly significant. Furthermore, no competition was possible in the supply of gas as Distrigaz had the exclusive legal right to transport and store gas in Belgium. Apparently, to solve the competition problem connected with the supply of gas to electricity producers, this part of Distrigaz's business was transferred to a new company in which Tractebel's rights as a shareholder were no greater than they had been prior to the privatization. The European Commission cleared the amended transaction after a second notification.

PRIVATIZED ENTERPRISES AS STATE EMANATIONS

The transfer of an enterprise from state to private ownership also raises the question as to what extent a privatized enterprise should continue to be considered as being an organ or emanation of the state.

Concept of Emanation of the State

The distinction between public and private bodies has been primarily considered in the context of whether a body is bound by the terms of an EC Directive. The EC Court has traditionally held that Directives, which are addressed to Member States,[36] may only bind Member States and cannot impose obligations on private individuals which could be enforced before national courts.[37] This denial of so-called "horizontal direct effect" would appear to mean that Directives should not impose enforceable obligations on privatized enterprises. The case law of the EC Court has, however, somewhat blurred the distinction between private and public bodies with the result that the privatization of an enterprise does not necessarily mean that it will no longer be considered as an emanation of the state.

The EC Court considered this distinction when the question arose as to whether the provisions of a directly effective Directive could be relied on against the British Gas Corporation, the nationalized predecessor in title of British Gas Plc.[38] In its judgment, the EC Court laid down a general formula containing four conditions which should be considered when deciding whether a body constitutes an emanation of the state. That is:
(1) The body must provide a public service;
(2) It must provide this service pursuant to a measure adopted by the state;
(3) It must provide the service under the control of the state; and
(4) It must possess special powers beyond those normally applicable in relations between individuals.

The third condition requiring that the enterprise acts under the control of the state would appear to exclude most privatized industries. However, the final decision as to whether an enterprise constitutes an emanation of the state rests with the national court who must apply the criteria laid down by the EC Court. In the case of *Foster*, it was subsequently held by the House of Lords that the British Gas Corporation, when it was still nationalized, did fulfill the criteria and was an emanation of the state. It is much more doubtful whether the privatized British Gas Plc would also have fulfilled the conditions but this issue was not considered by the

---

36 EC Treaty, Article 189(a).
37 *Marshall* vs. *Southampton and South West Hampshire Health Authority (Teaching)* [1986] ECR 723.
38 *Foster* vs. *British Gas* [1990] ECR I–3313.

House of Lords. Furthermore, the criteria laid down by the EC Court in *Foster* have not always been perceived by national courts as providing an exhaustive test and bodies that are not apparently covered might be considered an emanation of the state on some other basis. For example, the English Court of Appeal has held[39] that the test was not intended to provide the answer to every category of case but provided a starting point and if one element was not present, the presence of another element might result in the enterprise still being considered an emanation of the state.

With regard to privatized enterprises, the main area of contention will be whether they provide a public service under the control of the state. This particular issue was considered by the English High Court in *Griffin & Others* vs. *South West Water Services Limited*.[40] This case raised the question as to whether a privatized water company could be bound by the terms of a Directive which had not been implemented into United Kingdom law. The High Court held that, although the company was privately owned, it required a state license to operate, which imposed far-reaching conditions on its operations which aimed to protect consumers. These restrictions included restrictions on tariff levels and tariff structure, restrictions on the disposal of assets, review of quality standards and an obligation to report. The power to implement the conditions was given to the Secretary of State as well as a special water industry body with regulatory powers. Both had far-reaching enforcement powers for breach of these conditions, including the possibility to apply to the court for a "special administration order" transferring the water and sewage functions of the company to another company. In these circumstances, it was held that the provision of the public service was under the control of the state and that the criteria laid down in *Foster* were fulfilled.

It is therefore evident that if a state retains a sufficient degree of control in a privatized enterprise it may still be considered as an emanation of the state. Consequently, a Community Directive which has not been fully implemented by a Member State may be enforced against such an enterprise. This may, in some circumstances, expose a privatized enterprise to applications for injunctions or even substantial claims for damages. Such an outcome may appear

---

39 *Doughty* vs. *Rolls-Royce* [1992] ICR 538, at 552.
40 High Court judgment of 25 August 1994, unreported.

to be unfair since the privatized enterprise is being made accountable for the default of a Member State. Any potential liabilities should, therefore, be considered by prospective purchasers of an enterprise which is being privatized. It might also be prudent to seek an indemnity from the Member State concerned covering any liabilities arising from the state's failure to correctly implement an EC Directive.

Public Procurement

The definition of the term "state" has particular importance in the field of EC public procurement rules. The fact that an application of the principles laid down in the *Foster* case might lead to a privatized enterprise being considered as an emanation of the state raises the question as to what extent such enterprises would be subject to the European Community public procurement Directives. The application of the said Directives would entail considerable financial implications for an enterprise. This is therefore a matter which should be carefully considered by prospective purchasers of a state-owned enterprise.

Public Authorities

Certain contracts with public authorities which do not provide public services in the water, energy, transport or telecommunications sectors are subject to the Works Directive,[41] the Supplies Directive[42] and the Services Directive.[43] The Works Directive defines public authorities as:

> ". . . the state, regional or local authorities, bodies covered by public law, associations formed by one or several of such authorities or bodies governed by public law".[44]

---

41 Council Directive 93/37/EEC OJ 1993 L199/54.
42 Council Directive 93/36/EEC OJ 1991 L199/1.
43 Council Directive 92/50/EEC OJ 1992 L209/1.
44 Works Directive, Article 1(b).

Similar definitions are contained in the Supplies and Services Directives. It was made clear in the *Beentjes* case,[45] which related to the original Works Directive, that the word "state" must be interpreted in functional terms. The European Court held that a body must be regarded as being within the definition of the state where:

(1) Its composition and functions are laid down by legislation and it depends on the authorities for the appointment of its members and the observance of the obligations arising out of its measures; and
(2) It depends on the state for the financing of the public works contract which is its task to award.

Given the even broader definition of an emanation of the state adopted in the *Foster* case and later applied in the *Griffin* case, it remains to be seen whether this definition might be extended to the field of public procurement, in which case even some privatized enterprises might be considered subject to the Directives. In particular, the public procurement Directives might be applicable to concessions of public services and public works. The scope of the *Foster* case is, however, uncertain and it is possible that the definition adopted for an emanation of the state is limited to the application of the principle of direct effect to EC Directives.

Public Undertakings and Utilities

Many privatized enterprises will, however, come within the scope of the Utilities Directive[46] which, in addition to public authorities, also covers certain contracts with "public undertakings" and "utilities". Both provide services to the public in connection with the water, energy, transport and telecommunications sectors on the basis of special or exclusive rights granted by a Member State. The Directive defines public undertakings as undertakings where the public authorities exercise a dominant influence by virtue of ownership, financial participation therein, or the governing rules. Any nationalized or semi-state body would probably fall within the scope of "public undertakings".

---

45 *Gebroeders Beentjes BV* vs. *The Netherlands* [1988] ECR 4635.
46 Council Directive 93/38/EEC OJ 1993 L199/84.

The concept of utilities, however, is much wider and can cover both public and private bodies. Utilities are defined as entities in a relevant sector which are neither public authorities nor public undertakings, but which "operate on the basis of special or exclusive rights granted by a competent authority of a Member State".[47] The relevant Directive provides that the "special or exclusive rights" must result in the reservation for one or more entities of the exploitation of one of the relevant sectors.[48] If a privatized enterprise provides a service in one of the relevant sectors and operates on the basis of "special or exclusive rights" granted by the Member State, it will come within the scope of the Directive. Special or exclusive rights are rights which are derived from authorizations granted by a competent authority of the Member State concerned by law, regulation or administrative action.[49]

This concept of special or exclusive rights goes beyond the traditional association of these rights with monopolies and may, in time, be found to include a very large number of prerogatives given to private companies. For the European Commission, it would seem that the important criteria for deciding whether the entity is covered by the Utilities Directive is the consequence of the rights granted. The question will be whether these rights reserve for one or more entities the exploitation of a relevant activity for the purposes of the Directive. If other enterprises are free to carry out the same activities, either the entities will no longer be considered to be operating on the basis of special or exclusive rights or the activities will no longer be considered to be relevant activities. The Utilities Directive provides an illustrative list in Annexes I–X of entities in each of the Member States which are considered to fulfill these criteria, many of which are enterprises which have been privatized.

CONCLUSION

It is apparent from the above analysis that various aspects of EC law must be taken into account in structuring any privatization in

---

47 Utilities Directive, Article 2(1)(b).

48 Utilities Directive, Article 2(3).

49 Utilities Directive, Article 2(3).

the EC. It must be borne in mind that the EC Commission has significant powers to intervene should it consider that the applicable rules are not being respected. As yet, these powers appear to have been exercised primarily in selected areas, such as state aid and merger control. Furthermore, intervention by the Commission in privatization is undoubtedly limited by political constraints, given that the usual adversary of the Commission is liable to be a national government. However, in addition to regulatory action on the part of the Commission, EC law may also be raised in direct legal challenges related to privatization in the national courts. The developing concept of an "emanation of the state" may also have considerable financial implications for privatized enterprises. The lack of legal certainty in this field makes it very difficult for purchasers of a state-owned enterprise to assess the potential extent of their future liabilities.

INDEX

A

Africa
  Egypt 26
  Morocco 26

Argentina
  Deregulation 32
  Investments 38
  Legal framework 34
  Privatization 23, 31
  State-owned company deficit 30, 37
  Taxation 31, 32
  Transfer of assets 32

Asia
  China 24
  India 24
  Japan 24
  Malaysia 25
  Philippines 25
  Singapore 25
  Taiwan 25
  Thailand 26

Authorized investment companies
  Ownership certificates 208
  Slovenia 208

B

Brazil
  Collor Administration 46, 60
  Denationalization 23, 45, 50
  Directive Committee 49
  Foreign debt securities 55
  Industrial development 45
  Legal structure 47
  Ministry of Finance 50, 58
  National Privatization Council 58
  President 52
  Privatization certificates 55
  Privatization funds 55
  Privatization procedures 48

Bulgaria
  Compensation 76
  Evaluation of assets 69
  Foreign investment 67
  Investment bonds 80
  Investors 66
  Letting 77
  Management buy-outs 75
  Management contract 78
  Privatization 20, 63, 68
  Public auction 71
  State decision-making authorities 65
  Tenders 72

C

Companies
  Assets 94
  Authorized investment companies 208
  Employees 99, 107, 137, 203, 233
  Legal transfer 99
  Liabilities 217
  Limited company 63, 70, 104, 121, 202
  Management 138, 203
  Mergers 252
  Restrictions on shareholdings 248
  Restructuring 15, 123, 214
  Shares 49, 69, 89, 162, 191, 203
  Stock corporation 70, 202
  Subsidiaries 88
  Valuation 69, 163
  Winding-up and liquidation 50, 125

Compensation
  Bulgaria 76
  Cooperatives 200
  Croatia 84
  German Democratic Republic 112
  Hungary 122
  Ownership certificates 208
  Slovenia 200

Competition
  Benefits of 2
  Book-building 223
  European Community 103, 240
  Mergers 252
  Monopolies 36, 47, 60, 104, 240, 261
  Preferential rights 240

Index

265

    State aid 241
    Telecommunications 213
Confiscation
    GDR 112
    Restitution 88
    Slovenia 199
Cooperatives
    Agricultural 114, 200
    Compensation 200
    German Democratic Republic 200
    Slovenia 114
                                                              200
Croatia
    Compensation 84
    Croatian Privatization Fund 84
    Mixed ownership 85
    Pension funds 83
    Privatization 85
    Self-management 81
    Subsidiaries 82
                                                               88
Currency and scrip
    Brazil 54
    Forms of payment 54

D

Decision-making
    Authorities
    Bulgaria 65
    Hungary 65
    Process 129
    Relevant factors 134
Denationalization
    Aims 35
    Apartments 201
    Argentina 29
    Belgian energy sector 255
    Beneficiaries 199, 208
    Brazil 45
    Bulgaria 45
    Case-by-case programs 63
    Citizenship 8
    Compensation 199
    Compulsory privatization 200
    Confiscation 98
                                                             199

Cooperatives 200
Croatia 81
Delegation 251
Effects 37
Emanations of the State 256
European Community 231, 233, 239
Evaluation of assets 69
External auditing 57
Fast-track or multi-enterprise programs 6
Foreign debt securities 55
Fund manager 50
German Democratic Republic 107
Germany 6
IMF/World bank 3
Independent appraisals 53
Industrial efficiency 2
Liabilities 216
Management buy-outs 9, 11, 14, 75, 141, 224, 225
Mass privatization programs 7
Merger control 251
National property 95
Opposition 96
Ownership certificates 206
Private sales 13, 219, 224
Privatization certificates 55
Privatization funds 55
Public auction 71
Public procurement 259
Public undertakings and utilities 260
Regulation 157, 231
Restitution 200
Restrictions on shareholdings 248
Simplified privatization 137
Slovak Republic 8, 189
Slovenia 199
Socially owned companies 201
State aid 241
Tenders 53, 72, 131, 133
United Kingdom 1, 211
World War II 153, 199, 211

E

Eastern Europe
  Bulgaria 20
  Czech Republic 20
  Estonia 20
  Hungary 20
  Kazakhstan 21
  Latvia 21

Index

    Lithuania 21
    Poland 21
    Romania 21
    Russia 22
    Slovak Republic 22
    Ukraine 22

Employees
    Labor codetermination 101
    Retirement provision 100
    Shares 56, 141, 143, 204
    Transfer of company 99

European community
    Competition 240
    Delegation 251
    Discrimination 231, 249
    European Community Merger Regulation 253
    Free movement of capital 249
    Golden shares 249, 250, 255
    Market economy investor principle 242, 245
    Merger control 251
    Monopolies 104, 240, 261
    Preferential rights 240
    Privatization 239
    Public authorities 259
    Public procurement 259
    Public undertakings and utilities 260
    Restrictions on shareholdings 248
    Right of establishment 249

G

German Democratic Republic
    Agriculture 112, 114
    Compensation 113
    Cooperatives 114
    Liquidation of assets 109
    Principle of restitution 111
    Privatization 108
    Unification 106

Germany
    Privatization 18, 91, 93
    Public utilities 92
    Unification 106

Golden shares
    Brazil 57
    European Community 249, 250
    United Kindom 229

H

Hungary 122
    Compensation 132
    Competitive bidding 147
    Concessions 123
    Credit consolidation program 146
    Foreign investors 141
    Management buy-outs 132
    Minority shares 140
    Payment in installments 140
    Preferential privatization techniques 124
    Preferential shares 20, 117
    Privatization 140
    Privatization leasing 131
    Public auction 127, 131
    Public offer 137
    Simplified privatization 119
    State asset holding company 129
    State privatization and holding company 119
    State property agency 131, 133
    Tenders

I

Italy 169
    Amortization fund 159
    Economic public entities 162
    Interministerial committee 178
    Limits on share ownership 168
    Permanent Consultation Committee 153
    Political background 18, 153
    Privatization 165
    Public auction 157
    Public credit institutions 176
    Public interest companies 164, 174
    Public offer 180
    Public utilities 154
    State acquisitions 155
    State deficit 158
    Taxation

L

Latin America 22
    Argentina 23
    Brazil 23
    Columbia

Mexico 23
Peru 23
Venezuela 24

Liabilities
  Directors 218
  Disposal of 217
  Public offer 217
  United Kingdom 216

M

Marketing
  United Kingdom 227

Mergers
  Community dimension test 252
  Concentration test 252
  European Community 252
  European Community Merger Regulation 253

Ministry of Finance
  Authorization from 58
  Brazil 58

O

Ownership certificates
  Authorized investment companies 208
  Compensation 208
  Entitlement 207
  Slovenia 207
  Value 207

P

Private sales
  Globally 13
  Italy 167
  United Kingdom 218, 223

Property
  Beneficiaries 199
  Compensation 200
  Deregulation 32
  Expropriation 111
  In naturam 200
  Leases 200

Purchase of assets 125
　　Restitution 190, 200
　　Sale of assets 13
　　Slovenia. 200
　　Temporary utilization 145
　　Tenancies 200
　　Transfer of assets. 32, 126

Public auction
　　Bulgaria 71
　　Hungary 130
　　Italy. 165

Public offer
　　Bulgaria 75
　　Globally. 11
　　Hungary 127, 131
　　Italy. 164, 174
　　United Kingdom 213, 217, 221

Public undertakings and utilities
　　Agriculture 112
　　Airlines 16, 20, 39, 215, 240, 254
　　Banking. 16, 103, 158, 170
　　Coal 19, 234
　　European Community 260
　　Electricity 16, 18, 173, 181, 213, 225, 230, 235, 255
　　Gas 19, 102, 213, 225, 230, 257
　　Germany. 91, 103
　　Highways 38
　　Oil 18, 19, 38, 182, 215, 254
　　Post 97, 103, 235
　　Railways 105, 215, 234
　　Steel 215
　　Telecommunications. 18, 20, 38, 103, 184, 213, 225, 259
　　Television 34
　　Transport 259
　　United Kingdom. 256
　　Water. 18, 225, 231, 258

S

Shares
　　Assets 204
　　Back-end tender 223
　　Book-building 223, 235
　　Clawback. 223
　　Dividends 8, 206
　　Employees. 9, 56, 84, 136, 142, 204, 223, 225
　　Flotation 220, 225

Index

Golden shares 57, 229, 249, 250, 255
Incentives 226
International offers 222
Limits on ownership... 178
Management buy-outs 9, 11, 14, 75, 141, 224, 225
Marketing.. 227
Minority shares 132
Payment 86, 205
Preferential shares.. 124
Price 69, 86, 191, 205
Private sales... 10, 13, 213
Public auction.................................... 71, 86, 131, 165
Public offer 10, 11, 75, 86, 127, 131, 164, 205, 213, 217
Share shops... 226
Socially owned companies 203
Stagging 221
Voting rights... 205

Slovak Republic
  Direct sales... 197
  Investment funds 196
  Privatization.. 20, 189, 192
  Restitution 190
  Strategic Enterprises Act..................................... 194
  Voucher privatization... 191

Slovenia
  Authorized investment companies 208
  Cooperatives... 200
  Denationalization.. 199
  Law on Apartments 201
  Socially owned companies 201
  World War II... 199

Socially-owned companies
  Assets 204, 206
  Employees.. 204, 206
  Form 202
  Privatization.. 201
  Shares.. 203, 204
  Slovenia... 201
  Voting rights.. 205

State aid
  Automatic exemptions 244
  Conditions.. 246, 247
  Discretionary exemptions 245
  European Community 241
  General prohibition 241

U

United Kingdom
  Compulsory competitive tendering 232
  European Community 231, 233
  Flotation 220
  Golden shares 229
  Incentives 226
  Legislation 216
  Liabilities 216
  Management buy-outs 224, 225
  Policy considerations 220
  Private sales 219
  Privatization 211
  Public offer 217
  Restructuring 214
  Share shops 226

V

Voucher privatization
  Eligibility 191
  Globally 2
  Hungary 122
  National property fund bonds 193
  Slovak Republic 191

W

Western Europe
  Austria 16
  Belgium 17
  Denmark 17
  France 17
  Germany 17
  Greece 18
  Italy 18
  Netherlands 18
  Portugal 19
  Sweden 19
  United Kingdom 19